To continued peace along the American-Canadian border

Contents

Part Three: Legacies

Illustrations

Abbreviations

Askin Papers   Milo M. Quaife, ed., *The John Askin Papers*, 2 vols. (Detroit: Detroit Library Commission, 1928-31)

BHC   Burton Historical Collection, Detroit Public Library

City of Detroit   Clarence M. Burton, *The City of Detroit Michigan, 1701-1922*, 5 vols. (Detroit and Chicago: S.J. Clarke, 1922)

MPHC   Michigan Pioneer and Historical Society, *Michigan Pioneer and Historical Collection*, 40 vols. (Lansing: Michigan Historical Commission, 1877-1929)

WCM   Windsor's Community Museum, Windsor, Ontario

Style

In most areas, this volume conforms to the *Chicago Manual of Style*. Quotations are rendered as faithfully to the original sources as possible, including capricious spellings and capitalizations. To retain the spirit of language from the early nineteenth century, the term *sic* has been avoided. Instead, the editors have inserted brackets when an original term is unclear.

The book uses the terms Indian and Native American interchangeably, recognizing fully the fallacies of both names. Whenever possible, authors have tried to refer to native peoples by their tribal or village names. Outside of historical quotations, Ojibwa is used for Ojibwe, Ojibway, Chippewa, and Chippeway; Wyandot for Wendat and Huron; Potawatomi for Pottawatomie and Pottawatomi; and Odawa for Ottawa.

Geographical and historic place names in Michigan and Ontario can be confusing. Therefore, the historical name is used whenever possible with parenthesis identifying its present-day equivalent. There are two important exceptions. Because of their repeated use, the current locations of Upper Canada (Ontario) and Sandwich (Windsor, Ontario) are not given after the Introduction. Michigan did not become a state until 1837. References to "Michigan" before this date should be assumed to mean Michigan Territory. Likewise, Canada did not become a self-governing country within the British Empire until 1867. References to "Canada" and "Canadians" before this date should be assumed to mean the British colonial territory and British colonial subjects, respectively.

The names of forts in Upper Canada and Michigan Territory can also be vexing. This volume uses the original name Fort Amherstburg for the British garrison opposite Bois Blanc Island at the mouth of the Detroit River, although it is known today as Fort Malden. Founded in 1796, the fort was known officially as

Amherstburg and the surrounding township as Malden. Following the Battle of Lake Erie in September 1813, the Americans occupied the fort until the end of the war. They generally referred to the garrison as "Fort Malden," and the name stuck. Meanwhile, the community that grew up next to the fort became known as Amherstburg, effectively reversing the original names for the fort and town.

The fort at Detroit during the War of 1812 was originally built by the British and named Fort Lernoult, after the officer who supervised its construction. The Americans officially changed the name to Fort Detroit in 1805. After they reclaimed Detroit in September 1813, the Americans renamed the installation Fort Shelby in honor of Kentucky Governor Isaac Shelby, who had contributed men for the operation. The fort, which was located at the current intersection of Fort and Shelby streets in downtown Detroit, should not be confused with Fort Wayne, which was built southwest of the earlier fort in 1845. Finally, this volume uses the official name Fort Mackinac to describe the garrison on Mackinac Island in the Straits of Mackinac, which connect lakes Huron and Michigan and divide Michigan's upper and lower peninsulas. Founded by the British in 1781, Fort Mackinac often was called "Michilimackinac," even after the Americans assumed control in 1796. Michilimackinac was the name of the earlier mainland French fort and trading post (today Mackinaw City, Michigan).

Acknowledgments

By definition, a community history project depends on a community of people to make it happen. We have been fortunate in this project to have support from a wide range of community partners. *Border Crossings* started as a group of graduate and undergraduate students at Wayne State University working in archives under Professor Denver Brunsman in the summer of 2011. It blossomed into a graduate seminar that fall, became a mixed graduate-undergraduate class in the spring of 2012, and turned into a public symposium at the Detroit Historical Museum in late 2012. All the while, the students worked closely with Joel Stone and the superb staff at the Detroit Historical Society and Douglas D. Fisher, an expert on the War of 1812 and a managing editor at Crain Communications Inc. in Detroit.

The editors thank all the individuals and groups who contributed their time and resources to make this volume possible. Community*Engagement*@Wayne, a program of the Irvin D. Reid Honors College at Wayne State University, provided generous seed money. Jerry Herron, dean of the college, has been a champion of the project from the start. Elizabeth Barton, the past director of Community*Engagement*, and Monita Mungo, its current director, deserve credit for sponsoring this innovative form of service-learning. At the Detroit Historical Society, we are most grateful for the support of the Society's Board of Trustees and its president, Thomas C. Buhl. Several departments and staff members made this collaboration between an academic institution and a public history organization so successful. We thank, in particular, the Society's executive director, Robert A. Bury; chief operating officer, Michelle Wooddell; as well as Peter Poulos, Tobi Voigt, Tracy Irwin, Alease Johnson, Bill Bryan and, especially, Rebecca McDonald, manager of programs. We also gratefully acknowledge Grace Bliss Smith for a generous contribution on behalf of her two organizations, the Louisa St. Clair Chapter of the Daughters of the American Revolution and the Michigan State Society of the United States Daughters of 1812. Robert Olender, Scott Cortese, and the family of student Joshua Zimberg also provided thoughtful financial assistance for the project.

Professor Brunsman accepted a position at The George Washington University near the completion of *Border Crossings*. He thanks his former colleagues at Wayne State University, particularly Marc Kruman, chairman of the History Department, for continuing to support the project. Professor Brunsman also appreciates the enthusiasm shown by his new colleagues at George Washington. The Eisenberg Institute for Historical Studies at the University of Michigan in Ann Arbor hosted him as a visiting scholar and provided exceptional office support during much of the project.

Numerous authorities on the War of 1812 have contributed in different ways. Alan Taylor, the preeminent scholar in the field, generously accepted an invitation to write the engaging Foreword to the book and to provide the keynote address at the symposium. Michigan's War of 1812 Bicentennial Commission and its secretary, Jim McConnell, have been tireless in promoting commemoration efforts in the state, including this project. Commission members Brian Leigh Dunnigan of the University of Michigan and Dennis Moore, public affairs officer of the Canadian consulate in Detroit, have cheerfully provided further assistance. Larry L. Nelson, editor of *Northwest Ohio Quarterly*, has been generous in sharing his expertise of the Great Lakes region.

Additional help came from numerous places. Under the leadership of Jane Hoehner, Wayne State University Press has partnered with the Detroit Historical Society in distributing the book. Heather B. Wendt and Margaret F. Booras of Uproar Communications have overseen the book's elegant typesetting and design. Dr. Gerald Dreslinski's generous scholarship fund in early American history at Wayne State University has advanced research by several of the volume's authors. Librarians, archivists, and curators across Michigan and Ontario were extremely helpful, especially those at the Burton Historical Collection of the Detroit Public Library; Purdy/Kresge Library at Wayne State University; Elmwood Cemetery, Detroit; St. Clair Shores Public Library; William L. Clements Library and Bentley Historical Library at the University of Michigan, Ann Arbor; Archives of Michigan, Lansing; Windsor's Community Museum; Leddy Library at the University of Windsor; North American Black Historical Museum, Amherstburg; and John Marsh Historical Collection, Amherstburg. Special thanks to John MacLeod and the Fort Malden National Historic Site of Canada for graciously hosting us and aiding our research. We also offer sincere appreciation to the Very Rev. Philip M. Dinwiddie and the staff of St. James Episcopal Church, Grosse Ile, Michigan. The Circa 1890 Saloon in Detroit and Café Ambrosia in Ann Arbor provided nourishment and good cheer for marathon editorial sessions.

Several of Professor Brunsman's students provided valuable research that added to the overall success of the project: Len Adams, Jonathan Colo, Patrick Deng, Michael Franco, Adam Geffen, Steve Goudreau, Eric Haddon, Matthew Kastely, Jason Masopust, Jim McCoy, Paul Mengel, Larry Rosenberg, Tracy Smith, Steve Steinhardt, Amy Weiss, and Devon Wilbur. Justin Wargo served as the editorial assistant, spending numerous hours helping the editors and his fellow students with sources. As our chief "border crosser," Justin also acted as our liaison to research depositories in Canada.

Finally, the editors thank their families for their love and understanding when the concerns of 1812 took us away from the pressing matters of 2012.

Foreword

Alan Taylor

On the eve of the War of 1812, the two sides of the Detroit River presented a particular combination of differences and similarities along the boundary between the American territory of Michigan on the west and the British colony of Upper Canada on the east. That border derived from the 1783 peace treaty that concluded the War of the American Revolution, which spawned a new republic while preserving Canada within the British Empire. The border became effective thirteen years later when the British belatedly evacuated their fort at Detroit on the northern (American) side of the river. Thereafter, the boundary divided the closely related Francophone and Catholic peoples, who had far more in common with each other than with the British and American officials sent to govern them by the rival regimes. A mix of traders, artisans, and farmers, the inhabitants derived from French colonists of the early eighteenth-century. Some had intermarried and many traded with the native peoples, who still comprised a majority in the region.

Needing those natives as military allies and trading partners, the British officials treated the Indians with greater diplomatic respect and more generous presents than did the American officials on the north bank. Indeed, the Americans conducted native diplomacy with a grudging, bad grace that reflected a determination eventually to dispossess and subordinate the Indians in a new domain of settlements created by newcomers:

Protestant farmers from the United States. And those American officials distrusted most of the inhabitants as allegedly corrupted by their Catholic faith and their Indian connections. Led by the territorial governor, William Hull, the Americans longed to break the British alliance with native peoples which reached across the border to promote resistance to the expansion of the American settlements. In sum, the two halves of the region combined similar inhabitants (Francophones and natives) with starkly dissimilar political regimes (American republic and a British colony) pursuing radically different relations with the natives.

The British alliance with native peoples contributed to the American decision to declare war in June 1812. That animus toward the British-native alliance also led the James Madison administration to give priority to the Detroit River region in the first campaign of the war. Sound strategy called instead for attacking Montreal, but politics trumped military considerations in this highly political war. Indeed, the influential politicians of Ohio and Kentucky demanded an aggressive advance into Upper Canada via the Detroit River as the best means to break up the British alliance that might otherwise unleash Indian raids on the American settlements. More ambitious than realistic, Governor Hull also pitched an invasion under his leadership as the best means to win the war quickly and most cheaply. Instead, he bungled the invasion and reaped a British counterattack that culminated in his abject surrender of Detroit in August 1812. Led primarily by Tecumseh, native warriors proved critical to the victory by intimidating Hull into a quick surrender. Making the most of their military importance, the natives solicited a British promise to retain Michigan as a native buffer zone, rather than return the conquest to the Americans in an eventual peace treaty. In the meantime, the native warriors plundered many of the inhabitants, particularly the minority who came from the United States. Instead of breaking up the British-Indian partnership, Hull's attack had bolstered that alliance at the expense of the

American vision of a settled land that marginalized the natives.

It took another year of fighting and a naval victory on Lake Erie for the Americans to recover Michigan Territory from the British and their Indian allies. In October 1813, William Henry Harrison's American army occupied both sides of the Detroit River. Now the shoe was on the other foot, as the American military mistreated the Francophone inhabitants of the British side, arresting some leaders and compelling all to sell their produce at a loss to the occupiers. Dropping the pose of liberators, the American troops treated the Canadians as an enemy. Indeed, the war ended just in time to preempt an American plan to burn out all of the settlements on the Canadian side of the river in order to discourage the British from attempting another attack on Detroit.

As a consequence of first the British-Indian conquest of Michigan Territory and then the subsequent American occupation of western Upper Canada, the War of 1812 gave clearer definition to the previously porous border. After the war, most of the people in Michigan, Francophones as well as Anglophones, felt more alienated from the British and the Indians. Defining themselves against their wartime enemy, the Michigan people became Americans. The same process played out on the Upper Canadian side of the border, where the people felt stronger ties to other Canadians, who shared their wartime resentment of the Americans. On both sides of the border, differences came to outweigh similarities during the War of 1812. But both sides also learned an important lesson from the conflict: that conquering and retaining the other would cost too much in blood and treasure. Whatever their new differences, majorities on both sides wanted to keep the peace with one another, which was the very best outcome of an otherwise tragic war.

In this collection of essays, students from Wayne State University explore the diverse aspects of war and peace in the Detroit River region. Under the adept leadership of Professor Denver Brunsman, they have illuminated the kaleidoscopic array of peoples derived from Europe, Africa, and North America who lived and fought in this region. Readers will learn about fires, banks, officials, natives, militias, wives, sailors, outlaws, diplomats, and historians. The essays deftly reveal the mix of folly and courage and of persistence and adaptation that characterized a border region at war.

Alan Taylor
Professor of History at the University of California at Davis and author of *The Civil War of 1812: American Citizens, British Subjects, Irish Rebels, & Indian Allies*

Introduction

Denver Brunsman

This volume is the product of a year-long collaboration between the Detroit Historical Society and Wayne State University to commemorate the bicentennial of the War of 1812 in the Detroit River region. The project builds on the success of a similar community history project between the two institutions in 2009 that resulted in the book *Revolutionary Detroit: Portraits in Political and Cultural Change, 1760-1805.* My graduate and undergraduate students have again devoted themselves to educating the public about the area's early history as a form of service-learning. Thanks to Detroit's centrality in the War of 1812 and the current bicentennial, however, they have not faced as steep a learning curve for this project. National news coverage of the bicentennial has largely focused on the American public's apathy for the commemoration, compared to the avid interest of the Canadian people. The level of engagement in southwestern Ontario has matched or exceeded that in the rest of Canada, but attention has been equally high in Michigan. The state has a War of 1812 Bicentennial Commission dedicated to commemoration efforts that has sponsored or helped to publicize lectures, symposia, essay contests, historical markers, battle reenactments, and a documentary film. In addition, a National Battlefield Park has been dedicated at the River Raisin, and replica "tall ships" from the war have navigated the Great Lakes and anchored in the Detroit River.[1]

The impressive list of activities begs the question: How is this project different? Whereas most bicentennial commemoration efforts have a particular national emphasis, either American or Canadian, this volume is transnational in focus. The international boundary running down the middle of the Detroit River was the fundamental reason for the region's importance during the War of 1812. This book's title, *Border Crossings: The Detroit River Region in the War of 1812*, underscores our attention to the shifting control, divided loyalties, and emerging identities on both sides of the river border. The goal throughout is not to rehash familiar events from the war – General William Hull's surrender of Michigan Territory, the battles at the River Raisin, the Battle of Lake Erie, and the Battle of the Thames – but to recapture, as much as possible, the lived experience of the border for regular people in the era. In so doing, we aim to highlight extraordinary everyday experiences from the period, while also providing new perspectives on more famous people and events. The student essayists featured in the volume have themselves become intrepid "border crossers" to tell these stories by traveling to archives and libraries in Canada and the United States. Our community partners and my talented co-editors, Joel Stone, senior curator at the Detroit Historical Society, and Douglas D. Fisher, historian and a managing editor at Crain Communications Inc., have helped to ensure that the students' findings are presented in a professional manner.[2]

The book is divided into three parts, "Frontiers," "War," and "Legacies," which together trace border relations from peace to conflict to reconciliation. The Canadian historian R. Alan Douglas once observed that "the international boundary running invisibly through the Detroit River community is invoked by the residents of the two shores when it is convenient to do so – but otherwise it is only a line in the water."[3] In its first generation, the boundary separating British Canada from the United States along the Detroit was indeed no more than "a line in the water." The border was created by the Treaty of Paris signed at the end of the American Revolutionary War (1775-83). But the line was ignored from the start in the Canadian-American borderlands by residents and the British administration, which continued to occupy Detroit and other posts in the American Northwest. The British cited the U.S. government's failure to compensate loyalists for their losses in the Revolution as the official reason for staying. Local inhabitants did not complain. At the time, Detroit covered both the north and south sides of the river, which acted more as a highway than as a barrier. Native Americans constituted a majority of the population in the region, with particularly dense concentrations of Wyandots, Obijwas, Odawas, and Potawatomis. French *habitants* and their descendants from the first colonial regime in the region remained the most numerous European group. A British military, merchant, and administrative elite governed on both sides of the river. A small African population, both enslaved and free, and other European traders contributed to the mix. The one constituency not represented in early American Detroit was American citizens.[4]

That changed in July 1796, when the British at last evacuated Detroit and other American possessions in the Northwest in accordance with Jay's Treaty of 1794. For the first time, the Stars and Stripes flew above the fort at Detroit. The British moved their military presence and Indian Department across and downriver in founding Fort Amherstburg, opposite Bois Blanc Island at the mouth of the Detroit River. The community directly opposite Detroit on the south shore of the river became known as Sandwich (today Windsor, Ontario).[5]

Over the next several years, the residents of the Detroit River region endured several additional administrative changes. The Constitutional Act of 1791 (also known as the Canada Act) created Upper Canada (today Ontario) and Lower Canada (today Quebec) out of the former province of Quebec. Within Upper Canada, Sandwich and Amherstburg belonged to Essex County in the Western District. By 1800, the district included Essex and Kent counties, which covered the territory between Lake St. Clair and Lake Erie roughly from present-day Windsor to London, Ontario. Meanwhile, on the American side of the border, Detroit initially belonged to Wayne County within the Northwest Territory. In 1802, the community was incorporated as a town governed by a local board of trustees. The following year, Detroit became part of Indiana Territory after Ohio was admitted as a state to the Union. In the fall of 1804, Detroiters petitioned the U.S. Congress to form their own territory. The effort was successful, and on July 1, 1805, Detroit became the capital of the newly created Michigan Territory. The original boundaries included the lower peninsula of present-day Michigan, the eastern third of the upper peninsula, and a northern strip of present-day Ohio, following a line due east from the southern tip of Lake Michigan.[6]

Into the early 1800s, regardless of their exact governmental jurisdiction, the residents of Detroit and Sandwich remained above all friends and neighbors. Commercial and personal relations transcended the international boundary, and many families kept residences and other property on both sides of the border. The communities were so closely linked that people described crossing the river as simply "going over," without further explanation.[7] It helped that the new American regime initially created a light imprint on the region. The non-Indian population of the Detroit area never exceeded the approximately 2,500 people at the time of the American takeover – and generally remained much lower – until years after the War of 1812.[8] Early attempts at enforcing national divisions were mostly counterproductive. Several prominent British merchants, including John Askin, moved across the river rather than pledge loyalty to the United States, but remained close to American family and friends. Some British subjects stayed, including Askin's close friend and brother-in-law Commodore Alexander Grant. Both Askin and Grant married into Detroit's French Barthe family. The onetime administrator of Upper Canada, Grant commanded the Royal Navy's fleet on the upper Great Lakes from his home in Grosse Pointe – on American soil – until his death in 1813. Grant's service and burial in Sandwich made evident that his regional identity coexisted easily with his national loyalty.[9]

The essays in Part One, "Frontiers," provide vivid portraits of the Detroit River region in the years between the formation of Michigan Territory in 1805 and the outbreak of war in 1812. The dominant concern in Detroit during the period was recovering from the devastating fire that consumed the town on June 11, 1805. The town's rebuilding effort is the topic of the first essay in the volume by Keith A. Killoran. The situation was greatly complicated by the timing of the blaze, exactly three weeks before the arrival of the territory's first governor, William Hull. As outlined in the Northwest Ordinance of 1787, Hull was to govern the territory with the assistance of three judges and a secretary. The most influential of the judges was Augustus B. Woodward, who often clashed with Hull over decisions large and small. Killoran argues that, contrary to common perception, Woodward deserves only limited credit for the rebuilding of Detroit. However visionary, the judge's plan for a new frontier metropolis was too complicated to execute in the existing environment. Instead, an ad hoc process involving aggressive action by local residents, assistance from the new territorial leadership, and approval by Congress began to remake Detroit in an American image.

John Paris's essay on the fraudulent Detroit Bank shows that inhabitants of the town had concerns other than recovering from the fire. The region's trade, particularly in furs, suffered from an acute lack of currency. Hence, residents and leaders alike supported the establishment of the Detroit Bank in the fall of 1806. The brainchild of Boston financier Andrew Dexter Jr., the bank was sold as a way to pump currency into the fledgling economy of Michigan Territory. In reality, the institution printed notes that benefited Dexter and his investors, who could sell them at a discount at their eastern exchange houses. Among those taken in by the scheme was Elijah Brush, a rare misstep for one of the most prominent lawyers in early American Detroit. In her essay, Sharon Tevis Finch presents Brush as a case study in how the border operated before the war. He lived a particularly transnational life by marrying into the Askin family and conducting his father-in-law's business on the American side of the Detroit River after the family moved to Sandwich in 1802. Brush's life also demonstrates the tragedy of the hardening of the border and national differences during the War of 1812. After the British occupied Detroit in August 1812, he was exiled. Brush returned later that fall, only to be exiled again. He died from an epidemic disease after returning home a second time in the fall of 1813.

For Brush and other early leaders of Detroit, much of the town's official business was transacted in taverns. Kristen Harrell likens taverns to a "town hall" because of their popularity with frontier elites, who had few other options for public meeting places. Tavern owners, such as James Donaldson, ran establishments on both sides of the river, and patrons "went over" frequently to their favorite spots to imbibe, socialize, and conduct business.

An issue of particular concern for leaders in Michigan Territory and Upper Canada was managing relationships with the region's Indian groups. Steve Lyskawa looks closely at Governor Hull's diplomacy with natives in the years preceding the War of 1812. The governor faced a losing proposition by being the local representative of a national government that cynically took Indian lands in treaties and then often failed to follow through on even the meager compensation promised in the agreements. In the Treaty of Detroit in November 1807, the Odawas, Ojibwas, Wyandots, and Potawatomis ceded a huge swath of land, the southeastern quarter of Michigan Territory, in exchange for goods and annuities. It is no wonder, according to Lyskawa, that most of the region's Indians sided with the more generous British in the War of 1812.

Charlie Keller's essay on Detroit's first black militia closes Part One. The militia, for which records are scant, was founded by Hull in response to the *Chesapeake-Leopard* Affair of June 1807. Off the coast of Virginia, the HMS *Leopard* fired a broadside into the USS *Chesapeake* after it refused to surrender British deserters; the action killed three American sailors and injured eighteen others (one of whom died soon thereafter). The incident nearly caused war between Britain and the United States. Locally, it demonstrated how quickly the normally peaceful border separating Michigan Territory and Upper Canada could become militarized. For Hull, the benefits of a black militia were twofold: It contributed manpower necessary for Detroit's fortifications, while also irritating Canadian slave owners to no end. The laws concerning slavery in the region were confusing and contradictory. Although provisions in both the Northwest Territory and Upper Canada banned new cases of slavery, existing cases were legally protected. The discrepancy allowed enslaved Africans to attain freedom by crossing either side of the border. The runaways and other members of Detroit's black militia never fought together, as the unit was disbanded before the War of 1812. Regardless, the militia's brief existence demonstrated that of all the different uses and meanings attached to the international boundary, the most powerful was as a pathway to freedom.

Part Two, "War," details the War of 1812 in the Detroit River region from an array of perspectives. Entire books have been devoted to debating the causes of the war. In truth, there were many. The conflict served as the American theater of the larger French Revolutionary and Napoleonic Wars (1793-1815) between Britain and France. As a neutral, the U.S. was caught between the two more powerful European nations, but suffered especially from ongoing depredations at sea by the British Royal Navy. The navy seized American ships to prevent them from trading with Napoleonic Europe and impressed (or forced into service) American seamen suspected of being British deserters.

The British alliance with Indian groups on the North American frontier, including the Detroit River region, further incensed the administration of President James Madison, members of Congress, and ordinary citizens. War came to the frontier much earlier than to the eastern seaboard. In November 1811, Indiana territorial Governor William Henry Harrison led an American force to victory against a pan-Indian alliance established by the Shawnee warrior Tecumseh and his brother Tenskwatawa (known as "the Prophet"). The Battle of Tippecanoe, as it became known, took place at Prophetstown, near the confluence of the Tippecanoe and Wabash rivers (today near Lafayette, Indiana). The American triumph proved temporary as Tecumseh reassembled his alliance and forged stronger ties to the British Indian Department at Fort Amherstburg. On June 18, 1812, Congress responded to the long-simmering tensions at sea and on the frontier by declaring war against Britain.[10]

The Detroit River region figured prominently in the Madison administration's war plans. Britain's Canadian provinces provided the most convenient way for the Americans to strike at the British Empire. Although some politicians no doubt wanted to take Canada as a prize, most scholars agree that the U.S. sought to use the colonial territory as leverage to force concessions on impressment and other grievances.[11] In the opening months of the war, the Americans planned a three-pronged attack on Canada: at the Detroit River, Niagara River, and Lake Champlain. All three failed miserably. Hull's experience as a Revolutionary War officer won him the command of the Army of the Northwest and the task of leading the first invasion. General Hull's campaign started in Ohio, where he took command of three militia regiments and the 4th U.S. Infantry and proceeded to march to Detroit. On July 1, 1812, still not aware of the war declaration, Hull put sick men and baggage aboard the schooner *Cuyahoga* at the foot of the Maumee River, to be transported across Lake Erie to Detroit. The next day, news of the war declaration finally reached Hull's army, but not soon enough to stop the *Cuyahoga*. The British command at Fort Amherstburg learned about the war a day earlier and easily captured the vessel as it neared the fort on July 2. Among the captured belongings was sensitive information outlining Hull's plans for attacking Upper Canada.[12]

The setback did not stop Hull from invading. On July 12, his forces faced minimal resistance in crossing the border and occupying Sandwich. The initial success was followed by a drumbeat of disturbing news. Skirmishes at the Canard River between Sandwich and Amherstburg made clear that the fort would not fall without a fight. In early August, Hull learned that on July 17, the British had captured Fort Mackinac, on Mackinac Island between lakes Huron and Michigan. The loss instantly raised fears of Indians in northern Michigan Territory traveling south to attack Detroit. On August 5, a more immediate Indian threat came to light as dozens of native warriors ambushed one of Hull's detachments in the Battle of Brownstown, south of Fort Detroit. Days later, Hull received word that a combined British-Indian force would soon reinforce Fort Amherstburg.

The cumulative weight of the news convinced the general to retreat to Detroit. General Isaac Brock, the British commander in Upper Canada, led the reinforcement of Amherstburg. Like the Americans, he saw control of the Detroit River region as key to success in the war. With Detroit and Mackinac, the British could protect all of Upper Canada as far east as Kingston, where the Saint Lawrence River flows out of Lake Ontario. Brock thus planned a quick invasion of Detroit. On August 16, 1812, after sustaining British cannon fire for a day and a half and fearing an attack by Indian warriors, Hull surrendered to Brock without a fight. "Detroit is ours, and with it the whole Michigan Territory," Brock reported triumphantly to Major Thomas Evans.[13] In the words of the historian Henry Adams, it was "the greatest loss of territory that ever before or since befell the United States."[14] As a result, Hull was court martialed, found guilty of cowardice and neglect of duty, and sentenced to death – an outcome prevented only by President Madison commuting the sentence based on the general's service in the Revolution. Debate continues to this day over whether Hull was indeed cowardly in surrendering or responsible for saving lives given the likely loss of civilians in an attack on Detroit by the British and their Indian allies.[15]

The first trio of essays in Part Two, by Justin Wargo, Kerri Jansen, and Daniel F. Harrison, each explore the fall of Detroit from a different viewpoint. Wargo uses the home of François Baby, a prominent British Canadian politician and militia officer of French descent, to explore the respective American and British invasions. Hull turned Baby's house into his headquarters during his three-week occupation of Sandwich. Soon after, Brock used the same grounds for his artillery assault on Fort Detroit. Although both generals damaged the property, Baby blamed the Americans and ended the war, like many residents of the Western District, bearing characteristics of an emerging Canadian identity. Jansen's essay depicts the travels on the Northwest frontier of Lydia Bacon, the New England wife of U.S. Army officer Josiah Bacon. Bacon accompanied her husband to the Battle of Tippecanoe, was aboard the *Cuyahoga* when it was captured by the British, and took shelter in Fort Detroit as cannons fired from the Baby home in Sandwich. Daniel F. Harrison looks at the American defeat by using a rare narrative from the Odawa oral tradition. The account describes the Odawa alliance with the British and events from the skirmishes at the Canard to the raising of the British Union Jack in Detroit. From the Odawa perspective, the victory belonged to them as much as it did the British.

The next three essays, by Timothy Marks, Carly Campbell, and Scott A. Jankowski, illuminate broader aspects of the war in the region. Marks traces the multiple ways that the war touched a single family, the Askins of Sandwich. The family's patriarch, John Askin, had four sons, three sons-in-law, and ten grandsons fight in the War of 1812. Askin kept close tabs on the Detroit, Mackinac, and Niagara fronts and received news of events as far away as the British Isles by corresponding with his sons and daughters. Campbell explores the heroism of women during the British occupation of Michigan Territory. With men often exiled, women such as Elizabeth Anderson of Frenchtown (today Monroe, Michigan) had to protect homesteads, especially against Indian raids. The low point of the occupation came in the aftermath of the battles at the River Raisin in January 1813. After the Americans failed to retake the Detroit area, Britain's native allies killed between thirty and sixty wounded prisoners – an event invoked by U.S. troops for the rest of the war in the battle cry, "Remember the Raisin!" Jankowski uses the River Raisin massacre, as it became known, as one of several examples of the treatment of casualties in the war. He shows that combatants on the frontier practiced rudimentary forms of medicine and ignored international protocol for the handling of prisoners. The result, evident in all three essays, was that the war took a heavy toll on the people of the Canadian-American borderlands.

The final essays in Part Two, by Meghan McGowan, Rebecca Russell, and Joshua Zimberg, uncover dimensions of the American reconquest of the Detroit River region between September 1813 and July 1815. McGowan profiles the Upper Canadian turned American Andrew Westbrook. Considered a traitor by some and a patriot by others, Westbrook was a border crosser *par excellence*. He used his intimate knowledge of the Western District to lead devastating raids on his former neighbors after the Americans recaptured Detroit in September 1813.

The American triumph in the Battle of Lake Erie that month made the retaking of the region possible. Russell shows that the victory, often attributed to the heroics of Master Commandant Oliver Hazard Perry, was equally due to the contributions of uncommon and unsung sailors in his fleet, including frontiersmen and African Americans. U.S. control of Lake Erie and the Detroit River led directly to the occupation of Fort Amherstburg, the subject of Zimberg's essay. The accomplishment, never matched in the Niagara region, was a high point of the war on the American side. The U.S. Army under General William Henry Harrison killed Tecumseh and defeated the retreating British and Indians at the Battle of the Thames (also known as the Battle of Moraviantown) in Upper Canada in early October 1813. Yet, as Zimberg shows, the ensuing American occupation of the Western District was anything but joyous. The army confronted food shortages, epidemic disease, hostility from Canadian civilians, and ongoing fears of a counterattack by the British and natives. In late December 1814, the Treaty of Ghent officially ended the war and returned relations between the U.S. and Britain to *status quo ante bellum* (the state before the war), but the Americans' uneasy occupation of Amherstburg persisted until July 1815.

Part Three, "Legacies," highlights several different outcomes of the war. On the American side, the most significant result was fully opening the trans-Appalachian West to white settlement following the defeat of Tecumseh's pan-Indian alliance. Tim Moran evaluates the growth of the Tecumseh legend in the nineteenth century, showing how a talented leader in life was transformed into a superhuman figure in death. All sides in the War of 1812, particularly the Americans, benefited from the outsized image of Tecumseh, whose death inflated the nation's standing and the reputations of battlefield participants, including a future president, Harrison, and vice president, Richard M. Johnson.

The return of peace to the Detroit River region is the subject of the next two essays by Merry Ellen Scofield and James M. Shuryan. In mid-February 1815, word of the Treaty of Ghent reached the area. Detroit's civic and military leaders soon began planning a celebration of the peace. The town's festivities, highlighted by a dinner and ball on March 29, differed in two important respects from similar celebrations in other towns: They were referred to as "pacification," not "peace," events, and former enemies were invited. Both exceptions reflected the peculiar nature of the conflict in the region. The war had been hard fought, and with Amherstburg still occupied by the Americans, pacification was a more appropriate term than peace. At the same time, the two warring sides had been formerly united for so long that it only seemed natural to invite residents of Sandwich. Shuryan's essay demonstrates that Detroit's leaders had reason to commemorate the peace cautiously. After the war, the British Royal Navy continued to stop and search American merchant vessels – an original cause of the War of 1812 – on the Great Lakes and connecting waterways, particularly at the mouth of the Detroit River off of Fort Amherstburg. Complaints by Michigan territorial Governor Lewis Cass helped to expedite diplomatic talks between the U.S. and Britain about disarming their navies on the lakes. The negotiations resulted in the Rush-Bagot Agreement of 1817, ratified the following year by the U.S. Senate as the Rush-Bagot Treaty. The treaty, still active in modified form with Canada today, severely limited the number of armed vessels that the U.S. and Britain could maintain on the Great Lakes.

The final trio of essays in the volume, by Kaitlin Cooper, Matthew R. Thick, and Charles Wilson Goode, explore the growth of Detroit and Michigan Territory in the shadow of the War of 1812. In August 1817, James Monroe became the first president to visit the territory as part of a national goodwill tour following his election. As Cooper argues, Monroe's visit allowed Detroit's leaders to imagine Michigan, which had been maligned even before Hull's surrender, as an eventual equal member of the Union. In 1818, the territory took the next step in this goal by having its population recognized as meeting the 5,000 free male inhabitants necessary to send a nonvoting delegate to Congress. John R. Williams, the subject of Thick's essay, could have used this political representation earlier. After the British occupied Detroit in August 1812, Williams moved his family and trading business to Albany, New York, and lost two large trunks of belongings in the process. Williams spent years lobbying the U.S. government for compensation, but to little avail. The failure did not keep him from later success, however, as he rebuilt his business and filled numerous important public positions, including as Detroit's first mayor under the city's amended charter of 1824.

Williams's recovery from his personal losses represented a micro version of a larger process in Michigan Territory after the war. Goode's essay explores how the territory shed its dismal reputation for its supposedly poor soils, marauding Indians, British interference, and capitulation in the war. He finds the answer in an often overlooked treatise written by the influential geographer William Darby, who toured Michigan Territory in 1818. Darby praised the territory's agricultural potential and dispelled myths about its social ills by extolling the refinement of the border region. The timing of his treatise could not have been better. In 1818, the *Walk-in-the-Water* became the first steamship to reach Detroit, the U.S. government opened a land office in the town, and the Erie Canal stretching from the Hudson River to Lake Erie had begun construction. By 1825, the completion of the canal turned the already steady stream of migrants to Michigan Territory into a flood. Twelve years later, Michigan at last became a state long after surpassing the population of 60,000 free residents (male and female) necessary to join the Union.

Although the growth of Windsor (as Sandwich became known in the mid-nineteenth century) did not keep pace with Detroit, it shared in the region's success while continuing to forge its own political identity. In December 1838, the community rallied against an invasion by more than one hundred Americans and British Canadians who crossed the Detroit River in a failed attempt to bring republican government to Upper Canada. The invaders burned several structures before many were detained on the property of none other than François Baby. Nearly 70, Baby had last endured a republican incursion at his home a quarter-century earlier. The Battle of Windsor, part of the Patriot War of 1837-38, was also related to the unsuccessful Rebellions of 1837-38 against oligarchic government in the Upper and Lower Canadian provinces. The rebellions were the last major disturbances before Canada became a self-governing country within the British Empire in 1867. Canadians today hail the War of 1812 for setting in motion the events that resulted in Canada's independence.[16]

As the following essays attest, the war's bicentennial also offers the opportunity to celebrate the transnational ties that connect the Detroit River region. The War of 1812 proved an aberration in the long history of peaceful cooperation in the Canadian-American borderlands, yet one that demands remembering. John Askin called the conflict "this destructive war" for a reason: It nearly ruined the communities on both sides of the river. Recalling this destruction helps to negate the complacency that naturally comes from sharing the world's longest undefended border for generations. Along that border, the Detroit-Windsor crossing is the busiest in North America in terms of trade volume. In fact, the amount of traffic is so heavy that the two sides are currently collaborating on a third crossing to relieve the Ambassador Bridge and Detroit-Windsor Tunnel. The thriving partnership is a legacy of the reconciliation that followed the War of 1812. This volume is dedicated to another two hundred years and more of peaceful border crossings.[17]

NOTES

1 For national coverage of the bicentennial, see Thomas Kaplan, "For War of 1812 Bicentennial, Indifference from Albany," *New York Times*, November 25, 2011; James M. Lundberg, "Happy 200th Birthday, War of 1812!," *Slate*, May 25, 2012; Rick Hampson, "War of 1812 Bicentennial: USA Shrugs as Canada Goes All Out," *USA Today*, June 14, 2012; and Alistair MacDonald, "Along the U.S.-Canadian Border, Skirmishes Persist over the War of 1812," *Wall Street Journal*, June 18, 2012. For efforts in Michigan, see the bimonthly issues in 2012 of *Michigan History*; quarterly issues in 2012 of *Michigan's Habitant Heritage: Journal of the French-Canadian Heritage Society of Michigan*; Matt Helms, "Downriver War of 1812 Trail Gets Its Due," *Detroit Free Press*, April 11, 2011; Zlati Meyer, "Navy Ships Sail in for Gala," *Detroit Free Press*, July 26, 2012; Tony Horwitz, "War of 1812: Remember the Raisin!," *Smithsonian* (June 2012): 28-35; and War of 1812 Bicentennial Commission, Department of Natural Resources, State of Michigan, www.michigan.gov/war1812 (accessed September 2, 2012).

2 This volume builds on earlier transnational approaches to the region, including Alan Taylor, *The Civil War of 1812: American Citizens, British Subjects, Irish Rebels, & Indian Allies* (New York: Knopf, 2010); David C. Skaggs and Larry L. Nelson, eds., *The Sixty Years' War for the Great Lakes, 1754-1814* (East Lansing: Michigan State University Press, 2001); John J. Bukowczyk et al., *Permeable Border: The Great Lakes Basin as Transnational Region, 1650-1990* (Pittsburgh: University of Pittsburgh Press, 2005); Gregory Wigmore, "Before the Railroad: From Slavery to Freedom in the Canadian-American Borderland," *Journal of American History* 98 (2011): 437-54; R. Alan Douglas, *Uppermost Canada: The Western District and the Detroit Frontier, 1800-1850* (Detroit: Wayne State University Press, 2001); Dennis Carter-Edwards, "The War of 1812 along the Detroit Frontier: A Canadian Perspective," *Michigan Historical Review* 13 (1987): 25-50; Sandy Antal, *Invasions: Taking and Retaking Detroit and the Western District during the War of 1812 and Its Aftermath* (Windsor, ON: Essex County Historical Society, 2011); Albert B. Corey, *Canadian-American Relations along the Detroit River* (Detroit: Wayne State University Press, 1957); and the essays in Nora Faires, ed., "Emerging Borderlands," special issue of *Michigan Historical Review* 34 (2008): vii-117.

3 Douglas, vii.

4 Denver Brunsman and Joel Stone, eds. *Revolutionary Detroit: Portraits in Political and Cultural Change, 1760-1805* (Detroit: Detroit Historical Society, 2009); Philip P. Mason, *Detroit, Fort Lernoult, and the American Revolution* (Detroit: Wayne State University Press, 1964).

5 Amherstburg Bicentennial Book Committee, *Amherstburg, 1796-1996: The New Town on the Garrison Grounds* (Amherstburg, ON: Amherstburg Bicentennial Book Committee, 1996); Mark A. Mallia, "From Detroit to Fort Malden: The Transfer of Sovereignty and Subjects," in *Revolutionary Detroit*, 128-32.

6 Douglas, 5-10; Brian L. Dunnigan, *Frontier Metropolis: Picturing Early Detroit, 1701-1838* (Detroit: Wayne State University Press, 2001), 102-3; Reginald Horsman, *Frontier Detroit: 1760-1812* (Detroit: Michigan in Perspective Conference, 1964), 14-15; Frederick C. Bald, *Detroit's First American Decade, 1796-1805* (Ann Arbor:

University of Michigan Press, 1948), 207-49. For the evolution of Michigan Territory, including its changing boundaries, see Alec R. Gilpin, *The Territory of Michigan* (East Lansing: Michigan State University Press, 1970).

7   Variations of the phrase appear throughout John Askin's correspondence. For examples, see *Askin Papers*, 2:531-63, 570-71, 581, 600, 729, 769. I thank Sharon Tevis Finch for sharing these references.

8   Dunnigan, 102, 148; "The 1796 Census of Wayne County," in *Michigan Censuses, 1710-1830, under the French, British, and Americans*, ed. Donna Valley Russell (Detroit: Detroit Society for Genealogical Research, 1982), 59-74; "Census of Michigan Territory, 1811," in *MPHC*, 36:235; "Official Census of the City from 1810 to 1880," in *MPHC*, 5:536.

9   Arthur M. Woodford, *This Is Detroit, 1701-2001* (Detroit: Wayne State University Press, 2001), 36; *City of Detroit*, 1:242-53; Bald, 115-16, 197; Douglas, 21, 66.

10 For overviews of the different causes of the war, see Bradford Perkins, ed., *The Causes of the War of 1812: National Honor or National Interest?* (New York: Holt, Rinehart and Winston, 1963); Reginald Horsman, *The Causes of the War of 1812* (Philadelphia: University of Pennsylvania Press, 1962); and Donald R. Hickey, *Don't Give Up the Ship! Myths of the War of 1812* (Urbana: University of Illinois Press, 2006), 12-47.

11 J.C.A. Stagg, *Mr. Madison's War: Politics, Diplomacy, and Warfare in the Early American Republic* (Princeton: Princeton University Press, 1983), 7; Hickey, 36-39.

12 My discussion of the war in the Detroit area in this and following paragraphs is informed by the excellent literature on the subject, including Anthony J. Yanik, *The Fall and Recapture of Detroit in the War of 1812: In Defense of William Hull* (Detroit: Wayne State University Press, 2011); Sandy Antal, *A Wampum Denied: Procter's War of 1812* (Ottawa: Carleton University Press, 1997); Philip P. Mason, ed., *After Tippecanoe: Some Aspects of the War of 1812* (1963; reprint, East Lansing: Michigan State University Press, 2011); Alec R. Gilpin, *The War of 1812 in the Old Northwest* (East Lansing: Michigan State University Press, 1958); Ralph Naveaux, *Invaded on All Sides: The Story of Michigan's Greatest Battlefield Scene of the Engagements at Frenchtown and the River Raisin in the War of 1812* (Marceline, MO: Walsworth, 2008); and the essays in "The War of 1812," special issue of *Michigan Historical Review* 38 (2012): 1-154.

13 Isaac Brock to Thomas Evans, August 17, 1812, in *The Documentary History of the Campaign upon the Niagara Frontier*, ed. E.A. Cruikshank, 9 vols. (Welland, ON: Tribune Office, 1896-1907), 3:186.

14 Henry Adams, *History of the United States during the Administrations of James Madison* (New York: Library of America, 1986), 528. I thank my student Paul Mengel for this reference.

15 For the controversy surrounding Hull's actions and trial, see Yanik.

16 Douglas, 157-69.

17 John Askin to his children, November 12, 1813, in *Askin Papers*, 2:773.

Part One:

Frontiers

A View of Detroit and the Straits, taken from Huron Church June 22nd. 1804.
Painting by Edward Walsh, surgeon with the 49th British Regiment of Foot.
Lithograph of watercolor on paper. Detroit Historical Society Collection.

Burned! The Fire of 1805 and Rebuilding of Detroit
Keith A. Killoran

On January 11, 1805, President Thomas Jefferson approved a congressional act that divided Indiana Territory in two, giving Michigan its own territorial status as of June 30. On June 11, 1805, while the newly appointed Michigan territorial governor, William Hull, was still en route with his family, Detroit burned to the ground in a fire whose origins are lost to history. The most commonly accepted story is that the fire was accidentally started by a town baker named John Harvey or his assistant, Peter Chartrand, by carelessly emptying out a tobacco pipe. Whatever the origin, most of the town burned, leaving a large segment of the population essentially homeless. To make matters worse, the first territorial government in the new capital of Michigan would be seated in nineteen days.[1]

Although catastrophic to Detroit's infrastructure, the fire took no lives and caused few injuries. From the destruction came an opportunity: Detroit could reinvent its physical layout from the previous cramped conditions of a village huddled along a river into something much grander. Yet, by as late as 1825, ambitious plans for expanding the town were not realized, and the settlement was still limited to the 2,500 or so feet of riverfront property between the Cass and Brush family farms. What happened? This was certainly not the vision of the territorial administration, specifically Judge Augustus B. Woodward, who has traditionally been credited with conceptualizing what Detroit would become.

In reality, Woodward's vision was premature and not practical for the town. His stubborn adherence to his grand blueprint actually delayed the rebuilding. Detroit recovered from the fire, but not through strict adherence to Woodward's or anyone else's lofty plan. Instead, a new Detroit emerged through an ad hoc process of conflict, compromise, and innovation that transformed the European and Native American fur-trade outpost into an American city.

Prior to the fire, Detroit was still a small frontier town whose location within the Great Lakes made it a key point in the northwestern fur trade. The town was situated on the north bank of the Detroit River across from the British Canadian town of Sandwich. It consisted of a collection of about three hundred primitive houses and buildings, including "sheds, stores, outhouses, barns, and sties," made mostly of wood and spaced closely together on approximately three acres of land.[2] Detroit followed a common grid pattern of east-west main streets that were extremely narrow: as little as ten feet wide in places. A wooden stockade surrounded the settlement with a west gate downriver and a gate to the east named after the Indian warrior Pontiac, who unsuccessfully laid siege to the town in 1763. The north-south walls of the stockade extended to the base of the fort to the north. Separated from the town by a commons and garden area, Fort Detroit (formerly Fort Lernoult under the British) was built to the rear of the town and housed a couple of hundred soldiers mostly performing "caretaking" tasks.[3]

Outside of the town was a procession of narrow farms owned mostly by French farmers whose families had occupied the properties for several generations after receiving land grants from the French crown. Some of these farms were also occupied by farmers under land grants issued by the British after taking over in 1760 and through various Indian treaties. Although these land titles had never been in dispute before, the fire brought about a new sense of urgency for the American government to validate

Detroit's patchwork of land claims.

The fire posed the first and one of the most lasting challenges to Michigan's unique territorial governing structure of a governor and judges. Nearly three weeks passed between the fire and the arrival of Governor William Hull and Woodward. Woodward arrived first, on June 30, 1805, making him the de facto authority figure. But when he realized the complexity of the situation, he convinced the townspeople to wait for Hull. The governor arrived the next day and quickly recognized how crowded the original settlement had been along the river. The most obvious way to expand would require encroaching on the commons between the fort to the north and the old town to the south. The only problem was that Secretary of War Henry Dearborn had different ideas. Dearborn sought to clear the area between the fort and river for defensive purposes and relocate the town away from the river, adjacent to the fort.[4]

Impatient, the displaced townspeople began rebuilding before the local or national government reached any decisions. Residents built lean-tos and other temporary shelters on the commons between the fort and the old town, found shelter up and down the river in barns or farmhouses, or left altogether. Those who wanted to rebuild immediately could not agree on the best way to begin. Some proposed building on their old sites, while others wanted more room and debated expanding onto the commons.[5]

Hull and Woodward agreed on little, but did come to a similar conclusion that the commons between the fort and old town had to be allocated, at least in part, in order to rebuild properly. In a report submitted to the United States Congress in October 1805, on the "unfortunate fate of the new Government," they made clear that the "folly of attempting to rebuild the town, in the original mode, was obvious to every mind; yet there existed no authority . . . to dispose of the adjacent ground."[6] Ultimately, Congress had the final say on all land allocations. Neither Hull nor Woodward had the authority initially to either authenticate existing land claims or officially grant new ones. It would not be until a congressional act in the spring of 1806 that land and titles could be officially recognized by the governor and judges of Michigan Territory.[7]

In the meantime, all parties involved did their best to muddle through. The town's proprietors and residents, outlying farmers, and military personnel all had conflicting goals. Prior to the fire, sixty-nine proprietors owned most of the buildings, not including military structures and Indian stores. A survey of the losses was taken on June 24, 1805, by a committee made up of Matthew Ernst, François Lasalle, and Charles Moran "at the request of a number of Proprietors." The survey listed dimensions and values, as well as estimated valuations of their square footage. No doubt that aside from having shelter, Detroit's merchants wanted to get their businesses running again as quickly as possible.[8]

By contrast, the fire did not reach Fort Detroit nor did it affect the dozens of predominantly French farms that existed for miles up and down the river from the charred town. Although rebuilding was certainly in the best interest of the countryside, expanding beyond the commons area would either mean allocating land in the wilderness beyond the fort or encroaching upon farmland. The neighboring farms, mostly in the French "ribbon" style, generally consisted of small waterfront homestead lots extending away from the river for various distances. Descendants of the original claimants often had no documentation to prove their claims. Land grant documents, when they did exist, were often dubious, contradictory, and overlapping.[9]

In short, the fire added confusion to an already confusing situation. The process of validating land claims in the Detroit River region began before the fire, in 1804; the land commissioners did not present their preliminary reports until December 1805. Without the authority to recognize claims, Hull and Woodward could only make promises. As Hull later explained to Secretary of State James Madison, "When I was with them [residents of Detroit] I gave them promises. It was all I could give them. They were satisfied. I cannot again repeat them. An honest and fair adjustment of their claims would have given more strength and security to the Country, than a thousand disciplined troops."[10] In lieu of such "security," Hull and Woodward made emergency provisions to see to the immediate needs of Detroit's residents. A new town was laid out with the express understanding that Congress would need to authenticate any claims that were doled out in the interim. The territorial government distributed lots to both original landowners and tenants; no money was due for a year since no legal titles could be given out immediately. The government also commissioned a survey to determine how much public land would be needed to append to the original town footprint.[11]

Detroit's leaders and residents all recognized that their ad hoc process of rebuilding could only go so far without sanction from the national government. In October 1805, therefore, Hull, Woodward, and Detroit's proprietors determined that the governor and chief justice would travel to Washington to explain the situation. The town needed a land act to allow for the settlement of private claims in question. Woodward brought a report addressed to Congress and President Jefferson that detailed the state of affairs and urged quick action on behalf of the territory. In essence, the report asked Congress to confirm the land titles that the governor and judges had tentatively approved.[12] Hull and Woodward spent the winter of 1805 and early spring in 1806 lobbying members of Congress. On April 21, 1806, Congress at last gave the Michigan territorial government free rein to "lay out a town, including the whole of the old town of Detroit, and ten thousand acres adjacent." The act also provided all persons over age 17 "not owning or professing allegiance to any foreign power," as of June 11, 1805 (the day of the fire), a grant of land where territorial authorities "shall judge most proper, a lot not exceeding the quantity of five thousand square feet."[13]

Back in Detroit, Woodward assumed the task of expanding on the simple survey that was presented in Washington and detailing a new plan for the town. Woodward had resided in Washington during its infancy and was deeply influenced by Charles L'Enfant's elegant design for the capital. L'Enfant's plan focused on public areas and circular parks, or "circuses," from which major thoroughfares radiated like the spokes of a wheel. Woodward likewise envisioned Detroit as a "new metropolis" that would rise from the ashes of the fire to become one of the great cities of the young republic. With the help of Abijah Hull, the governor's nephew, Woodward worked for a year and a half completing what would be known as the "Governor and Judges Plan," or more simply, the "Woodward Plan."[14]

A number of complications made Woodward's plan impractical from the start. Unlike L'Enfant, who worked with mostly open, uninhabited space, Woodward had to contend with Detroit's existing residents. To the judge's dismay, the townspeople did not share his vision for a sprawling new metropolis. "All the attachment of the inhabitants is to the old spot," Woodward lamented. "They value all the ground within the vicinity of the old town enormously rich, and all the rest at scarcely worth anything."[15] Woodward's plan was a tough sell to the displaced inhabitants of Detroit, who craved a return to normalcy with quick recognition of their land claims. In its simplest form, the plan consisted of a mesh of equilateral triangles, at four thousand feet per side, which could be repeated in any direction and expanded as needed. Where these triangles intersected, large circular plazas were envisioned with eight major avenues radiating from each. These plazas were to be the site of public buildings, such as schools, or large parks with ornate landscaping.

Woodward's blueprint for an expanding metropolis proved to be too ambitious and was mostly ignored. After returning from Washington, Hull and Woodward – and their respective factions – fought over the more basic question of how to proceed with approving lots. In a letter to Madison in November 1806, Hull expressed his frustration with the pace of land allocation: "The donees contended that it was the intention of Congress that they should have the most valuable lots, and all who had purchased lots from this Government, insisted on those lots being considered as donations. The Governor and Judges have now agreed on a system, which I believe will give general satisfaction. The storms seem to have abated, and I presume everything will be tranquil."[16]

The rancorous debate, to which Hull alluded, mostly defused when the territory's land board grouped Detroit's residents into multiple classes to determine the size of their donation lots. The classes reflected relative wealth (proprietor or not), family status (head of household or not), citizenship (U.S. citizen or British subject), and legal status (free or slave). Under the system, the primary losers were resident aliens, all British subjects, who were denied donation plots. Although French land owners outside town remained annoyed by the slow recognition of their land claims, the distribution of lots and the rebuilding of Detroit finally proceeded with relative calm.[17]

By late 1807, Detroiters completed most of the rebuilding from the devastating fire. The town remained concentrated on the riverfront, but increasingly filled the commons that had separated the fort from the main settlement. Woodward's plan, after being neglected, was officially abandoned in 1817. Traces of his design can still be seen in the heart of downtown Detroit, particularly in Campus Martius and Grand Circus Park and the major boulevards that radiate from them. Yet, in most cases, his ideas were out of touch for the times, particularly leaving the fort out of his plan. In March 1806, Woodward wrote to President Jefferson: "The Fort itself or the garrison in it are of no view of importance to the place, and will inevitably be abandoned by the government." Hull took the opposite view, which America's escalating tensions and eventual war with Britain proved correct.[18]

Ultimately, Detroit did not resemble the sprawling metropolis that Woodward imagined until the population boom spawned by the Erie Canal in the mid-1820s and 1830s. Until then, the rebuilding of Detroit after the great fire of 1805 was a collective, messy process among competing interests. Longtime inhabitants of the old town and landowners for miles up and down the river had much different visions of what the town should be than did eastern elites and military men. Woodward's vision for Detroit was particularly fantastical and impractical for the conditions under which it was proposed. The town's inhabitants needed homes and assurances of their land titles, not a European-inspired metropolis featuring the latest trends in city planning. Detroit did not rebuild as a result of a single plan, act of Congress, or foresight of a small group of men. Detroit rebuilt through a complicated but very American process in which local leaders and, especially, ordinary residents took matters into their own hands to do what was needed.

NOTES

1 For standard treatments of the fire, see *City of Detroit*, 1:304-9; Frederick C. Bald, *Detroit's First American Decade, 1796-1805* (Ann Arbor: University of Michigan Press, 1948), 235-42; George B. Catlin, *The Story of Detroit* (Detroit: The Detroit News, 1923), 115-19; Willis F. Dunbar and George S. May, *Michigan: A History of the Wolverine State* (Grand Rapids: Eerdman, 1980), 195-96; Silas Farmer, *The History of Detroit and Michigan: Or the Metropolis Illustrated* (Detroit: S. Farmer, 1884), 489-91.

2 Frank B. Woodford and Arthur M. Woodford, *All Our Yesterdays: A Brief History of Detroit* (Detroit: Wayne State University Press, 1969), 107.

3 John W. Reps, "Planning in the Wilderness: Detroit, 1805-1830," *Town Planning Review* 25 (1955): 240-50; Bald, 24; Farmer, 222-24. Estimates of the number of soldiers stationed at Fort Detroit before the War of 1812 vary widely; two hundred is the most commonly cited figure.

4 Frank B. Woodford, *Mr. Jefferson's Disciple: A Life of Justice Woodward* (East Lansing: Michigan State College Press, 1953), 7-8; Brian L. Dunnigan, *Frontier Metropolis: Picturing Early Detroit, 1701-1838* (Detroit: Wayne State University Press, 2001), 114, 116; Henry Dearborn to William Hull, July 23, 1805, in *The Territorial Papers of the United States*, ed. Clarence E. Carter and John P. Bloom,

27 vols. (Washington, DC: Department of State and National Archives and Records Service, 1934-69), 10:23-24.

5 Dunnigan, 114, 118; Dunbar and May, 137; Woodford, 7.

6 "Report of the Governor and Judges of Michigan Territory to Congress," October 10, 1805, in *MPHC*, 36:103-4.

7 "An Act to Provide for the Adjustment of Titles of Land in the Town of Detroit and Territory of Michigan, and for Other Purposes" (1806), in *Statutes at Large of the United States of America*, 17 vols. (Boston: Little, Brown, 1845-73), 2:398-99.

8 "List of Real Estate Owners and Values at the Time of the Detroit Fire in 1805," in *MPHC*, 36:114-15.

9 Woodford, 42.

10 William Hull to James Madison, April 30, 1806, in *MPHC*, 31:559.

11 "Report of the Governor and Judges of Michigan Territory to Congress," October 10, 1805, 36:103-11.

12 "Report of the Governor and Judges of Michigan Territory to Congress," October 10, 1805, 36:103-11.

13 "An Act to Provide for the Adjustment of Titles of Land in the Town of Detroit and Territory of Michigan, and for Other Purposes" (1806).

14 Woodford, 36-52, remains the most detailed discussion of the Woodward Plan. See also Dunnigan, 114-19; and Buford L. Pickens, *Early City Plans for Detroit: A Projected American Metropolis* (Detroit: Detroit Institute of Arts, 1943).

15 Woodward quoted in Woodford, 39.

16 William Hull to James Madison, November 13, 1806, in *MPHC*, 31:570.

17 For the donation of land plots, see "Allotment of Lands after the Detroit Fire of 1805," in *MPHC*, 31:574-83, 578 (quote); Mary Agnes Burton and Clarence M. Burton, eds., *Governor and Judges Journal: Proceedings of the Land Board of Detroit* (Detroit: Michigan Commission on Land Titles, 1915); and the essay in this volume by Charlie Keller. For the controversies concerning the French and resident aliens, see Woodford, 42, 47-50.

18 Woodward quoted in Woodford, 37.

Detroit Bank note
Engraving, 1806. Ink on Paper. Detroit Historical Society Collection.

Fraud on the Frontier: The Detroit Bank
John Paris

In March 1806, Michigan territorial Governor William Hull
returned home to Boston to attend to his affairs. During the visit,
old friends presented him with a petition requesting permission
to establish a bank of "discount and deposit" in Detroit. Hull
championed the project, which culminated with the establishment
of the Detroit Bank on September 19, 1806. By March 1807,
the United States Congress disallowed the bank as a complete
and obvious scam. Two months later, Hull acknowledged that
the bank had been a swindle. In the historian Frank Woodford's
estimation, the affair was possibly "the most serious error
committed" by Michigan's early territorial administration.[1]

According to the Boston petitioners, the bank was to finance
Detroit's fur industry, yet the petitioners never traded in furs
or provided any significant financing for the Detroit business
community. Instead, the Bank of Detroit (as it was also known)
was a tool of Andrew Dexter Jr., the greatest con man of his
generation. The bank's true purpose was to print notes that could
be traded at a discount on Dexter's Boston Exchange Bank (BEB)
either for more secure notes or to purchase goods and services.
Previous works have emphasized a shift in Dexter's activities from
dishonest to illegal by the spring of 1808, but a close study of the
Bank of Detroit reveals that the criminality began in 1806. The
Detroit Bank was a criminal enterprise from its inception.[2]

Hull had long ties to the Dexter family. He also had financial problems that were well known. The governor owned five shares in the Detroit Bank, and, according to Judge Augustus B. Woodward, had sought election as the bank's first president (the position eventually went to Woodward).[3] Some of Hull's actions, such as dispatching workers originally hired to build his home to construct the bank instead, created the appearance of impropriety. Although Hull was widely criticized for his conduct, he was not corrupt. The governor held that a legitimate bank was in Detroit's public interest and championed it for that reason. He was not a part of Dexter's criminal enterprise, but a victim of it.[4]

In the early American republic, there was no legal tender, no universal medium of exchange. What existed were bank notes, printed by state-chartered private corporations. Bank notes were IOUs from the issuing banking corporation. They were a promise by the corporation's president and directors to pay the bearer the sum of the note when presented in specie or other notes. No one was required to accept them. Their value, or lack of it, was based on the confidence that the holder of the note had in the institution's promise to pay.[5]

In a commercial center like Boston, merchants received notes from local banks and distant banks. The risk inherent in accepting local notes was easy to determine. The soundness of notes from distant banks, called "current money," was not. Dexter's Boston Exchange Bank, founded in 1804, formed an active trading forum for current money. Current money traded at a discount to par value on the exchange at known, published rates. The existence of the BEB ensured that there was a liquid secondary market for out-of-town notes, thus making local merchants more willing to accept them. By creating the secondary market, the BEB gave current money much more value than it would have had otherwise.[6]

The BEB made conservative bankers, those who still expected notes to be backed with specie or other valuables, nervous. Dexter knew that the farther away a bank was from Boston, the less likely it was that the notes would ever be returned to the issuing bank for payment. His business strategy was to gain control of country banks, notably the Berkshire Bank in Pittsfield, Massachusetts, the Farmers' Exchange Bank in Gloucester, Rhode Island, and the Bank of Detroit, which were all remote from Boston and one another. By controlling the BEB, Dexter controlled the market for current money in Boston and could create an inflated value for the country notes. By owning the remote banks themselves, he controlled the supply of current money as well. Dexter and his group of investors approached Hull with the notion of founding a bank in Detroit specifically because it was remote and the danger of its notes ever being returned for payment in substantial amounts was small.[7]

Dexter's scheme did not leave this possibility to chance. As soon as notes were issued, they were circulated as far away from the issuing bank as possible. In Detroit, Farmers' Exchange notes were circulated instead of Detroit notes and vice versa. It was akin to a game of lock-and-key, with the object being to keep the lock and key as far from each other as possible. In late September 1806, Nathaniel Parker, BEB director and a stockholder in the nascent Detroit venture, left the town for Boston with a large cargo of freshly signed Detroit Bank notes. The notes were discounted in Boston, but this hardly mattered. Save the costs of printing and transport, the transaction was pure profit.[8]

To complete the illusion, all of Dexter's banks printed notes on the latest stereotype printing presses to make them look upstanding and reliable. In the *New England Palladium*, "A Friend of the Public" wrote that the notes were a facade "calculated to deceive."[9] They were, in fact, almost worthless. For example, Dexter's Farmers' Exchange bank in Rhode Island issued more than $580,000 in notes against specie reserves of $86.49 before it failed in 1809. Dexter traded this nearly worthless script either at the BEB, where he controlled the rates, or so far from the issuing source that the original notes would rarely, if ever, be exchanged for hard currency. His operation was the definition of a confidence game: If it looked like money and felt like money, it was money.[10]

Dexter's use of the ill-gotten funds ultimately brought the scheme down. His fraudulent rural bank notes financed the construction of the Boston Exchange Coffee House (BECH), a mammoth institution that was to not only house the Boston Exchange Bank but a hotel, reading rooms, shops, and restaurants. At the time, the BECH was the largest commercial building in the United States, and it consumed cash like a black hole, forcing Dexter's banks to issue more and more notes. By 1809, the large volume of notes being issued alarmed Boston merchants and bankers so much that they bound together to systematically return notes from Dexter's banks to their origin for payment. Since Dexter's banks could not pay, he fled to Nova Scotia for safety. William Flanagan, Dexter's associate and cashier of the Detroit Bank, observed, "I do not think his affairs can ever be put right."[11]

Hull's involvement with the Bank of Detroit emerged from a longer pattern of poor financial decisions and connections to the Dexter family. Alexander Dexter Jr.'s uncle Samuel was a longtime ally and benefactor of Hull. On at least one occasion, Samuel Dexter came to Hull's financial rescue by lending him money, with Hull's home as security. Prior to the Detroit Bank, Hull was a large shareholder in the New England Mississippi Land Company (NEMLC). He and other New Englanders, including Alexander Dexter Jr. and Sr., held what became known as "Yazoo Shares," fraudulent land titles passed off by Georgia development interests. Alexander Dexter Jr.'s older brother, Samuel, served as an attorney for NEMLC claimants when the state of Georgia reversed its earlier decision and attempted to invalidate the sale of the disputed land. The state's action threatened to hurt investors even more than the original fraud. In 1810, the case reached the United States Supreme Court, resulting in the famous *Fletcher v. Peck* decision in which the court upheld the sanctity of private contracts, even those made under dubious circumstances.

Unfortunately, the decision came too late and provided too little to help Hull. By then, he was five years into his governorship of Michigan Territory, a job that he had accepted largely because he needed the money.[12]

Despite his financial difficulties, Hull agreed to help establish the Detroit Bank to advance the public's interest. He accepted Dexter's cover story that it would help to pry the fur trade from British to American traders by establishing a medium of exchange. In first describing the bank to Woodward in April 1806, Hull wrote, "A very rich & respectable Company of Merchants, in Boston, have agreed to make an establishment in our Territory to carry on the fur Trade."[13] Detroit River region merchants had bemoaned the lack of currency for trading. However, Dexter and members of his organization never intended to benefit the fur trade or other Detroit interests. Of the approximately $100,000 in notes initially issued by the Detroit Bank, a few thousand dollars at most circulated in the region. In truth, the bank was created to supply notes for the Boston Exchange Bank, which in turn aided the construction of the Boston Exchange Coffee House. The Bank of Detroit was "Detroit" in name only.[14]

After meeting with Dexter and his associates in March 1806, Hull gave them "such assurances that they will immediately make all their arrangements."[15] This, they quickly did. In May, Flanagan was named cashier to run the bank's day-to-day operations. He had previously served as cashier of the BEB. Dexter's men issued him a bond of $15,000 as part of the specie to capitalize the bank and sent him to Detroit, lugging both the specie and iron bars to build the vault. With Flanagan came two of the bank's new directors, Nathaniel Parker and Dudley S. Bradstreet, who also served as directors of the BEB. They were along to sell 25 percent of the stock left for purchase in Detroit. Hull's backing had inspired such confidence that 75 percent of the stock was already subscribed in Boston before the Michigan territorial legislature authorized the bank in September 1806.[16]

By late July 1806, eastern newspapers from Baltimore to Vermont reported the appearance of Detroit Bank notes in Boston – two months before the bank legally existed! Dexter's organization printed its bank notes at a shop in Newburyport, Massachusetts, with special dyes. The BEB's directors secured the dies and delivered them to the shop only when notes were ready to be printed. For the Bank of Detroit's notes to be official, they had to be signed by the cashier, Flanagan, and the yet unnamed bank president. Flanagan left Boston in June 1806, so it is possible he signed the first batch of notes. Any notes signed by the bank's president, though, were fraudulent because the position was not yet filled. These illegal notes represented the endemic criminality behind the Detroit Bank from its outset.[17]

In Detroit, construction began on the bank in July 1806. Detroit's devastating fire the year before left Hull with poor accommodations. He once complained, "There is not a barn in Massachusetts more open, than the room I have slept in this winter."[18] Therefore, people noticed when Hull diverted his homebuilders sent from Boston to construct the bank. There was nothing unethical in delaying work on his house, but the decision provided tangible evidence of his connection to the Dexter network.[19]

On September 6, 1806, the first day of the legislative session, the Michigan territorial legislature introduced the petition to establish the Detroit Bank. On September 19, the charter was approved, thus finally and legally establishing the bank. The charter had some irregular characteristics. In the words of the historian William Jenks, "The wildest promoter could not have asked for more."[20] There was no restriction on the value of notes that could be issued, no provision for redeeming bills, and no restrictions on loans or debts. At the insistence of Woodward, the term of the charter was upped from 20 years to 101 years, and the maximum capital increased from $400,000 to an amazing $1 million. To put these figures into perspective, most bank charters lasted ten years, and Michigan's total annual commerce in 1805 was about $40,000.[21] Of the charter, Hull later explained to Secretary of State James Madison: "I did not approve in all its parts – It seemed to be the only one in which we could all agree."[22] While territorial laws were to be adopted wholly from laws of existing states, the Bank of Detroit charter circumvented this rule. The charter mixed provisions from multiple states and included outright fabrications. According to Jenks, the terms were so favorable that the promoters must have drafted the bill themselves, only to be enhanced by Woodward. The deal was almost too good to be true.[23]

Dexter's organization sought to profit on the bank at every turn. The Detroit Bank's charter authorized 10,000 shares. Bostonians purchased their initial 75 percent stake (7,500 shares) at $2 a share. According to Detroit resident John Gentle, Nathaniel Parker attempted to dupe some Detroiters into paying as much as $50 per share for the remaining 25 percent stake. The eastern banker had few takers, especially because the charter allowed less than a week for the local sale of shares. As a result, Bostonians ended up owning approximately 95 percent of the bank's stock by late September 1806. Still, Parker was not done. On his way back to Boston in November 1806, the industrious banker tried to sell additional shares of the Bank of Detroit to Albany merchants, most notably John Jacob Astor. Parker failed to mention one important detail: The shares technically did not exist since nearly all had already been sold to interests connected to Dexter's Boston Exchange Bank.[24]

In the fall of 1806, Gentle drew national attention to the fraud surrounding the Detroit Bank in a widely circulated newspaper essay. Gentle's fourteen-point tirade emphasized three majors criticism of the bank: (1) that the Dexter organization swindled Hull into supporting the Detroit Bank; (2) that the bank's true purpose was to flood Boston with dubious paper that would profit Dexter; and (3) that the Michigan territorial government had no business being involved in a private enterprise without the citizenry's consent.[25] In January 1807, "A Friend of the Public," writing originally in the *Boston Centinel*, condemned Hull for misusing "all the power that he has been given by the President and Congress: and it cannot be thought they would let him make laws against common sense by establishing a bank which could do as much good as one on the Lake of Ontario?"[26]

Congress could not ignore the charges being leveled against the Bank of Detroit. Under the law establishing Michigan Territory, all subsequent territorial laws were subject to congressional approval, and the bank's charter had obvious flaws. On March 4, 1807, the last day of its session, Congress struck down the charter with lightning speed. The *Portsmouth Gazette* published an eyewitness account of congressional action by "a Gentleman from Washington to his Friend in Boston." "The scheme had always seemed to me an improper speculation," the gentleman reported, "I am now convinced of it." Members of Congress heard some of the basic facts connected to the Detroit Bank's charter: The bank had an established capital of $1 million for a territory with fewer than 5,000 inhabitants; the charter only allowed five days for the stock subscription, one of which was a Sunday; and the bank's term extended for 101 years, with the right to establish branches anywhere in the U.S. Once the case had been presented, according to the gentleman, "there appeared to be but one sentiment on the subject a bill disapproving the act and declaring it null had passed the house unanimously." The lack of a single backer in Congress made clear that the Detroit Bank was indefensible.[27]

The bank's swift collapse compelled Hull to defend his role in the venture. In May 1807, he explained to Madison that he was "of the opinion that a small bank, conducted on fair and proper principles, would be promotive of the public Interest. Yet under the circumstances this has been conducted I rejoice that Congress has disapproved the law." The reactions of other Detroiters to the scandal supported Hull's position that the bank had local backing and was considered in the public interest, at least initially.[28]

Hull also maintained that he never sought to profit personally from the bank. His only interest was the five shares that he had purchased. Valued at $10, this was hardly a large interest or one that would be likely to corrupt Hull's motives. In a letter to his friend and fellow American Revolutionary War officer, Henry Dearborn, Hull declared, "I am not desirous of wealth or any kind of splendor – I wish to procure fame by promoting the prosperity of the Country."[29] Hull's actions backed up his words. Notwithstanding his money problems, he was motivated by fame, not greed, throughout his career. This ambition was not uncommon for his generation.[30] In a speech commemorating his nomination for a second term as governor in May 1808, Hull defended his approval of the bank charter as "done from the same motives which have influenced all my public conduct. I believed it would give facility to the commerce and business of the country, and promote the public interest."[31] Hull's public devotion could wear on both him and his family. In a touching letter written by his wife, Sarah, in April 1809, she encouraged him to step away from public service: "Lay your commission at their feet, return to private life and obscurity, if poverty is the result, I will share it with you with cheerfulness and contentment RENOUNCE ALL POLITICS, BE NEUTRAL!" Always the public servant and seeker of fame, if not riches, Hull ignored his wife's sage advice.[32]

As for Andrew Dexter Jr., he was not one to be troubled by legality. He managed to keep the Bank of Detroit running as a private corporation with Detroiter James Henry as president until late 1808. Henry and his associates petitioned the Michigan territorial legislature, claiming that they had "no knowledge that anything improper has taken place, hitherto, in conducting the affairs of the bank." Ultimately, the legislature passed a law making it illegal to engage in banking in Michigan. The law, combined with the earlier action by Congress, forced the Detroit

Bank to close its doors for good.[33]

The Bank of Detroit was the ultimate misnomer. It was not so much a bank as a facade to advance Andrew Dexter Jr.'s interests. The bank created notes that looked like money and felt like money, but never had the backing of real money. The few notes that were returned to Detroit were either denied payment or paid only after long and extensive shenanigans.[34] The Bank of Detroit was never a Detroit operation. It was owned almost exclusively by Bostonians to provide notes to trade at Dexter's Boston Exchange Bank, which in turn facilitated the construction of his Boston Exchange Coffee House. In short, everything about the Detroit Bank was a lie. The founders lied about its purpose and about the price of its shares. They printed notes before the bank was chartered, and, at least twice, they tried to sell shares that did not exist. Dexter's organization carried on the bank even after Congress declared it illegal. It was a criminal enterprise from start to finish.

In hindsight, Hull's support of the Bank of Detroit is understandable. He was in a job he needed rather than wanted, in the most remote area imaginable. Detroit represented obscurity to Hull. When old friends approached him to create a bank, he naturally listened. As Hull expressed many times, a properly conceived bank would have been beneficial to the local community. In the aftermath of the Detroit Bank's failure, President Thomas Jefferson provided a fitting epitaph of Hull's conduct: "The Governor committed a great error in the bank institution, and at first a suspicious one. but we have found that he took a very small interest in it, and got out of it as soon as he found he was wrong. In every thing else, his conduct has been correct & salutary. that there was much roguery in the institution of the bank, I believe, of which he was the dupe."[35]

NOTES

1   Frank B. Woodford, *Mr. Jefferson's Disciple: A Life of Justice Woodward* (East Lansing: Michigan State College Press, 1953), 55. For Hull's explanation of his trip to Boston, see Hull to James Madison, October 11, 1805, in *MPHC*, 31:540. For Hull's acknowledgment of the fraud, see "William Hull to James Madison, on the Subject of the Bank of Detroit," May 26, 1807, in *MPHC*, 36:196-97.

2   The leading work on Dexter, Jane Kamensky, *The Exchange Artist: A Tale of High-Flying Speculation and America's First Banking Collapse* (New York: Viking, 2008), portrays him as an aggressive speculator who only edged into illegality in 1808. For the most complete study of the Bank of Detroit, see William L. Jenks, *The First Bank in Michigan: The Detroit Bank* (Port Huron, MI: First National Exchange Bank, 1916). Jenks views the bank as a cautionary tale about the need for strong banking laws and regulations (no page numbers in book). See also Woodford, 55-59, which is typically sympathetic of Woodward and critical of Hull's role in the bank.

3   Augustus B. Woodward to Ephraim Pentland, January 1, 1808, Box 3 (1806-1809), Augustus Brevoort Woodward Papers, BHC.

4   "William Hull to James Madison, on the Subject of the Bank of Detroit," 36:196-97.

5   Kamensky, 15-16; Jenks.

6   Kamensky, 17, 52-60, 144; Jenks.

7   Kamensky, 58-70, 132-35.

8   Kamensky, 59-70; Jenks; Arthur M. Woodford, *Detroit and Its Banks: The Story of Detroit Bank & Trust* (Detroit: Wayne State University Press, 1974), 32.

9   "Detroit Bank," *New England Palladium*, December 23, 1806.

10 Kamensky, 9, 14-18, 61, 140, 144, 160; Jenks.

11 William Flanagan to Solomon Sibley, July 20, 1809, Box Z7 (1809-1819/Flanagan Papers), Solomon Sibley Papers, BHC. For the fall of Dexter's scheme, see also Kamensky, 132, 147-49; and Jenks.

12 For Hull's financial predicament and ties to the Dexter family, see Kamensky, 38-39, 45, 63; and Sarah Hull to William Hull, April 10, 1809, Box 3, Woodward Papers.

13 William Hull to Augustus B. Woodward, April 1, 1806, in *The Territorial Papers of the United States*, ed. Clarence E. Carter and John P. Bloom, 27 vols. (Washington, DC: Department of State and National Archives and Records Service, 1934-69), 10:48.

14 For Hull's misjudgment, see "William Hull to James Madison, on the Subject of the Bank of Detroit," 36:196-97; Silas Farmer, *The History of Detroit and Michigan: Or the Metropolis Illustrated* (Detroit: S. Farmer, 1884), 858; Jenks; Kamensky, 63-64, 69-70; Charles Moore, *Governor, Judge, and Priest: Detroit, 1805-1815. A Paper Read before the Witenagemote, on Friday Evening, October the Second, 1891* (New York: De Vinne Press, 1891). For the lack of currency within the fur trade, see Robert Sanders to John Sanders, December 11, 1806, Robert Sanders Papers, BHC. See also letters of January 11, February 2, and February 13, 1807. Estimates for the amount initially issued by the Bank of Detroit ranged from William Hull's $80,000 to John Gentle's $163,000.

15 Hull to Woodward, April 1, 1806, 10:48.

16 Kamensky, 65-66; Jenks; Bond of William Flanagan, May 27, 1806, in *MPHC*, 8:572-73.

17 The news first appeared in the *American Commercial Advertiser* (Baltimore) on July 29, 1806, and was soon reprinted in several newspapers. Kamensky dismisses the reports about Detroit notes appearing in the East because no bank yet existed (67).

18 William Hull to Henry Dearborn, March 4, 1807, in *MPHC*, 40:105. For the Detroit fire of 1805, see the essay in this volume by Keith A. Killoran.

19 Farmer, 855; Kamensky, 65-67.

20 Jenks.

21 Augustus B. Woodward to the *Pittsburgh Commonwealth*, January 12, 1808, Box 3, Woodward Papers, BHC; Kamensky, 65.

22 "William Hull to James Madison, on the Subject of the Bank of Detroit," 36:197.

23 Jenks.

24 Farmer, 855-58; Nathaniel Parker to Augustus B. Woodward, November 18, 1806, in *MPHC*, 8:573-74.

25 Farmer, 857-58.

26 "Serious Reflections Respecting Detroit Bank Bills," *Green Mountain Patriot* (from *Boston Centinel*), January 13, 1807.

27 "Extract of a Letter from a Gentleman in Washington to his Friend in Boston," *Portsmouth Gazette*, March 21, 1807.

28 "William Hull to James Madison, on the Subject of the Bank of Detroit," 36:196-97. For the reaction of local Detroiters, see James Henry to William Henry, April 19, 1810, James Henry Papers, BHC; and Robert Sanders to John Sanders, December 11, 1806.

29 Hull to Dearborn, March 4, 1807, 40:105.

30 Douglass Adair, "Fame and the Founding Fathers," in *Fame and the Founding Fathers: Essays by Douglass Adair*, ed. Trevor Colbourn (Indianapolis: Liberty Fund, 1974), 3-37.

31 "An Address to the Citizens of Michigan Territory, by Governor Hull," *National Intelligencer* (Washington, DC), July 1, 1808.

32 Sarah Hull to William Hull, April 10, 1809.

33 James Henry, William Brown, and William Flanagan to the Legislative Board for the Territory of Michigan, December 12, 1808, in *MPHC*, 8:577.

34 Farmer, 856.

35 Thomas Jefferson to William Duane, February 7, 1808, in *Territorial Papers of the United States*, 10:197.

Portrait of Colonel Elijah Brush
Artist unknown, c. 1812. Oil on canvas. Detroit Historical Society Collection.

Elijah Brush, Transnational American
Sharon Tevis Finch

Elijah Brush, Died Dec. 14, 1814. Aet. 42.
Loyal Soldier, Eloquent Advocate,
Loving Husband, Devoted Father
At Thy Hearthside Unforgotten Ever

– gravestone, Elmwood Cemetery, Detroit, lot 73A

In 1798, a young lawyer named Elijah Brush arrived in
Detroit. Twenty-six years old, born in Bennington, Vermont,
educated at Dartmouth, Brush was one of the first American
pioneers in the Detroit River region, a true transnational
American. Brush epitomized these earliest American migrants
who came to seek their fortunes in a place that had until lately
been only a small fur-trading *entrepot* and French agricultural
settlement – a far outpost of the British and French empires, a
primitive frontier of European civilization. There were only five
hundred European descendants in Detroit in 1796, when the
Americans assumed control from the British. They lived side-by-
side, sometimes uneasily, with hundreds of Native Americans who
still clung to their lands. Brush came to this multicultural frontier
environment and thrived because he was willing to shed the
traditional habits of the East Coast, ready to flex and grow with
his new country.[1]

What did this young man do in Detroit in the fifteen years
before his untimely death? He developed a successful law practice,

was on the cutting edge of every public matter, was elected a trustee of the town of Detroit in 1803, was appointed the second mayor of the newly incorporated city of Detroit in 1806, was appointed the second treasurer of the territory of Michigan in 1806, served as the second attorney general of the territory during the period from 1808 to 1813, led local militias, helped mobilize the troops before the War of 1812 when General William Hull was absent, and served as commander of Detroit under Hull during the invasion of Upper Canada and occupation of Sandwich in July and August 1812. The significance of his accomplishments is concealed within this listing. In essence, he wove the vividly separate threads of his environment into a masterful tapestry of interculturalism – a microcosm of the new America.

Behind Brush's public persona and accomplishments lay a rich personal life with deep roots in the Detroit River region. He and his wife created a transnational space for themselves and their descendants. In 1802, Brush married Adelaide Askin, daughter of John Askin and Marie Archange Barthe Askin. John Askin was a leading British trader, merchant, and landowner in the Detroit River region. His first wife was Indian; his second was French. Foreshadowing his son-in-law Elijah, Askin had married out of his cultural background, wedding the daughter of one of the most land-rich men in the area. This acceptance of cross-cultural marriage was common in the region, starting when the French *coureur de bois* (fur traders) cohabitated with Indian women and fathered their *métis* children. Adelaide Brush spoke and wrote French as easily as English, and all her letters to her "*chere mere*" Archange were in French, as were those of her sisters. Elijah and Adelaide had four children who lived to adulthood, Edmund Askin, Charles Reuben, John Alfred, and Archange (known as Samantha or Sumantha). Two children who perished in early childhood, Charles Brush and John Askin Brush, are buried on the family plot in Detroit's historic Elmwood Cemetery with the rest of the family. Adelaide, called "Alice" or "Allice" by her family in letters, remained close to her parents, despite their removal to Sandwich in Upper Canada in 1802. Elijah thereafter conducted Askin's business on the American side of the Detroit River.

Brush's life was a living illustration of how the region and its border operated. Until the British turnover of Detroit in 1796, there was effectively no border to local residents. The new political division of the Detroit River region did not affect the lifestyles of its inhabitants, who were intermarried, interrelated, intercultural, and international. When the border was affirmed, most became transnational figures, moving easily back and forth across the river both by private craft and ferry. Letters from Elijah Brush, John Askin, and many others demonstrate the fluidity and porousness of this border, as they referred to trips to the other national territory simply as "coming over" and "going over."[2]

However, the growing political tensions between Britain and the United States before the War of 1812 turned that porous border into a barrier that limited free association and trade for both sides. In 1807, when relations were strained, Askin wrote to his friend and business associate Isaac Todd in Montreal that he was unable to get to "the other side" for some weeks and could not "untill the present disturbance . . . blows Over."[3] When war finally broke out in 1812, it caused many families, including Askin's, to divide not only geographically and nationalistically, but also in battle. Every young male in the Askin family except Brush fought on the British side. Brush fought as an officer on the American side. This painful result of the heightened recognition of the border is one of the reasons why the historian Alan Taylor calls this conflict a *civil war*.[4]

Askin respected Brush from the start. In an early estimation, Askin wrote, "My daughter Alice married to Mr. Brush – a lawyer who has a good deal of practice and well liked." To another associate, Askin beamed, "[Brush] bids fair to be an able Lawyer has considerable practice is sober and industrious therefore I believe Allice has made a good choice."[5] Throughout the years,

Askin continued to describe Elijah in glowing terms – as a "warm hearted fellow," "as kind & Fri[e]ndly a man, as ever was" – and commended "the goodness of Mr. Brush's heart, & good I believe it to be."[6] Askin also apprenticed his son Alexander to read law with Elijah, remarking, "I believe Mr. Brush's professional knowledge at least equal to any lawyer we have."[7]

In 1806, Brush bought the Askin farm in Detroit. It was important to both the Askins and the Brushes that the farm stay in the family, since it had been purchased from Askin's father-in-law, Charles Andrew Barthe, a French *habitant* settler. Brush's title was only fourth in line from the original land grant from the king of France. The agreement was that Brush would make payments upon a debt to Askin's creditors in Montreal, Todd and James McGill, until he could pay off the purchase price. Brush also bought other lands from Todd and McGill on credit. However, times were tough before the war, and Brush was soon unable to marshal funds in Detroit or sell enough property to make timely payments. Askin reassured Todd and McGill repeatedly that Brush would pay his debts when he could. In October 1808, Askin wrote to Todd: "Mr. Brush is certainly a regular, industrious, sober man, and except in improvements is by no means extravagant for a man who *earns so much by his profession*."[8] At the time, there was little specie available on the frontier. This deficiency in available cash is one reason the 1806 Detroit Bank scheme was so popular and why Brush subscribed for one hundred shares of the fraudulent institution. Brush was not alone in being taken in by eastern "sharpies." Many leading residents of Michigan Territory fell for the scam, including Governor Hull and Judge Augustus B. Woodward.[9]

Brush worked hard to support his family and pay his debts. He was the second lawyer admitted to practice in the Michigan territorial Supreme Court and had a busy private legal practice, in addition to his public work as attorney general representing the territorial government. Brush was in court almost daily, appearing on nearly every page of the territory's early court records.[10]

His most famous cases are the two Michigar
in 1807 that set the legal standard for slavery in tl
Territory. Although he held slaves – according to one ac
to twenty at a time – Brush, like any good lawyer, could ser
either side of a case. He represented both slaves and owners in the
landmark cases. In one, he championed the black Denison family
of Detroit, some of whom were already free, in their lawsuit to
have their still-enslaved adult children declared free. The law
was clearly against Brush, and he lost the case; the Northwest
Ordinance of 1787 banned new cases of slavery, but did not
provide the authority to manumit existing slaves. In the second
case, the same judge, Woodward, declared that blacks who were
legally enslaved in Upper Canada but managed to escape to the
United States could not be extradited to their Canadian masters.
Doing so violated the provision in the Northwest Ordinance that
barred new cases of slavery in the territory. Moreover, British law
did not accord such a return to American slave owners. In this
case, Brush represented the British-Canadian slaveholder James
Pattinson, who was married to Adelaide's sister. In each instance,
there was a happy ending for the slaves. The Denisons crossed the
river to Upper Canada where they could not be extradited to the
United States, lived with the Askins and worked for the family's
friends. They remained in Canada for years, eventually returning
to the U.S. without challenge after the War of 1812. The Pattinson
slaves, meanwhile, remained in Michigan Territory, where they
could not be extradited to Upper Canada. Together, the cases,
particularly the Pattinson decision, made slavery untenable in the
Detroit River region.[11]

The slave cases were representative of the multicultural and
transnational character of Brush's business and legal affairs. In
July 1805, he went on a trip as Askin's agent to represent Indian
chiefs in their sales of tribal lands to Americans, a scheme the
scholar Milo Quaife called "the Cuyahoga Dream." Askin was to
receive a percentage of the Indians' profits. Brush wrote to Askin

ᴴe had returned exhausted from his trip and would "come ᴼver" later to report in depth on how an American Indian agent would not cooperate in letting the Indian chiefs negotiate away their lands. At the end of the letter, Brush lightened the tone by wishing "to beg Some Cellery plants from Mrs. Askin as many as She can well Spare."[12]

Beyond his public affairs, this domestic detail highlights the essential qualities of Brush's life as a transnational American. Consumer goods and household necessities were in short supply on the Detroit frontier. Throughout their correspondence, Brush was called upon by Askin to secure and bring an assortment of household items across the river: tea, grapevines, a dining room table (which had to be built), boots (which took months and almost got lost in transit), and "shoes for Mrs. Askin." Not only merchandise went across the river. The custom before the war was to send letters to Canadians in care of Detroit residents who would then deliver them across the river, since the official international post had not developed. Endorsements on many letters show this forwarding chain.[13]

Within the Askin family, Brush participated in a larger regional trade of various domestic goods and foodstuffs. John Askin Jr., the firstborn child of John Sr.'s Indian wife, also participated in the network from his post as an interpreter and storekeeper on St. Joseph Island, a British possession in northern Lake Huron near Fort Mackinac. John Jr. often asked his father to send household necessities such as apple trees and onion plants from the Detroit River region, and he shipped British merchandise southward. As the relationship between Britain and the United States hardened before the war, numerous trade restrictions were put in place – including an American embargo on British goods. Although British-American trade was illegal, it went on briskly in the northern borderlands, far from Detroit. John Jr. explained smuggling methods in 1808 in a note that also expressed frustration with Brush:

Brush disappointed me. he was to have sent me a Barrl of Cyder
if not two. he could as well Smuggle Cyder to our side as wine
to his. If he had sent it to Makina addressed to Doct[or] Mitchel
& wrote the Doct[or] that it was intended for me it would
have been in my store House long ago. We have a method in
this Quarter, unknown below how to import & export into the
U.S. Per the *Nancy* youll receive a keg of Sugar marked in your
Name which I send you & one keg mark'd P address'd to your
Care which is intended for Mrs Peltier & Several things which
are intended as addressed in a Bundles marked in your Name[.][14]

During the war, restrictions on travel, shipping, and communication
in the Detroit River region, once so easily navigated, increased.
After the Americans occupied Amherstburg in late September
1813, John Jr., a militia officer in the British-held Mackinac region,
feared that his letters home would be intercepted and John Sr.
would be accused of illicit correspondence with the enemy army.[15]

 Brush's transnational family and business activities did not
keep him from being a committed American citizen. Indeed,
he was a civic force, an advocate for the causes and people of
Detroit. In 1805, Brush was appointed one of two fire inspectors
for the town. He was frequently in the lead on writing petitions
about public matters. After the calamitous fire of 1805 destroyed
Detroit, he joined James May and John Anderson in writing to
President Thomas Jefferson for assistance. The following year, the
French inhabitants of the "Potawatomi Coast," downriver from
Detroit, petitioned (in French) for tax relief; they asked that Brush
be on the supervising committee. In 1811, Brush reported to the
judges of Michigan Territory on the handling of financial matters.
On the eve of the War of 1812, Brush and other community
leaders marshaled the militia. On May 8, 1812, Brush joined a
subscription paying 16 shillings of his own money to purchase
gunpowder for the defense of Detroit. After the town fell, the
British put an occupation government in force. Brush was the first
of thirty-one signatories to a petition asking Judge Woodward to
stay and help them in their time of trouble. The petition explained

the difference between public servants who cared and those who didn't. Brush was of the first sort, consistently at the forefront of any civic action.[16]

That civic-mindedness extended to military affairs. With the rank of colonel, he commanded the First Michigan Militia, which was charged with guarding the northern perimeter of Fort Detroit. Just after the war broke out, Brush wrote to Askin in a touching blend of formality and intimacy:

> Dear Sir I am going to send my family to reside at Mr. Meldrums. I know not what maybe the destany of this country. my family are dear to my heart. will you receive some money in Keeping for them, and if so, would you prefer to have it in bills on our Government, or Cincinnati Bank notes as to specie there is none here. Adieu and may God bless you E. Brush If at any time hereafter you think proper to send for Alice & the children, they will go over.

The letter shows the fluidity of the river region, where one could just "go over," and Brush could expect his wife and children to safely cross in wartime. Adelaide and the couple's children likely spent the opening of the British occupation with the family of Detroit merchant George Meldrum, as Elijah had arranged; they may have also "gone over" at different times to stay with her parents in Sandwich.[17]

After Hull surrendered Michigan Territory in August 1812, Brush, as the acting commander of Fort Detroit, unhappily signed the capitulation document. The responsibility, along with his transnational family background, perhaps explains the rumors that soon circulated that Brush was complicit in the surrender. Immediately after the capitulation, Brush wrote to Askin asking for a copy of these charges so that he could respond, saying that he wanted "an opportunity to contradict any representations derogatory to my character." An eyewitness later recalled Brush's "anger and chagrin" at the hoisting of the white flag over Fort Detroit.[18]

Although Brush was critical of Hull's leadership and

benefited from his family ties with Askin, he was no traitor. Days before the surrender, the colonel was a co-signer, with several other officers, of a letter to Ohio Governor Return Jonathan Meigs Jr. warning of Hull's weakness and asking for a new commander. There are conflicting accounts of what happened to Brush after the British victory. The strongest evidence suggests that the British held him as a prisoner for a brief period at Fort George on the Niagara front before paroling him from Kingston to the U.S., perhaps as a result of assistance from his father-in-law.[19]

By early November 1812, Brush had returned to the Detroit area. In a letter to his children, John Askin reported, "We hear Every two or three days from Mr. Brush & Allice who with their dear Children are all well."[20] In January 1813, Brush and other community leaders performed a dramatic act of citizenship by attempting to get permission from British Colonel Henry Procter to ransom American captives who were being held by Britain's Indian allies following the battles at the River Raisin. Procter offered to pay $5 a head for the captives, while the Indians received up to $80 from inhabitants on both sides of the river. He was so displeased with the pressure by the American group that he banished all twenty-nine of them in early February 1813 – Brush's second exile of the war. He did not return to his home and family in Detroit until the British occupation ended following the American victory in the Battle of Lake Erie on September 10, 1813. A few months after his return, Brush died.[21]

A faithful soldier, a colonel in the Michigan territorial militia and the Legionary Corps (a branch of the militia), Brush died from a disease contracted during the war. A cholera-like illness raged through Detroit soon after the British occupation ended in September 1813. Nearly 1,300 military personnel fell ill, of whom as many as 800 died. The epidemic was so severe that the city ran out of coffins, and a mass grave of soldiers was created at the present intersection of Washington Boulevard and Michigan Avenue in downtown Detroit. Unlike many, Brush did have a coffin and a gravestone, but his stone today incorrectly marks the date of his death as December 14, 1814 (see epitaph at the opening of this essay). Letters indicate that Brush died at the height of the epidemic a year earlier, on or around December 14, 1813. In February 1814, Askin's longtime business partner Isaac Todd offered his condolences on "the loss . . . I am told [of] Mr. Brush."[22]

Brush's probate estate file valued his personal property at $2,666.66. In five pages of elaborate script, a man's life is laid out – the pioneer scarcity, the intellectual quotient, the measure of the man. This inventory graphically demonstrates the simplicity of life in Detroit at the time of the War of 1812. Brush was a successful attorney, a landowner, and a community leader, yet his material goods were few, with the striking exception of his books, his professional stock in trade. Accounts owed to him totaled $7,337.94½, illustrating the difficulty everyone had in paying their debts when there was little money in circulation. Adelaide stated that the family had $500 cash on hand when Brush died, which was soon spent on family necessities.[23]

Even in death, Brush was a transnational figure. He left Adelaide a life estate in his property, to devolve equally to their four children. This meant she could occupy and use the property as she saw fit, but could not sell or encumber the real estate. Brush also designated Adelaide as his executrix – the person who would officially handle his estate. The totality of this legal arrangement reflected the gender attitudes of multiple cultures in the Detroit River region. There was the British method of leaving the estate to the children, with the wife holding dominion until her death. There was the French approach of treating the wife as a business partner, by making her the executrix and not tying up the estate during her lifetime, as the British might have done. And, finally, there was the American style of treating all children equally, regardless of gender or birth order. Adelaide, as executrix of his will, faithfully pursued the estate claims and ensured the family's financial stability after Elijah's death, assisted by their son

Edmund, also a lawyer. This property, the Brush Farm, became some of the most valuable in Detroit. It enveloped much of the eastern portion of what became the downtown area and was kept in one piece for a long time by Edmund. Rather than sell portions of the property, he used what was dubbed the "Brush lease." A long-term lease was offered at a low rate, with the lessee or tenant to pay all of the real estate taxes and other assessments. Eventually, the portion near present-day Comerica Park and the Detroit Medical Center was subdivided into an area of luxurious Victorian mansions known as Brush Park.[24]

Elijah Brush could not have foreseen the rich future for Detroit and his family when he wrote, "I know not what maybe the destany of this country," shortly before his beloved town fell. His short life in Detroit bore out its pioneer promise of building a new and successful territory, one that mixed old and new cultures. He was a natural border crosser, moving with ease through the region's multicultural population and across its porous border. He strung together the diverse threads of Native Americans, French inhabitants, British subjects, African Americans, and other American settlers. He was both a true transnational figure and a true American.

NOTES

1 There are only short biographical portraits of Elijah Brush, all of which contain some inconsistencies or incorrect information. See *Askin Papers*, 1:15, 207 n48; *City of Detroit*, 2:1361; Silas Farmer, *The History of Detroit and Michigan: Or the Metropolis Illustrated* (Detroit: S. Farmer, 1890), 1031; and Judy Jacobson, *Detroit River Connections: Historical and Biographical Sketches of the Eastern Great Lakes Border Region* (Baltimore: Clearfield, 1994), 59-63. For Detroit at the time of Brush's arrival, see Frederick C. Bald, *Detroit's First American Decade, 1796-1805* (Ann Arbor: University of Michigan Press, 1948).

2 For the border after the American Revolution, see Denver Brunsman and Joel Stone, eds., *Revolutionary Detroit: Portraits in Political and Cultural Change, 1760-1805* (Detroit: Detroit Historical Society, 2009). For descriptions of crossing the border, see *Askin Papers*, 2:531-63, 570-71, 581, 600, 729, 769.

3 John Askin to Isaac Todd, September 4, 1807, in *Askin Papers*, 2:571.

4 Alan Taylor, *The Civil War of 1812: American Citizens, British Subjects, Irish Rebels, & Indian Allies* (New York: Knopf, 2010). For the participation of the extended Askin family in the war, see the essay in this volume by Timothy Marks.

5 John Askin to Isaac Todd, February 23, 1802, in *Askin Papers*, 2:370 ("My daughter"); John Askin to Robert Hamilton, April 8, 1802, in *Askin Papers*, 2:374 ("[Brush] bids fair").

6 John Askin Sr. to John Askin Jr., July 5, 1809, in *Askin Papers*, 2:627 ("warm hearted"); John Askin to James McGill, July 17, 1812, in *Askin Papers*, 2:709 ("as kind"); John Askin Sr. to John Askin Jr., July 5, 1809, in *Askin Papers*, 2:641 ("the goodness").

7 John Askin to Isaac Todd and James McGill, March 25, 1807, in *Askin Papers*, 2:546. Apprenticeship to a practicing lawyer was the law school of the time. Alexander Askin later removed himself and his legal studies across the river, since he did not intend to practice in the U.S. and Upper Canadian law required a five-year apprenticeship in the province. The decision provides another example of the border's new importance. Alexander Askin to Charles Askin, April 28, 1808, in *Askin Papers*, 2:600.

8 John Askin to Isaac Todd, October 8, 1808, in *Askin Papers*, 2:612.

9 For an example of the lack of currency in trade, see Joseph Guy to John Askin, June 26, 1806, in *Askin Papers*, 2:525. For the Detroit Bank, see *City of Detroit*, 1:622-27; "The Detroit Bank," in *MPHC*, 8:571-78; and the essay in this volume by John Paris.

10 See the first two volumes of *Transactions of the Supreme Court of the Territory of Michigan*, ed. William W. Blume, 6 vols. (Ann Arbor: University of Michigan Press, 1935-40).

11 For records in the slave cases, see *Transactions of the Supreme Court*, 1:87-88, 414-18; and "Relative to the Subject of Slavery," in *MPHC*, 12:11-22. For the impact of the cases on slavery in the Detroit River region, see Gregory Wigmore, "Before the Railroad: From Slavery to Freedom in the Canadian-American Borderland," *Journal of American History* 98 (2011): 437-54; and the essay in this volume by Charlie Keller.

12 Elijah Brush to John Askin, July 8, 1805, in *Askin Papers,* 2:471-72; 472 (quote).

13 For references to different items to be secured and transported, see *Askin Papers*, 2:475, 480, 583, 606, 677 ("shoes").

14 John Askin Jr. to John Askin Sr., June 17, 1808, in *Askin Papers*, 2:606.

15 John Askin Jr. to John Askin Sr., May 1, 1815, in *Askin Papers*, 2:780.

16 Bald, 237; "Memorial of Elijah Brush, James May and John Anderson to the President of the United States" [1805 or 1806], in *MPHC*, 8:549-53; "Subscription to Raise Powder. 1812," in *MPHC*, 8:620; "Address of the Citizens of Detroit to A.B. Woodward" (January 6, 1813), in *MPHC*, 36:271.

17 Elijah Brush to John Askin, August 11, 1812, in *Askin Papers*, 2:729. The Meldrum farm was just east of what is now Mt. Elliot Street on Detroit's near east side, coincidentally the eastern boundary of Elmwood Cemetery. For George Meldrum, see Charles Wilson Goode, "Meldrum & Park: Commerce, Society, and Loyalty in Frontier Detroit," in *Revolutionary Detroit*, 133-39.

18 Elijah Brush to John Askin, September [?], 1812, in *Askin Papers*, 2:730; "Shubael Conant," in *MPHC*, 28:631. For the fall of Detroit, see Taylor, 164-65; and Anthony J. Yanik, *The Fall and Recapture of Detroit in the War of 1812: In Defense of William Hull* (Detroit: Wayne State University Press, 2011), 93-102.

19 For internal opposition to Hull, see *City of Detroit*, 2:1035-36; and Yanik, 81-82. For Brush's release, see Mr. Scott to Colonel Gardner, October 8, 1813, in *MPHC*, 15:406. Several sources mistakenly state that Brush was paroled to Ohio and never returned home. The error has possibly resulted from confusing Elijah with another Brush in the northwest theater, Captain Henry Brush from Chillicothe, Ohio. Henry Brush brought reinforcements to the River Raisin at the time of the capitulation. He refused to surrender and went back to Ohio.

20 John Askin Sr. to his children, November 12, 1813, in *Askin Papers*, 2:773.

21 *City of Detroit*, 2:1042. For the aftermath of the massacre, see also the essays in this volume by Carly Campbell and Scott A. Jankowski.

22 Isaac Todd to John Askin, February 3, 1814, in *Askin Papers*, 2:776. For reasons unclear, Clarence M. Burton recorded Brush's death as April 1, 1814 (*City of Detroit*, 2:1361), a mistake duplicated in *Askin Papers*, 1:207 n48. The editor, Milo M. Quaife, later corrected the error (*Askin Papers*, 2:370 n6). For Askin's illness, see John Anderson to Solomon Sibley, December 6, 1813, in Clarence M. Burton, *History of Detroit, 1780 to 1850: Financial and Commercial* (Detroit: Burton, 1917), 63. This work lists Brush's death as December 14, 1813 (65), which is consistent with the timing of Brush's illness and the closest approximation that we have. Writing to Solomon Sibley on December 31, 1813, Benjamin Chittenden reported on Brush's recent illness and death (Box 37, Solomon Sibley Papers, BHC). For the epidemic that likely took Brush's life, see *City of Detroit*, 2:1050; and the historical marker at the mass grave site (www.hmdb.org/marker.asp?marker=21745, accessed August 5, 2012). Brush was first buried on family land before he was finally laid to rest in Elmwood Cemetery on November 14, 1849. The error on his gravestone could be due to a mistake when the stone was prepared after the tumult of the war and epidemic. It is also possible that a new gravestone was made around the time of his body's removal to Elmwood. I thank Michael Shukwit of Elmwood Cemetery for graciously assisting me with its archives.

23 The Wayne County Probate Court files of Elijah and Adelaide Brush are found on microfilm in the Archives of Michigan, Lansing. Elijah Brush, File 108, Roll 6616.28. Adelaide Brush, File 3100, Roll 6660. I thank the archivists at the Archives of Michigan for their unstinting personal assistance.

24 Wayne County Probate File 108, Petition to Close Estate, May 12, 1912, Archives of Michigan. For the "Brush lease," see Friend Palmer et al., *Early Days in Detroit* (Detroit: Hunt & June, 1906), 513. In 1824, the U.S. Congress allotted $500 in response to a petition by Adelaide to reimburse the family estate for pickets destroyed during the war. An Act for the Relief of the Representative of Elijah Brush, *Public Statutes at Large of the United States 1789 – March 3, 1845* (Boston: Little & Brown, 1846), vol. 6, 18th Congress, 1st sess., 17 May 1824, ch. 74, p. 300. Adelaide died on July 20, 1859.

Town Hall: Taverns in Early Detroit
Kristen Harrell

Alcohol played an integral part in forming early Michigan. References to intoxicating substances appear as early as 1701, when Antoine Laumet de La Mothe, Sieur de Cadillac, settled Detroit. According to Cadillac's testimony in a trial at Quebec in 1705, brandy was commonplace in Detroit; one trader had 400 quarts, which was used for trading and corrupting Indians. Alcohol also played a key role in the fur-trade industry of the eighteenth century, as spirits remained one of Native Americans' favored means of payment for pelts. By 1800, taverns were scattered about Detroit's main streets with little regulation or organization. Some were well known public establishments. Others were merely parlors in homes where drinks and conversation flowed. Detroit's taverns may have developed organically, but their purpose in the frontier town was more than entertainment. Taverns functioned as the setting for important meetings of business and government.[1]

For early Detroiters, alcohol was a common element of daily life in a time when drinking water was suspect. Many medicines contained alcohol, including treatments for children, and it was eventually used as a disinfectant. Spirits also went hand-in-hand with militia service. Militiamen's hard drinking habits caused instances of insubordination and often rendered the men unfit for duty. Even without available taverns, alcohol found its way to the hands of servicemen in the form of daily rations. Many commanders felt as if their men could more easily survive without food than without alcohol. When militiamen were home, rather than on assignment, there was rarely an empty tavern in town.[2]

As today, early taverns were popular gathering places. In the late eighteenth century, James Donaldson was one of the Detroit River region's most prominent tavern owners. Donaldson ran four taverns between Detroit and his home in Amherstburg – all lavish establishments for which he spared no expense. John Askwith, an indentured servant to Detroit merchant John Askin, frequented Donaldson's tavern in Detroit. By spending up to twenty-seven days per month partaking in punches and brandy, Askwith left behind a substantial tab when he died in 1795. Fortunately for Donaldson, Askin helped to settle his former servant's estate.[3]

While still popular meeting spots, many taverns also had deep political significance. The best example is the tavern kept by John Dodemead in his Detroit home at the turn of the nineteenth century. Married with ten children, Dodemead was an affluent member of the community and later served as a judge for Wayne County, as a member of Detroit's Board of Trustees, and as a coroner for the town. His home was located on St. Anne Street and extended for fifty feet to St. Louis Street. The home had two separate entrances: the St. Anne entrance, which led to the family's private quarters; and the back door on St. Louis Street, which opened to the saloon that Dodemead kept with his wife, Jane. The county courts used the second floor of the Dodemead tavern to conduct general judicial business and legal affairs. The mixture of politics and spirits, all in a semi-private setting, was neither uncommon nor disputed by Detroit's residents. The tavern itself was available for boarding visitors at night and featured billiard tables for a small fee per game. John Dodemead kept busy with all the responsibilities of running a court and a tavern from his home. Owning a tavern was rarely a person's sole occupation.[4]

Dodemead's tavern also hosted local elections. The 1798 census indicated that at least 5,000 free male inhabitants lived in the Northwest Territory, meaning that the territory was entitled to a legal governing body. The territory's governor, Arthur St. Clair, called for an election in Detroit to select a delegate for the new territorial legislature in Cincinnati.[5] Dodemead's tavern was a natural setting for the contest between Solomon Sibley and James May. The election began on Monday, December 17, 1798, with both candidates entering the tavern and voicing their choice to two judges seated at a table, and ended that Wednesday with Sibley as the victor. May complained that Sibley and his friends were guilty of taking several persons "to the houses where these liquors were provided, and induced to drink till they became intoxicated, and in that state were taken to the poll and their votes received for Mr. Sibley." With alcohol commonly used as a bartering tool and social lubricant, May's argument found little traction.

The election was not the last controversy associated with Dodemead's tavern. By 1799, the tavern had become such a popular location for military personnel that Major David Strong requested that a sentinel be stationed at the St. Louis entrance to deter any soldiers from drinking while on duty. The military presence at the door to the "courthouse" alarmed Dodemead, who worried about the possible influence on legal proceedings.[6] Local judges sent notice of this possible infringement of their independence to Governor St. Clair in Cincinnati. Meanwhile, in a letter to Sibley, Strong suggested that he was simply "taking measures to put a stop to Drunkennes, which has been the cause of the Desertions which has so frequently taken place, owing entirely to those Evil minded Persons who are constantly selling Liquors to the men" rather than trying to inhibit the work of the court.[7] Dodemead and his fellow judges provided a temporary solution to the conflict by moving the court to Major William Winston's tavern while waiting for an official response from St. Clair. By January 1800, Dodemead succeeded in having the sentinel removed from his post, allowing his home and tavern to once again double as a courthouse.[8]

Long the setting of government business, taverns were eventually subject to government oversight. In 1802, when Detroit began the formal process to incorporate as a town, the Board of Trustees (which included John Dodemead as treasurer) began to create a unified set of laws and regulations. These laws included formal procedures for obtaining a license to operate a tavern. The regulations stipulated that no taverns could operate on the Sabbath, and that "minors, apprentices, Servants or Negroes" were not permitted to receive "any Strong drink without Special order & allowances of their parents or masters." Tavern owners who violated the latter rule faced a possible fine of up to $10 and the loss of licensure.[9]

In March 1802, the first official tavern license recorded under the new rules was granted to Ann Coates. Coates was the daughter of James Donaldson, who left one of his taverns to her in his estate. The Board of Trustees decided to grant only five tavern licenses that first year. Yet, in late December, it made an exception to grant a license to John Dodemead. His tavern was likely overlooked because it was such a familiar setting for government business. Much like the sessions of the court, meetings of Detroit's Board of Trustees occasionally met in local houses where drinking occurred. Thus it is possible that the board met on occasion in an unlicensed tavern to decide the fate of individuals petitioning for tavern licenses.[10] The local process of licensing taverns continued into August 1805, when the new Michigan territorial legislature passed additional laws regarding tavern-keeping and the sale of alcohol. The legislature set the cost of obtaining a license to operate a tavern between $10 and $25, depending on other uses of the building.[11]

The fire of 1805 further changed Detroit's tavern industry. Dodemead lost everything in the fire, including his tavern. By the next year, he built a new home, with a tavern and rooms to let, and returned to hosting court sessions. Still, Dodemead never fully returned to his previous status as one of Detroit's most prosperous men. The fire prompted the United States government to construct a stone building, known as the Council House, which was intended for public business. The building lessened the dependence on private accommodations for official proceedings and reduced the use of public funds for alcoholic beverages. When a court met in a tavern, the bill for the alcohol consumed was often sent to the public treasury. The Council House also decreased the opportunity for malfeasance that could take place in a private setting.[12]

Despite the new stone building, political gatherings continued to take place in taverns. Following the fire in 1805, the tavern of choice was an establishment run by Richard Smyth near the corner of Woodward and Woodbridge streets. Smyth's inn served as Detroit's unofficial town hall, much as Dodemead's tavern had in past years. In the period leading up to the War of 1812, men in town convened in Smyth's tavern to discuss matters of the day and to consider rumors of the impending struggle. Smyth's was not only a place to find local gossip, but an established inn that met the needs of travelers with beds, food, and a stable. Over time, the tavern expanded and changed names to the Sagina Hotel in 1823 and then the Michigan Hotel when it was sold to John Brunson in 1830.[13]

On the night of October 19, 1807, the usual revelry in Smyth's tavern turned violent. James Heward arrived in Detroit from Upper Canada that afternoon to give testimony on behalf of Matthew Elliott for the purpose of reclaiming Elliott's two slaves who had run away. James Dodemead, son of the late John Dodemead, met Heward by the dock, and the two young men returned to Dodemead's lodgings. By 7 p.m., Heward was intoxicated and decided to venture out and visit another of his Detroit acquaintances. Along the way, he saw Smyth's tavern and decided to enter. Dodemead advised him not to, suggesting that he had already had enough to drink. Heward persisted that he should "Stop there, and get a drink of grog." Being a loyal friend, Dodemead accompanied Heward inside Smyth's tavern, and a verbal altercation with other intoxicated patrons ensued. After being called "a damn'd british rascal," Heward ran outside and headed home, fearful of fighting an angry, drunken mob. Dodemead also went toward home, until he heard a young boy call out that Heward was being killed. Upon returning to Smyth's yard, Dodemead found that his friend had been tarred and feathered. Heward's wig was found the following day on a street corner hanging by a nail. Although the court indicted several men for Heward's attack, the attorney general decided against prosecuting. The territory's officials dropped the matter to keep harmony along the American-British border.[14]

During the post-fire era, the very role of taverns also shifted in the town's affairs. What once was a smattering of tiny businesses primarily operated in the owners' homes evolved into the modern hospitality industry. Michigan territorial laws outlined regulations requiring new taverns to provide more than beverages to their patrons; taverns were required to offer "suitable entertainments for man and horse."[15] This new requirement made it more difficult to operate a legal tavern from the comforts of home. The first major hotel and tavern owner that set out to meet the needs of the people on a grand scale was Benjamin Woodworth. A carpenter by trade, Woodworth came to Detroit to do woodworking on the house of Governor William Hull. Woodworth considered himself a patriot, led an artillery company in the War of 1812, and even managed to publish a weekly newsletter titled "The War" in 1812. Woodworth established his hotel in 1812, as a simple structure at the corner of Woodbridge and Randolph streets.[16]

Woodworth's tavern was used for official city business, much like the taverns that preceded it. But his establishment catered to political events on a grand scale. Woodworth's tavern hosted dinner parties with dancing, including the Pacification Ball in 1815 and the welcoming reception for President James Monroe in 1817. Following Woodworth's success, many other prominent Detroiters followed suit and either expanded their businesses to include lodgings or opened new, similarly structured establishments.[17]

In 1818, Woodworth rebuilt his business on the same plot and named it the Steamboat Hotel. When it reopened in 1819, the hotel hosted tourists and travelers arriving on ships and the new steamboat, *Walk-in-the-Water*. The famous "long room" was rented out for public and political events, and the upper story had the requisite bedrooms to let for travelers. This hotel, from humble tavern beginnings, eventually expanded to become one of the most frequented hotels in the city during the mid-nineteenth century. Due largely in part to the legal requirements of such businesses to provide full accommodations for rent as well as spirits and other entertainments, the words hotel, inn, and tavern became nearly synonymous. Most all hotels included a tavern of sorts. In fact, taverns were eventually not listed as such in the city directory, only as hotels.[18]

In an article in 1877, George C. Bates recalled his memories of Woodworth and the Steamboat Hotel. Bates wrote that the building was two stories tall atop a basement. Upon entering the hotel, one encountered the stage office, then the bar, followed by a large sitting area that was modestly and comfortably furnished, and, finally, a large dining room. The second floor held a ladies parlor and several large rooms that were used for Whig party meetings and legislative council sessions. It was not uncommon to find at least eight legislative councilmen living and sleeping in these upstairs rooms. Bates explained, "The furniture was very substantial, not wahongnay; the forks were steel, not silver, and the knives had bone instead of ivory handles; but every room and bed in that hotel was full, year in and year out." Bates remembered Uncle Ben, as Woodworth was known by all, as "mild in his outward seemings, but when enraged a perfect volcano . . . [an] old-fashioned Yankee, whose heart was open as the day." The Steamboat Hotel was a beacon for travelers and locals alike, and Uncle Ben was their welcoming proprietor.[19]

Taverns helped to shape the early growth of Detroit. From their beginnings as small establishments in the private homes of their owners to their growth into proto-modern hotels, taverns hosted legal proceedings, political gatherings, and served as a stand-in for Detroit's town hall. Taverns doubled as courthouses until proper edifices existed and still held grand political balls and other ceremonies even after the construction of official government buildings. The availability of alcoholic drinks in an intimate setting encouraged political discussions, both big and small. From these safe havens where the grog flowed freely, the city of Detroit was born.

NOTES

1 For all their importance, there is surprisingly little written on Detroit's early taverns. See Amy Elliott Bragg, *Hidden History of Detroit* (Charleston: History Press, 2011), 65-69; Victoria J. Ross, *Detroit's Historic Drinking Establishments* (Chicago: Arcadia, 2008); Julia Roberts, *In Mixed Company: Taverns and Public Life in Upper Canada* (Vancouver: University of British Columbia Press, 2009); John Fitzgibbon, "King Alcohol: His Rise, Reign, and Fall in Michigan," *Michigan History* 2 (1918): 737-80; and Joel Stone, "Taverns of Early Detroit," *Michigan History* 92 (2008): 48-53. For Cadillac and alcohol in the fur trade, see Fitzgibbon, 738.

2 *Detroit Journal Year-book* (Detroit: Detroit Journal Company, 1891), 35, 59; Fitzgibbon; Alan Taylor, *The Civil War of 1812: American Citizens, British Subjects, Irish Rebels, & Indian Allies* (New York: Knopf, 2010), 343.

3 Roberts, 11-12; "Tavern Bill of John Askwith," in *Askin Papers*, 1:598-603; Clarence M. Burton, ed., *Corporation of the Town of Detroit: Act of Incorporation and Journal of the Board of Trustees 1802-1805* (Detroit: Detroit Public Library, 1922), 14. For Askwith, see also Kimberly Steele, "'Will Diligently and Faithfully Serve': Mr. Askin's Indentured Servants," in *Revolutionary Detroit: Portraits in Political and Cultural Change, 1760-1805*, ed. Denver Brunsman and Joel Stone (Detroit: Detroit Historical Society, 2009), 140-46.

4 For Dodemead's tavern, see Clarence M. Burton, *History of Detroit, 1780 to 1850: Financial and Commercial* (Detroit: Burton, 1917), 36-37; Mary Agnes Burton and Clarence M. Burton, eds., *Governor and Judges Journal: Proceedings of the Land Board of Detroit* (Detroit: Michigan Commission on Land Titles, 1915), 189; and "John Dodemead to Solomon Sibley, receipt for games of billiards," September 26, 1804, Solomon Sibley Papers, BHC.

5 *City of Detroit*, 152; Frederick C. Bald, *Michigan in Four Centuries* (New York: Harper, 1954), 103.

6 Burton, *History of Detroit*, 37-39.

7 David Strong to Solomon Sibley, January 24, 1799, Box 10 (Jan.-July 1799), Sibley Papers.

8 Frederick C. Bald, *Detroit's First American Decade, 1796-1805* (Ann Arbor: University of Michigan Press, 1948), 148-49.

9 Burton, ed., *Corporation of the Town of Detroit*, 40-41. For more on slavery in Detroit, see the essay in this volume by Charlie Keller.

10 For tavern licenses, see Burton, ed., *Corporation of the Town of Detroit*, 14, 17, 25, 33, 45. For Coats, see Roberts, 11-13.

11 *Laws of the Territory of Michigan*, 4 vols. (Lansing: W.S. George, 1871-84), 1:42-44.

12 For the fire of 1805, see the essay in this volume by Keith A. Killoran. For the mixing of courts and alcohol, see Frank B. Woodford, *Mr. Jefferson's Disciple: A Life of Justice Woodward* (East Lansing: Michigan State College Press, 1953), 66. For the Council House, see Silas Farmer, *The History of Detroit and Michigan: Or the Metropolis Illustrated* (Detroit: S. Farmer, 1884), 473-74; and *City of Detroit*, 348-49.

13 For the evolution of Smyth's tavern, see Farmer, 480; George W. Stark, *City of Destiny: The Story of Detroit* (Detroit: Arnold-Powers, 1943), 204; George B. Catlin, *The Story of Detroit* (Detroit: Detroit News, 1923), 206-7. For the location of taverns, see *Governor and Judges Journal*, 183.

14 "Affidavit of John Dodemead Relative to James Heward and the Fugitive Slaves of Matthew Elliott," in *MPHC*, 36:182-85 (quotes). For the incident from Heward's perspective, see Affidavit of James Heward, October 27, 1807, James Heward Papers, BHC. For Elliott's slaveholding, see Woodford, 88; and Keller.

15 *Laws of the Territory of Michigan*, 1:43.

16 For Woodworth, see J.C. Holmes, "The American Hotel, Detroit," in *MPHC*, 1:433; Robert B. Ross, *The Patriot War* (Detroit: MPHC, 1890), 88; and *City of Detroit*, 2:1404.

17 For the use of Woodworth's hotel for major public events, see Farmer, 103; and the essays in this volume by Merry Ellen Scofield and Kaitlin Cooper. For the later growth of the hotel industry in Detroit, see Farmer, 479-89; and James J. Mitchell, *Detroit in History and Commerce: A Careful Compilation of the History, Mercantile and Manufacturing Interests of Detroit* (Detroit: Rogers & Thorpe, 1891), 88-95.

18 Friend Palmer et al., *Early Days in Detroit* (Detroit: Hunt & June, 1906), 215-18; Farmer, 480; James Dale Johnston, *The Detroit City Directory and Advertising Gazetteer of Michigan for 1855-56* (Detroit, 1855).

19 Bates quoted in Palmer et al., 218 ("furniture"); 216 ("mild"). Woodworth operated the Steamboat Hotel until selling it to Milton Barney in 1844 and retiring to St. Clair, Michigan. The hotel was destroyed in a fire in 1848.

"Feeding them when hungry": William Hull's Failed Indian Relations

Steve Lyskawa

On August 16, 1812, after sixteen years under American control, Detroit was again in British hands. Michigan territorial Governor William Hull abandoned the post with minimal resistance a few weeks into the War of 1812. Hull's unwillingness to fight the British, who had fewer soldiers, was due largely to the prospect of having to also engage Indian warriors. Capitalizing on the Indians' fearsome reputation on the frontier, British General Isaac Brock sent Hull a letter warning that "the numerous body of Indians who have attached themselves to my troops, will be beyond controul the moment the contest commences." When British troops landed on Detroit shores the morning of August 16, Indians in their company caused such a panic that one observer wrote that he was "standing at the entrance to Hell, with the gates thrown open to let the damned out for an hour's recreation on earth!" Hull feared that his family inside the fort would suffer "under the Tomahawk of a Savage!"[1]

The surrender of Detroit has been questioned from the moment Hull signed the articles of capitulation. Court martialed for treason, cowardice, neglect of duty, and unofficerlike conduct, the historical debate over Hull's actions is as conflicted as the initial dispute. While some blame Hull for giving up without a fight, others praise him for saving innocent lives. Regardless, to appreciate why he abandoned Detroit in the summer of 1812, we must understand the longer history of his failed relations with the region's Indian groups.[2]

Warfare between Indians and white settlers was a defining feature of the American frontier. With frequent conflicts over land and power, popular stories of Indian "savagery" spread across the land from the colonial era through the early national period. Many reports were imagined or exaggerated, but some were grounded in brutal realities. Tales of Indian cruelty had a devastating effect on native populations as settlers often sought revenge. From colonial times, according to the historian Peter Silver, "local men of note were desperate to puncture what they saw as the myth of Indian military superiority, and the psychological edge that went with it." Fear of Indian savagery, justified or not, helped Native Americans to contest the ongoing incursion of white settlement on their lands.[3]

When he assumed the position as governor of Michigan Territory, Hull was surely aware of the reputation of Indians on the frontier. From the moment he arrived, Hull treated Native Americans as a threat. He viewed Indians as a problem to be managed as opposed to potential partners or allies. In doing so, he established relationships marked by mistrust on both sides. Loyalty was bought, and if payment was not made, allegiance waned. Seen from this perspective, Hull's surrender of Detroit was not an abrupt or irrational act, but a consequence of years of strained relations with the region's Indian population.

Hull arrived in Detroit on July 1, 1805, intent on rebuilding a viable American community recently destroyed by fire. The governor's early business included ending a land dispute involving the Wyandot Indians in the region. On July 30, Reverend Joseph Badger wrote to Hull from the Wyandot village of Lower Sandusky (today Fremont, Ohio) requesting help on behalf of the chief Tarhe ("the Crane"), who asked to send word to his "father at Detroit." At issue was an attempt by Isaac Williams, a settler who was part Wyandot, to encourage the village to resist an earlier treaty with the United States by visiting Washington, if necessary. Williams likely had his own interests in mind as he sought to defraud the Wyandots of land guaranteed by the agreement.[4]

Hull responded by attempting to establish power in the region. The governor asked Badger to "present my friendly regards to the Crane and the others, and inform them that the great Spirit will never look with approbation on them, if they listen to wicked people, who advise them to break their faith and their solemn treatie – That their Great Father the President of the U.S. always preserve the most inviolable good faith with them and he expects the same on their part." Hull also reported on a recent council that he held with a group of Wyandot chiefs: "There had appeared to be uneasiness with them[.] The Treaty was read and explained to them. At the close of the council they expressed unanimously their entire satisfaction."[5] On August 20, 1805, Badger agreed with Hull's assessment, noting that "the Chiefs expressed themselves well pleased with your observations and from what I can learn by Conversation with them or from any other quarter they are determined to abide faithfully by their agreement with the U.S." Faithful obedience is what Hull hoped for.[6]

The Williams affair provides important insight into Hull's approach to Native Americans. The governor never showed concern that Williams sought to defraud the Wyandots. Rather, his primary concern was that Indians would consider violating the terms of a treaty with the U.S. government. Hull later discussed the incident in a letter to Secretary of War Henry Dearborn. The governor expressed satisfaction at resolving the Williams incident by maintaining the loyalty of Indians and upholding the integrity of an American treaty. More generally, Hull indicated that he already considered diplomacy with Indians to be a burden, especially since native groups as far as the Sandusky River considered him their "Father." The governor complained that "the business of the indian department, I find is arduous and difficult" as "great circumspection and primness are necessary." According to Hull, Native Americans never forgot a promise favorable to them and "never forgive a breach of it."[7]

By the fall of 1805, Hull grew suspicious of Indian groups outside the Detroit River region. He worried about "Western Indians" sending messages to local Obijwas, Odawas, Potawatomis, and Shawnees. The western tribes referred to Americans as "natural Enemies" and considered "immediately" making war. Although local Indians assured Hull that the "hatchet was buried," he suspected that British officials and others who "have great influence with the Indians" encouraged conflict.[8]

In November 1805, while Hull visited his home state of Massachusetts, Michigan's acting territorial governor, Stanley Griswold, added to fears of Indian unrest. "Though a great majority of the Indians in our vicinity are believed to be peaceably disposed, and averse from a rupture with the United States," according to Griswold, "still it is apprehended that a spirit of discontent, if not of war, prevails among some tribes near the Mississippi, and that attempts have been made, and are making by them, to rouse their brethren near us, to join in hostilities." For the acting governor, the only way to stay safe was to remain vigilant at all times.[9]

In the immediate term, the concerns of Hull and Griswold about the British and western Indians corrupting Detroit-area Indians proved unfounded. Relations between the territorial government and the region's tribes remained stable into 1807. Hull's correspondence to Washington focused more on local treaties and annuities with Indians than on military issues. The relationship that Hull fostered with the Wyandots, based on economic support in exchange for submissiveness and potential land offerings, served as a blueprint for his relations with other native communities.[10] By May 1807, however, the situation changed rapidly. Captain Josiah Dunham of Fort Mackinac informed Hull that there "appears to be an extensive movement among the Savages of this quarter, which seems to carry with it a good deal of the *dark* and *mysterious*." Dunham shared rumors, which were exaggerated, that Fort Dearborn (today Chicago) had fallen to the western Indians and that mischief had spread along Lake Michigan to Lake Superior. While he did not know if an attack on Detroit was imminent, Dunham was worried enough to warn Hull.[11]

Dunham had legitimate reason to be suspicious of the Indians of the Mackinac region. He obtained a copy of a speech, which he shared with Hull, by the prominent Odawa warrior Le Maigouis ("the Trout"). Le Maigouis was a devoted follower of Tenskwatawa, the Shawnee Prophet, and spread the Prophet's message of native spiritual revival and resistance against American encroachment to Indian villages throughout northern Michigan Territory. In the speech obtained by Dunham, the Trout related that the Great Spirit had told him Indians must avoid white men and no longer partake of rum. La Maigouis further stated that the Great Spirit had made all white men, including the Spanish and English, but he did not make Americans: "They are not my *Children*. But the *Children of the Evil Spirit – They grew from the Scum of the great water, when it was troubled by the Evil Spirit – And the froth was driven into the Woods by a strong east wind. They are numerous – But I hate them – They are unjust – They have taken away your Lands which were not made for them*[.]"[12]

Hull never responded to this broad critique of American expansionism. Instead, he continued to emphasize the smaller issue of annuities and other obligations within treaty agreements between the U.S. and various Indian tribes. During the same period of the Trout's spiritual awakening, Hull delivered a message to "The Crane and other Chiefs and Warriors of the Wyandot Nation" in which he blamed missing American annuity payments on Indian miscommunication. The governor claimed he was told that tribes would be hunting and unavailable to receive payment until a later date. He then placed blame on New York banks that were initially going to pay in small bank bills. Finally, Hull explained that he had "stated to the Secretary of War the inconvenience of the orders" and hoped that future payments would be made in silver and gold, thereby eliminating delays. Most notably, Hull continued to reduce America's relationship with Indians to monetary compensation and civil obedience. Throughout the speech, he cited their "duty" to the United States. Offering a covert threat of military or economic reprisal, Hull maintained it was the "duty" and "interest" of the Wyandots to meet treaty expectations even if the U.S. failed to do so.[13]

In mid-June 1807, Dunham reported increasing tension with the northern tribes in Michigan. Hull had asked Dunham to invite Odawa and Ojibwa chiefs to a council at Detroit with the intent of acquiring northern lands. The chiefs refused the offer and were judged by Dunham "to be much alarmed on the subject and indicate a disposition by no means friendly." Dunham suspected tribes from outside the region had influenced the chiefs. After refusing to attend the council, tribal elders demanded promised annuities and threatened that if they did not receive full payment, they would consider Americans "*all liars*" and lose faith in the American government. Dunham pleaded with Hull to meet the demands: "Your Excellency will easily appreciate the importance of preventing an impression so derogatory to our National Character ever on the Minds of Unenlightened Savages."[14]

Hull held the six-day conference in June despite the absence of the Odawas and the Ojibwas. During the meeting, Hull first proposed the Treaty of Detroit. The treaty, which was not signed until November, forced the region's Indian groups to cede the southeastern quarter of Michigan Territory. In exchange, the U.S. pledged various goods and annuities. After first proposing the treaty, Hull reported that although the British still attempted to agitate the region's Indian communities, he predicted no hostility against the United States.[15]

Hull overlooked the growing division between the territory's northern and southern Indian populations. Dunham previously reported to the governor that the northern tribes blamed their southern brethren for "forgetting their Children" and that "if they are fools enough to throw away their hunting ground, let them do it – We however in this quarter will do no such thing."[16] In July 1807, Hull was confronted with the problem when several Saginaw chiefs refused to attend a council requested on behalf of President Thomas Jefferson; the meeting was likely intended to present details of the Treaty of Detroit. In their rejection, the chiefs indicated that they had been cheated of annuities and land. According to Hull, Saginaw's Indian elders stated that about thirty warriors "were in favor of taking up the Hatchet – That they were dancing the War-Dance, and in fact had the Scalp of a White Man." Hull responded by inviting Detroit-area Indian leaders to the fort to express regret at the behavior of the Saginaw Indians. The governor's guests viewed a military procession on the Fourth of July, for which he was "extremely gratified at the appearance and Soldierlike Conduct of the Troops."[17] Hull's mood improved still more a week later, when annuities finally arrived from New York. He immediately called for the chiefs of the Odawas, Obijwas, Wyandots, and Potawatomis and later sent word to Saginaw. The arrival of goods led the governor to reassess the earlier threats of the Indians at Saginaw as "very much exaggerated." He also took solace that all was quiet at Mackinac.[18]

In late July, Hull learned of the *Chesapeake-Leopard* Affair, and his favorable outlook reversed. Concerned that the incident would ignite hostilities in the region, Hull wrote to Dearborn: "You cannot be insensible to our situation here – In the neighborhood of a British Garrison, and settlements, and accessible to vast bodies of Indians, on whose friendship and fidelity, it is impossible to make any certain calculations, seperated by an extensive Wilderness from any settlements, which could reasonably afford us aid, We have only to depend on our own exertions for safety." Hull further informed the secretary of war of the northern Indians' discontent, which the governor blamed on the negative influences of the Prophet and the British.

Although the Odawas, Ojibwas, Wyandots, and Potawatomis near Detroit remained peaceful, experienced residents in the region advised Hull that the natives "will prove deceitful." Preparing for a possible attack, he asked for "Powder, Ball and flints" and requested the assistance of the governor of Ohio. Hull concluded his missive by asserting that a "very considerable addition to the force" was necessary to provide for public safety.[19]

Panic spread in the ensuing months. "The people in this country," Hull noted on August 4, 1807, "are in a high state of alarm on account of the Indians." Throughout the year, Hull had received intelligence regarding the influence of western tribes at Mackinac and Saginaw, but it was not until the late summer of 1807 that he started agreeing with others that Detroit River region Indians posed a direct threat. The governor had kept peaceful relations with local Indians by providing annuities and fulfilling other treaty obligations whenever possible. In August, however, he received information that local Indians had joined the northern and western tribes in preparing for war. To counter the threat, the governor reinforced the fort and asked Dearborn for "immediate and decided measures" to defend frontier settlements.[20]

Hull was not alone in fearing an attack. That same month, Judge Augustus B. Woodward reported that Indians on the Huron River and along Lake Erie "had abandoned their settlements in an unusual manner, plainly indicating hostilities," and he predicted that Fort Detroit was "to be attacked in the dead of the night by four hundred and fifty Indians" camped in the woods behind Fort Amherstburg. Woodward connected the disturbances to the "little revolution" that had been affecting the Indians in the Mackinac region.[21]

Days later, Hull replied to Dearborn's request for intelligence on Upper Canada. The governor estimated about 1,300 militiamen at Amherstburg with 800 to 1,000 additional British-Canadian subjects in the region who could take up arms against the Americans. Hull committed the last several paragraphs of his report to the subject of the region's native communities. He once again expressed faith in the peaceful intentions of local Odawa, Wyandot, and Potawatomi villages. But Hull found the threat of hostile natives to the north and west "so alarming" that he continued making Fort Detroit "as strong against Indians as possible." Should the post be lost, he wrote, it would "probably be attended with great Sacrifice of lives . . . the Indians would generally be encouraged to strike on our defenseless Settlements." As a result, "the Frontiers would suffer incalculable evils."[22]

By September 1807, even though Hull still observed that "every circumstance . . . indicates an expectation of War on the part of the British," his assessment of Detroit's Indian problem improved. This sudden optimism was due to pledges of loyalty on behalf of the region's native communities. These pledges were, in Hull's estimation, the direct result of a new round of annuities being offered to local tribes.[23] To sustain the positive relations, Hull stressed that American gift-giving had to continue. The flow of gifts indeed persisted, and in November 1807, Hull secured an estimated five million acres of native land in finalizing the Treaty of Detroit. For the Americans, the treaty signified not only Indian land, but loyalty. In the immediate term, at least, the region's native groups concurred. Hull learned that British officers informed Native Americans on the Canadian side of the Detroit River that "war would soon take place between them and the Americans." The Indians refused to support the British, however, explaining that the Treaty of Detroit placed them under U.S. protection.[24]

The British did not stop courting potential Indian allies. In March 1808, Colonel William Claus, who served as deputy superintendent of the British Indian Department in Upper Canada, met secretly with several Shawnee chiefs. Claus warned of American intentions to take more Indian land. The Shawnees responded with hope "to be relieved from our present distressed situation" and expressed gratitude to their British father. Claus and other British Indian officials did not have a hard case to make. American settlers continued to follow a pattern of encroaching on native lands, which were then secured in one-sided treaty negotiations. Following the Treaty of Detroit, the treaties of Brownstown (1808) and Fort Wayne (1809) passed millions of additional acres of land to the U.S. For their part, the British did not seek native alliances without wanting something in return. The *Chesapeake* Affair convinced the British that they needed Indian allies in any potential conflict with the United States. Like the French before them, the British viewed Indians as partners in a global conflict, while the Americans saw natives at best as an obstacle and at worst as a threat.[25]

By 1810, Hull predicted war with Britain and its Native American allies. America's deteriorating relations with Britain colored how he viewed Detroit's struggling Indian population. "While here, they must either starve or plunder the inhabitants," according to Hull, "in the present state of things with England, I consider it good policy not to refuse them bread." The governor recognized that refusing starving Indians food could invite aggression. The only recourse for America, therefore, was "*feeding them when hungry.*"[26] What Hull did not perceive is that his conduct, as part of America's larger Indian policy, had helped to push the region's native communities into this desperate state. From his arrival at Detroit in 1805 until this observation in 1810, Hull viewed Indians as a burden. He aided the Wyandots on occasion, but always within a framework of keeping them subservient to American power. As long as local Indians were offered enough to keep them docile, Hull viewed his efforts as a success.

Yet Hull ultimately failed to build strong relationships with Native Americans. Of course, the failure was not his own, for he carried out a larger policy of the U.S. government that cared little about their welfare. Hull was no visionary, but he knew natives of the region gave loyalty to those who offered needed supplies. This was the premise of the relations he established. But the supplies Hull requested never arrived in adequate amounts to ensure the Indians' loyalty. By 1812, the British filled the void by providing natives with a variety of goods. With American settlers continually seizing native lands and the U.S. government offering meager compensation, Indian loyalties were ripe for the taking.

Hull has been condemned as a coward and defended as magnanimous. Scholars will continue to debate whether he saved hundreds of lives or humiliated his country by surrendering Michigan Territory. Understanding why Hull surrendered, however, must include a careful examination of his relations with the region's Indian groups prior to the war. He feared Indian aggression and the effect it would have on the territory. Like other American frontier officials, he sought to create relationships of dependency with native groups. The policy had no chance of succeeding so long as the U.S. government did not support his efforts by providing even a basic level of sustenance. Hull did not surrender the territory out of cowardice or magnanimity. The region's Indians were starving, and it was the British who fed them.

NOTES

1 Quotes in Alan Taylor, *The Civil War of 1812: American Citizens, British Subjects, Irish Rebels, & Indian Allies* (New York: Knopf, 2010), 164.

2 For the most recent and vigorous defense of Hull, see Anthony J. Yanik, *The Fall and Recapture of Detroit: In Defense of William Hull* (Detroit: Wayne State University Press, 2011). Donald R. Hickey summarizes the argument against Hull in *Don't Give Up the Ship! Myths of the War of 1812* (Urbana: University of Illinois Press, 2006), 54-56. Few accounts give primacy to Hull's relationship with Native Americans.

3 Peter Silver, *Our Savage Neighbors: How Indian War Transformed Early America* (New York: Norton, 2009), 53.

4 Joseph Badger to William Hull, July 30, 1805, in *MPHC*, 40:63. The agreement referred to in the letter is the Treaty of Swan Creek, which appears to have been separate from later treaties of the same name. For Williams, see also William Hull to Henry Dearborn, September 19, 1805, in *MPHC*, 40:58-59; and October 28, 1805, in *MPHC*, 40:77.

5 William Hull to Joseph Badger, August 7, 1805, in *MPHC*, 40:65-66.

6 Joseph Bader to William Hull, August 20, 1805, in *MPHC*, 40:67.

7 Hull to Dearborn, September 19, 1805, 40:59.

8 Hull to Dearborn, October 28, 1805, 40:77-78.

9 Stanley Griswold, "General Orders," November 15, 1805, in *MPHC*, 36:159.

10 William Hull to Henry Dearborn, February 20, 1807, in *MPHC*, 40:100-3; May 6, 1807, in *MPHC*, 40:112-13.

11 Josiah Dunham to William Hull, May 20, 1807, in *MPHC*, 40:123-27; 123-24 (quote).

12 "Speech of Indian Chief to Various Tribes," enclosed in Dunham to Hull, May 20, 1807, 40:127-33, 129 (quote); R. David Edmunds, *The Shawnee Prophet* (Lincoln: University of Nebraska Press, 1983), 51. For Tenskwatawa, see the essay in this volume by Kerri Jansen.

13 William Hull to Wyandot Chiefs, May 6, 1807, in *MPHC*, 40:115-117; 116 (quote).

14 Josiah Dunham to William Hull, June 18, 1807, in *MPHC*, 40:142-43; 142 ("to be much"); 143 (*"all liars"* and "Your Excellency").

15 William Hull to Henry Dearborn, June 22, 1807, in *MPHC*, 40:139-142. For the Treaty of Fort Detroit, see also Hull to Dearborn, November 4, 1807, in *MPHC*, 40:212-14; and November 18, 1807, in *MPHC*, 40:219-20.

16 Dunham to Hull, June 18, 1807, 40:142.

17 William Hull to Henry Dearborn, July 4, 1807, in *MPHC*, 40:152.

18 William Hull to Henry Dearborn, July 11, 1807, in *MPHC*, 40:153-54; 154 (quote).

19 William Hull to Henry Dearborn, July 25, 1807, in *MPHC*, 40:159-62; 159 ("You cannot be"); 160 ("will prove deceitful"); 161 ("Powder"); 162 ("very considerable addition"). For the *Chesapeake-Leopard* Affair, see the Introduction to this volume.

20 William Hull to Henry Dearborn, August 4, 1807, in *MPHC*, 40:169-71; 169 ("people in this Country"); 171 ("immediate and decided").

21 Augustus B. Woodward, "Reports of Indian Alarms," August 14, 1807, in *MPHC*, 40:174-77; 174 ("had abandoned"); 175 ("a little revolution"); 176 ("to be attacked").

22 William Hull to Henry Dearborn, August 16, 1807, in *MPHC*, 40:182-86; 185 ("so alarming"); 186 ("probably be attended").

23 William Hull to Henry Dearborn, September 9, 1807, in *MPHC*, 40:197-203; 197 (quote). See also Hull to Dearborn, September 15, 1807, in *MPHC*, 40:204; and October 6, 1807, in *MPHC*, 40:205.

24 William Hull to Henry Dearborn, November 24, 1807, in *MPHC*, 40:224.

25 "Proceedings of a Private Meeting with the Shawenoes," March 25, 1808, in *MPHC*, 25:242-44; 244 (quote).

26 William Hull to William Eustis, January 25 1810, in *MPHC*, 40:311.

Portrait of Elizabeth Denison Forth
Photographer unknown, c. 1850. Original format unknown; adapted from a print.
Courtesy of St. James Episcopal Church, Grosse Ile, Michigan.

Detroit's First Black Militia
Charlie Keller

In 1807, fifty-six years before Michigan's African Americans formed the 102nd Regiment to fight in the Civil War, Detroit's first black militia was created by Michigan territorial Governor William Hull from a contingent of thirty-six men, many of whom were fugitive slaves from Upper Canada. Hull formed the militia as war fever spread across the United States in response to the *Chesapeake-Leopard* Affair of June 1807. In the Detroit River region, British Colonel Jaspar Grant at Amherstburg first mentioned Hull's black militia in a letter to Military Secretary James Green of Quebec on August 17, 1807: "There is, besides, a company of Renegade Negroes who deserted from Captain [Matthew] Elliott and several Gentlemen at this side. This company consists of, I am informed, 36 in number."[1] Word spread fast in Canada, as James Askin wrote the next day to his brother Charles about Detroit's "Company of Negroes mounting Guard."[2] In early September, John Askin wrote to Isaac Todd of Montreal that "our run Away Negroes have had Arms given them & Mount Guard."[3] British Canadians were already exasperated by the sharply escalating number of their slaves running away to Detroit; seeing some of their former slaves in a Detroit militia added fuel to the fire.

Hull's decision to create a black militia was ostensibly due to the shock of the *Chesapeake-Leopard* Affair, but there is also evidence that he wanted to give the Canadian fugitives a more secure status. In promoting the militia, the governor clashed with his frequent rival, Judge Augustus B. Woodward. Woodward's legal decisions for the territorial Supreme Court also supported the freedom of runaway slaves, but the judge drew the line at mobilizing an all-black armed militia. Hull was more pragmatic. With war between the United States and Britain seemingly imminent, he sought to increase the military forces in Detroit as well as to enhance the fortification of the town. The governor wrote a flurry of letters in 1807 to Secretary of War Henry Dearborn requesting more troops and military supplies. Hull, a Revolutionary War veteran from Connecticut, apparently saw no issue with enlisting local free blacks and fugitive slaves from across the Detroit River into a militia. Incorporating free blacks and slaves into the military was successful during the Revolutionary War (1775-83), when "most slave soldiers received their freedom with their flintlocks. Upon enlistment they were given certificates of manumission."[4] Before the War of 1812, the creation of the black militia combined with Woodward's legal decisions and the exodus of fugitive slaves each way across the border permanently weakened slavery in the Detroit River region.[5]

Detroit's black militia emerged out of the unusual slave culture in the area. After British rule ended in Detroit in 1796, Americans inherited what the historian Arthur Kooker calls "a slave dowry" from the French and British. Roughly one-quarter of Detroit's residents owned slaves in 1782; in 1796, there were at least 178 slaves in the town, approximately 8 percent of the population. Slaves comprised two groups: Native American *panis* and people of African descent. *Panis* had been captured in battles between native tribes and sold primarily to the French prior to the British and American eras, though British Canadians continued to possess *panis* into the early nineteenth century. Most of Detroit's early black slaves had been captured in Revolutionary War raids into Ohio and Kentucky or brought to frontier territories by British loyalists. Others were bought outright in Montreal,

Detroit, and other locales. Few people owned more than one or two slaves, and most slaves were used in the home or occasionally places of business. Only a few families held large numbers of slaves; William Macomb's will of 1796 lists the names of twenty-six.[6]

Although the scale of Detroit-area slavery paled in comparison with the American South, the cruelty and degradation related to the institution could be similar. The saga of Ann Wiley attests to desperate attempts for revenge and self-liberation. On June 24, 1774, Wiley, a slave owned by James Abbott, and a store employee named Jean Baptiste Contencineau stole furs, knives, and guns from the company Abbott and Finchley. Wiley and Contencineau were found guilty of petty larceny and publicly whipped. A few days later, Wiley and Contencineau returned to Abbott and Finchley and set fire to the warehouse. Caught again, and tried by a jury, their punishment was decided by Justice of the Peace Philip Dejean in the spring of 1776: death by hanging. On the appointed day, finding no one willing to be the executioner, Dejean offered to spare Wiley's life if she would hang Contencineau. Wiley agreed to the bargain and publicly executed her partner.[7]

After 1796, free and enslaved residents of the Detroit River region adjusted to laws governing slavery on each side of the border. On the American side, Article Six of the Northwest Ordinance of 1787 technically made slavery illegal in the Old Northwest. In reality, the law forbade bringing new slaves into the region. Preexisting slaves were allowed to be held as chattel property, an acknowledgment of earlier French and British customs and laws. Likewise, across the Detroit River, slavery was a small but enduring institution despite the 1793 Simcoe Act. Similar to the Northwest Ordinance, the act forbade new slaves from being brought into Upper Canada, without immediately freeing existing slaves. By the terms of the Simcoe Act's "gradual emancipation," adult slaves were property for life, while their children born after 1793 were to be freed at the age of 25. Only subsequent generations would be born free. When the Americans took over Detroit, Jacques (James) Baby and other British loyalists moved their families and slaves to homes in Sandwich. Matthew Elliott had already moved with his family and slaves to a 3,000-acre farm near Amherstburg in 1784. There, he would become notorious for publicly whipping his slaves. Under the Simcoe Act, Elliott and other British loyalists were allowed to keep their slaves.[8]

Even with legal protections for slavery in the Old Northwest and in Upper Canada, the international border at the Detroit River posed a special threat to the institution. American fugitive slaves crossed into Canada for freedom, and runaways also crossed the border in hopes of a free life in United States territory. The runaway slaves on both sides cleverly sought to take advantage of the provisions in the Northwest Ordinance and Simcoe Act that barred new slavery. They joined free black loyalists already residing in Canada and a growing free black population in Michigan Territory. According to the 1811 census of Michigan Territory, ninety-six nonwhite/non-Indian free persons lived in Detroit.[9]

After 1805, Michigan's territorial status and the Supreme Court at Detroit helped to protect the freedom of runaways, including those who ended up in Hull's black militia. Despite their famous rivalry, Hull's policies and Judge Augustus B. Woodward's decisions on the court worked together to open new possibilities for freedom-seeking slaves on both sides of the border. Of the two men, Woodward took longer to support the freedom of runaway slaves and never approved of the black militia. He initially viewed fugitive slaves and military deserters from across the Detroit River as legally similar. Both groups increased in the months following the *Chesapeake-Leopard* Affair in June 1807, but the growing numbers of runaway slaves provoked the most international consternation. As Woodward wrote to Secretary of State James Madison in July, "There is however one point on which the inhabitants of the different sides of the river are at variance.

This is the desertion of the slaves. I expect complaints will be made to you on this head by the British minister. I do not approve the temper, principles and conduct of the inhabitants of this side, on the subject. I thought something ought to be done to check it." Not only did U.S. and British Canadian officials disagree about what to do with military deserters and fugitive slaves, the leaders of Michigan Territory also took different positions. Woodward introduced a bill for the extradition of military deserters and fugitive slaves to Upper Canada, but it was opposed and ultimately defeated by Hull and Judge John Griffin.[10]

The different approaches to slavery were evident in how Hull and Woodward treated former slave Peter Denison. In August 1807, Hull made Denison the commander of Detroit's black militia. Denison had only recently been manumitted from slavery: In 1805, Detroit resident William Tucker emancipated Denison and his wife, Hannah, in his will. The couple spent a final year of bondage at attorney Elijah Brush's home. Sadly, the Denisons' four children, Elizabeth, Scipio, James, and Peter Jr., remained enslaved. Tucker bequeathed the Denison children to his sons, and they were held by his widow, Catherine. In September 1807, with Brush's legal representation, Peter and Hannah Denison sued Catherine Tucker for their children's freedom in the Michigan territorial Supreme Court. Woodward agonized over the case before deciding in favor of Tucker on September 23, 1807. The historian Reginald Larrie has referred to Woodward's verdict in the Denison case as "Michigan's Dred Scott Decision."[11]

Like Scott, the Denisons were defined as property – not people – and denied the freedom due to them according to the Northwest Ordinance. Woodward determined that, despite the antislavery clause of the ordinance, the second article of Jay's Treaty (1794) took precedent, protecting existing cases of slavery: "All settlers and traders within the precincts and jurisdiction of said post shall continue to enjoy, unmolested all their property of every kind and shall be protected therein they shall be at full liberty to remain there or to remove with all or any part of their effects."[12] According to Woodward, as Elizabeth, James, and Scipio Denison were born enslaved in British Detroit before the Simcoe Act of 1793, they were slaves for life. Their youngest sibling, Peter Denison Jr., was born after 1793 but before the Americans occupied Detroit in 1796. Therefore, he could be held as a slave until the age of 25. Elizabeth and Scipio Denison did not let the ruling deny their freedom. They promptly crossed the Detroit River to Sandwich, where they stayed with Brush's father-in-law, John Askin. At some point during or just after the War of 1812, Elizabeth and Scipio returned to Detroit, where they were befriended by esteemed white citizens and continued living in a free status.[13]

By then, Woodward's additional rulings on slavery protected the freedom of runaway slaves crossing from Upper Canada. In October 1807, one month after the Denison decision, Woodward redeemed himself in the cases of Richard Pattinson and Matthew Elliott. Pattinson, of Sandwich, issued a warrant for the arrest of his fugitive slaves Joseph Quinn and Jane in Michigan's Supreme Court. Woodward denied the extradition of Jane and Joseph on October 23, 1807. The next day, Woodward denied powerful Amherstburg slave owner Elliott the ability to apprehend "Sundry of his Slaves now within this territory."[14] Woodward's decisions were firmly respected. No slave owners from Sandwich or Amherstburg tried again to use legal channels to extradite runaway slaves from Michigan Territory. The court of Upper Canada followed Woodward's lead by refusing to return fugitive slaves who had escaped from U.S. territory into Canada. In this instance, Woodward viewed the fugitives as persons rather than property. He was very proud of his detailed opinion in the Pattinson case and circulated copies to eastern newspapers.[15]

Woodward did not support Detroit's first black militia, but his decisions not to return fugitive slaves to Upper Canada gave Hull the legal cover to use them as members of the militia.

The governor still had to overcome critics on both sides of the border. His initial defense of the black militia was written to calm the fears of Colonel Grant at Amherstburg. On September 3, 1807, Hull wrote to Grant: "And particularly the permission which I have given to a small number of Negroes, occasionally to exercise in Arms. This measure, I am informed has excited some sensibility among the Inhabitants on the British Shore. Be assured Sir, it is without any foundation, for they only have the use of their Arms, while exercising, and at all other times they are deposited in a situation out of their control."[16] The limits that Hull placed on the arming of blacks did not satisfy Woodward. On October 17, 1808, the day before departing for the East Coast, the judge drafted a list of thirteen resolutions on various topics to be examined by a committee of the territorial government. In Resolution IV, Woodward objected to the black militia, deeming it "injurious to the proprietors of slaves, both in his Britannic Majesty's province of Upper Canada . . . and in this Territory."[17]

Hull used Woodward's absence to solidify support for the black militia. As the only standing member of the committee at that time, Hull found it easy to refute Woodward's resolutions. Judge Griffin sent Hull's report to Woodward on December 23, 1808. Hull, as "the committee," stated: "The governor has given permission to the black male inhabitants to exercise as a military company; that he has appointed a black man by the name of Peter Denison to command them; though not in the form a military commission. It further appears that this company has frequently appeared under arms, and has made considerable progress in military discipline." Hull continued, "With respect to any of them being slaves, the committee only observes that they are black persons, who resided in the Territory, and were not claimed as slaves by any person or persons in the original States." The governor's usage of the word "persons" for blacks was highly unusual for the time period. The term implied the free status of members of the militia, which Hull made explicit in the following sentence: "They were persons residing in the Territory, subject to the laws and entitled to the protection of the government."[18]

Having defined blacks as persons, Hull used the committee's report to defend their right to military service. "They have ever conducted in an orderly manner, manifested on all occasions an attachment to our government and a determination to aid in the defence of the country whenever their services should be required," the governor wrote. Hull also reminded the Michigan territorial Supreme Court of Article Six of the Northwest Ordinance: "There shall be neither slavery, nor involuntary servitude in the said Territory." With bravado, Hull concluded that "the conduct of the executive . . . was not only proper but highly commendable; especially as it was at a period when the safety and protection of the Territory appeared to require all the force which could be possibly collected."[19]

Nonetheless, Woodward continued to oppose Detroit's black militia. On July 23, 1810, Woodward wrote to Hull objecting to "your embodying the runaway slaves belonging to the inhabitants of the adjacent province of his Britannic Majesty into a militia company, appointing a negro officer to command them, and supplying them with arms belonging to the United States." Woodward also leveled the "more serious" charge that Hull acted as a military dictator by ordering men to engage in martial activities when they were not members of Detroit's actual militia.[20] The following year, in June 1811, Woodward drafted a resolution, again berating the governor as "unauthorized" to organize fugitive slaves from Upper Canada into a military company.[21] The judge also used a legislative debate to censure Hull for "seducing negro slaves from gentlemen residing on . . . [the British] side of the river, and supplying them with arms and ammunition." Woodward's slanderous words offended Whitmore Knaggs, a Hull partisan, and resulted in a knock-down brawl between Knaggs and Woodward at a private social gathering.[22]

Woodward's critiques increasingly made clear that he mostly

opposed the black militia on military grounds, particularly for the added power that it gave to Hull. Woodward's mistrust of Hull's handling of military affairs dated to the governor's formation of a territorial militia in 1805. Hull appointed Woodward colonel of the First Regiment, made up of Detroiters, before quickly revoking the commission.[23] In other areas, the two leaders were in agreement on the free status of blacks in Detroit. The awarding of donation land plots to free blacks provides the best example of this consensus. After Detroit's 1805 fire, Hull and Woodward successfully urged the U.S. Congress to provide free land titles to Detroit residents to alleviate suffering as part of a new town plan. The donation plots were awarded gradually from 1806 until at least 1821. After the choicest titles went to those who could afford them, the remaining plots were allotted to three classes of people: property owners in Detroit before the fire, tenants or householders, and inhabitants who were neither owners nor tenants. In 1809, at least ten African Americans, as part of the third class, received donation plots. Most were probably very recently manumitted Detroit slaves: Pompey, Thomas Parker, Joseph Cooper, Cato, Harry, Hannah, London, Mary, Margrett, and Hannah. With the black militia and the decisions in the Pattinson and Elliott cases, the donation plots signaled a new status and respect for blacks in Detroit.[24]

Unfortunately, with the limited records available, we may never know the full history of Detroit's black militia. The last known reference to the militia appeared in a letter from Woodward to Secretary of War William Eustis on July 28, 1812. Writing in the past tense, Woodward criticized Hull for issuing "three commissions to captain Denison, lieutenant Burgess, and ensign Bosset, black men" without the legal authority necessary for an executive official to grant military commissions.[25] It is not clear when the black militia was disbanded or why it was not called into duty when the War of 1812 came to the Detroit River region, yet reactions in the area leave no doubt that the militia had considerable influence. In examining the history of slavery in the region leading up to the War of 1812, one sees a conflicted white view of slavery that swiftly transformed into manumissions, legal protections, and heightened status for blacks. Fugitive slaves from either side of the river started this series of events; local manumissions seem to have been granted under a sense of resignation that slavery was on its last legs in the area. The number of slaves listed in Michigan Territory censuses fell to twenty-four in 1811 and to zero in 1820.[26] Detroit's black militia, Woodward's decisions in 1807, and the awarding of donation land plots all reflected the improving status of Detroit's black residents and fugitive slaves from Upper Canada. Hull may be most remembered for surrendering Detroit to the British in 1812 and for the humiliating military trial that ensued. He should just as properly be remembered for upholding the dignity of Detroit's African-American population as a steadfast proponent of the town's first black militia.

NOTES

1 Jaspar Grant to James Green, August 17, 1807, in *MPHC*, 15:42. For the *Chesapeake-Leopard* Affair, see the Introduction to this volume.

2 James Askin to Charles Askin, August 18,1807, in *Askin Papers*, 2:566.

3 John Askin to Isaac Todd, September 4, 1807, in *Askin Papers*, 2:570.

4 Benjamin Quarles, *The Negro in the American Revolution* (Chapel Hill: University of North Carolina Press, 1996), 68-69.

5 For the most complete existing study of Detroit's black militia, see Norman McRae, "Blacks in Detroit, 1736-1833: The Search for Freedom and Community and Its Implications for Educators" (PhD diss., University of Michigan, 1982), 96-105. For broader works on blacks serving in the War of 1812, see Gerard T. Altoff, *Amongst My Best Men: African-Americans and the War of 1812* (Put-in-Bay, OH: Perry Group, 1996); and Donald R. Hickey, *Don't Give Up the Ship! Myths of the War of 1812* (Urbana: University of Illinois Press, 2006), 185-191. For references to African Canadians serving on the British side, see "War of 1812," www.eighteentwelve.ca (accessed March 16, 2012); and Daniel G. Hill, *The Freedom Seekers: Blacks in Early Canada* (Agincourt, ON: Book Society of Canada, 1981), 113-14. For the Hull-

Woodward rivalry, see Frank B. Woodford, *Mr. Jefferson's Disciple: A Life of Justice Woodward* (East Lansing: Michigan State College Press, 1953), 54-64.

6 Arthur R. Kooker, "The Antislavery Movement in Michigan 1796-1840: A Study in Humanitarianism on an American Frontier" (PhD diss., University of Michigan, 1941), 18. For slavery in the Detroit River region, see Gregory Wigmore, "Before the Railroad: From Slavery to Freedom in the Canadian-American Borderland," *Journal of American History* 98 (2011): 437-54; Afua Cooper, "The Fluid Frontier: Blacks and the Detroit River Region: A Focus on Henry Bibb," *Canadian Review of American Studies* 30 (2000): 127-48; J.A. Giradin, "Slavery in Detroit," in *MPHC*, 1:415-17; Denver Brunsman and Joel Stone, eds., *Revolutionary Detroit: Portraits in Political and Cultural Change, 1760-1805* (Detroit: Detroit Historical Society, 2009), 7-8; and Therese A. Kneip, "Slavery in Early Detroit" (master's thesis, University of Detroit, 1938). William Macomb ledger with inventory of slaves, R2:1796 (vault), Macomb Papers, BHC.

7 Errin T. Stegich, "Liberty Hangs at Detroit: The Trial and Execution of Jean Contencineau," in *Revolutionary Detroit*, 67-72; Kneip, 27-28; Giradin, 416.

8 For the overlapping, contradictory laws on slavery in the Detroit River region, see Kneip and Wigmore. For the movement of slaves to Canada, see Cooper, 129-32. Cooper states that thirty slaves were with the Baby Family and fifty were brought into Upper Canada by the Elliott family. See also William R. Riddell, "Slavery in Canada," *Journal of Negro History* 5 (1920): 333, which estimates the number of slaves held by Elliott at about sixty. For Elliott's move to Amherstburg, see Reginald Horsman, *Matthew Elliott, British Indian Agent* (Detroit: Wayne State University Press, 1964), 44-46. For Elliott's cruelty to slaves, see Riddell, "A Negro Slave in Detroit when Detroit was Canadian," *Michigan History* 18 (1934): 49-50; and accounts recorded in Elliott Family Chronology, Matthew Elliott Collection, Fort Malden National Historic Site of Canada, Amherstburg. For more visceral evidence, the lashing ring from Elliott's whipping tree is displayed at the North American Black Historical Museum in Amherstburg.

9 "Census of Michigan Territory, 1811," in *Transactions of the Supreme Court of the Territory of Michigan*, ed. William W. Blume, 6 vols. (Ann Arbor: University of Michigan Press, 1935-40), 1:5. One can safely assume that the ninety-six nonwhite/non-Indian free people in Detroit were free blacks. For emancipation by crossing the Detroit River, see Cooper, 129-31; and Wigmore.

10 Augustus B. Woodward to James Madison, July 18, 1807, Folder January-July, 1807, Box 1806-1808, Augustus Brevoort Woodward Papers, BHC. The letter is also transcribed in *MPHC*, 12:505-7.

11 Reginald R. Larrie, *Makin' Free: African-Americans in the Northwest Territory* (Detroit: Blaine Ethridge Books, 1981), 6. For Woodward's reasoning behind the decision, see *MPHC*, 12:511-18.

12 Jay's Treaty quoted in McRae, 91.

13 McRae, 89-92; Kooker 35-42. For Elizabeth Denison's case and life in Michigan after the War of 1812, see also Isabella E. Swan, *The Ark of God: A History of the Episcopal Church* (Grosse Ile, MI: Wardens and Vestrymen of St. James Church of Grosse Ile, 1968), 21-23; Swan, *Lisette* (Grosse Ile, MI: Swan, 1965); and Carol E. Mull, *The Underground Railroad in Michigan* (Jefferson, NC: McFarland, 2010), 13-14. For Brush's role in the case, see the essay in this volume by Sharon Tevis Finch.

14 See Blume, 1:414-18 for both cases (quote, 418). McRae identifies eight of Elliott's slaves who escaped in the winter-spring of 1806-7: Hanna, Abraham, Pompey, Candace, Fanny, Sipio, Thomas Chambers, and Capias. The first six persons were members of a family. Chambers and Capias escaped shortly after the family (94).

15 For the reasoning and influence of Woodward's decisions, see McRae, 93-94; and Wigmore, 451-52. For the absence of future Canadian slave cases in the Michigan Supreme Court, see Blume, 1:88-217. For Upper Canada's refusal to extradite U.S. fugitive slaves, see Wigmore, 454. For Woodward's opinion in the eastern press, see Woodford, 90.

16 William Hull to Jaspar Grant, September 3, 1807, in *MPHC*, 31:600.

17 "Judge Woodward's Resolutions," October 17, 1808, Folder October 15-December 1808, Box 3, Woodward Papers. *MPHC*, 12:462 dates these resolutions as December 31, 1806, which must be incorrect. Woodward departed on October 18, 1808, for the East Coast and did not return until October 5, 1809. See Blume, xxv, xxxix.

18 John Griffin to Augustus B. Woodward, December 23, 1808, in *MPHC*, 12:469.

19 Griffin to Woodward, December 23, 1808, 12:469 ("They have" and "There shall"); 470 ("the conduct").

20 Augustus B. Woodward to William Hull, July 23, 1810, Folder 1810-1811, Box 2, William Hull Papers, BHC.

21 Woodward's Resolution, June 14, 1811, Folder June-December 1811, Box 1809-1811, Woodward Papers.

22 Woodward described his censure of Hull and fight with Knaggs in a letter to British Colonel Henry Procter, January 29, 1813, in *MPHC*, 36:277-80; 278 (quote). For the Knaggs-Woodward fight, see also Woodford, 69-71.

23 Woodford, 54-55.

24 For donation plots given to Detroit African Americans, see McRae, 87-88; and Mary Agnes Burton and Clarence M. Burton, eds., *Governor and Judges Journal: Proceedings of the Land Board of Detroit* (Detroit: Michigan Commission on Land Titles, 1915), 20, 44, 47, 116, 162, 172, 207, 230-31, 268, 270, 280, 284. Of the land recipients, we have the most information for Pompey. He received the donation as Pompey Abbott, James Abbott being his final owner. He was sold at least five times, twice to John Askin. See *Askin Papers*, 1:58-59; Giradin, 417; McRae, 87; and Kooker, 8-9, 14. For the aftermath of the fire, see the essay in this volume by Keith A. Killoran.

25 Augustus B. Woodward to William Eustis, July 28, 1812, in *The Territorial Papers of the United States*, ed. Clarence E. Carter and John P. Bloom, 27 vols. (Washington, DC:

Department of State and National Archives and Records Service, 1934-69), 10:390.

26 Blume, ed., 1:5; Kooker, 47. Manumissions were also occurring in Sandwich and Amherstburg during the same timeframe, most likely out of frustration over fugitive slaves and gradual emancipation laws on both sides of the Detroit River. In 1806, there were only seventy-five recorded slaves in Sandwich and thirty-one in Amherstburg. Elliott listed no slaves in his will in 1814 (Wigmore, 453). His sons were antislavery men, and the Elliott house later became a refuge for fugitive slaves arriving in Amherstburg from the United States (Elliott Family Chronology, 1834, Elliott Collection).

Part Two:

War

François Baby House

Engraving by Lossing and Barritt. Published in Benson J. Lossing, *The Pictorial Field-Book of the War of 1812* (New York: Harper, 1869), 262.

Headquarters for Invasion: The François Baby House
Justin Wargo

On July 13, 1812, a sunny and pleasant Monday, American General William Hull stood in Sandwich, Upper Canada, and proclaimed to the gathering residents: "I promise you protection to your persons, property, and rights. Remain at your homes, pursue your peaceful and customary avocations; raise not your arms against your brethren." Even if Hull was sincere in his decree, there was one great inconsistency: He made his pronouncement while on the lands, and after commandeering the home, of François Baby.[1]

Baby was not present to hear Hull's declaration, due to his recently appointed role as assistant quartermaster general of the militia. The previous day, the entire Canadian militia situated in the Western District of Upper Canada followed a gentle southwesterly breeze in retreat to Fort Amherstburg after witnessing American forces prepare an invasion across the mile-wide Detroit River. Convinced Amherstburg was Hull's immediate destination, Baby's older brother, Jacques (known as James), colonel of the First Kent Militia, and younger brother, Jean-Baptiste, lieutenant colonel of the Second Division of Essex Militia, would join François after directing hesitant Canadian militiamen, primarily farmers and merchants, to the fort. General Hull and his assistant James Taylor Jr., quartermaster general and paymaster of the Northwestern Army, resided comfortably in François Baby's home, while hundreds of soldiers squatted upon his farmland and orchards. The Americans optimistically referred to Baby's property as "Fort Hope."[2]

The benefits of seizing Baby's property were twofold. First, Baby's home was logistically valuable for launching an assault on Fort Amherstburg while still within the maximum effective range of guns from Fort Detroit – an advantage Hull would later realize also worked the other way. Second, taking and eventually destroying Baby's home and property served as a warning to other inhabitants of the Western District. As influential Sandwich residents and fervent British subjects, the Babys represented the antithesis of the docile populace Hull hoped to encounter in Upper Canada. French-Catholic merchants, they increasingly held prominent parliamentary and social roles in Upper and Lower Canada, ultimately becoming part of the "Family Compact" that exerted aristocratic, oligarchic control over Upper Canada. The family's importance in the Detroit River region, due to a combination of its ethnic heritage, business success, and governmental positions, placed it directly within a cultural, commercial, and political British-French-Native trichotomy. At the start of the nineteenth century, the Babys in the Great Lakes region were French in blood, British in position, and both American and Canadian in property. After the War of 1812, and largely because of the economic, political, and social results of the conflict, the family reflected two significant consequences of war in the Detroit River region: a strengthening of the border between Michigan Territory and Upper Canada, and the beginnings of a Canadian national identity.[3]

The Baby family had deep roots in Detroit. Born near Montreal in 1731, Jacques Duperon Baby (known as Duperon) relocated to Detroit in the early 1750s to run the western sector of the family's business interests. Ardently French, he was recognized by King Louis XV for outstanding service at the final stand before Montreal fell to the British during the French and Indian War (1754-63). In 1761, Duperon pledged an oath of loyalty to Britain in order to remain in Detroit under British rule. On August 25, 1763, the legacy of the Baby family was assured when Duperon's wife, Susanne Reaume Baby, herself from an influential French family, gave birth to James on the south side of the Detroit River in what would become Sandwich. The remainder of the Baby children would be born inside Fort Detroit. Duperon maintained business interests on both sides of the river until his death in 1789.[4]

In December 1800, François Baby became the sole owner of the family's ribbon farm in Sandwich, known as *La Ferme*, after paying his mother and siblings ten shillings and one peppercorn. Years earlier, the land had been deeded to Duperon Baby by local Indians for his loyalty and friendship. The property that passed to François included a wood-frame home near the banks of the Detroit River that could have been built as early as 1760, when Duperon married Susanne. In early 1812, François began constructing a new house on the property. As much as a growing family influenced François's decision to build the home, an equally motivating factor was competition with his brother, James. In 1807, James purchased the impressive Sandwich mansion owned by merchant Alexander Duff. Partly in an attempt to outdo James, François chose to construct a brick home – the first on either side of the Detroit River – with double the number of fireplaces (four compared to James's two), a grand heating stove, and ten-foot ceilings on both the first and second floors. François's home was far from complete when the Americans arrived on July 12, containing little more than a shingled roof, laid floors, and windows. Yet, the structure still made an impressive headquarters for Hull.[5]

Soon after settling in at Fort Hope, the general made preparations for an advance on Amherstburg. Despite numerous attempts to push forward, Hull's efforts in the Western District amounted to a few indecisive skirmishes. His lack of significant progress, exacerbated by fears of Indian attacks and American losses sustained at Brownstown and Fort Mackinac, caused Hull to abandon the Upper Canadian campaign and return to Fort Detroit on August 7. Hull and the several hundred American troops who camped on François Baby's property showed utter disregard for his possessions, leaving little more than the two dwellings – the old wood-frame building and the new, incomplete brick house. The structures sat vacant for one day before British Colonel Henry Procter took command of the position and began installing armaments. On August 15, after convening at Fort Amherstburg, Major General Isaac Brock, Shawnee leader Tecumseh, and their respective fighters arrived at Baby's property to prepare to attack Detroit.[6]

The British Royal Engineers assembled their artillery under the cover of Baby's wood-frame house. New Englander Lydia Bacon, in Detroit while traveling with her husband, Lieutenant Josiah Bacon, described the view from the American side: "the enemy have been very busy building, as we suppose, a battery upon the opposite shore. The ends project beyond a large dwelling which conceals them while they work."[7] The British were prepared to bombard Detroit within hours of Brock's and Tecumseh's arrival. Prior to firing, though, Brock ordered Hull to peacefully relinquish the fort. As Hull nervously debated his next move, British soldiers across the river pulled down what remained of Baby's wood-frame home to unveil one 18-pound and two 12-pound cannons, as well as two 5½-inch mortars, trained on Fort Detroit. After Hull refused to capitulate, Brock ordered a bombardment of the fort on the evening of August 15. Even with having, in Brock's estimation, superior numbers and "well directed fire from seven 24 pounders," Hull ensured his legacy the following day by surrendering Detroit after snatching and unfurling a white tablecloth belonging to Jane Dodemead.[8]

The legend of Brock may have been born at the Baby house. One story states that Brock had his limited number of regulars march through the house in a perpetual loop, deceiving Hull into thinking a larger force opposed him than was actually present. The story has never been substantiated, but a letter from Brock to Major Thomas Evans indicates another form of trickery was certainly at play. Brock wrote, "Your thought of clothing the militia in the 41st cast off clothing proved a most happy one, it having more than doubled our own regular force in the enemy's eye."[9] Brock cleverly dressed his inexperienced band of fighting farmers as if they were the highly trained British redcoats so esteemed in military lore. Regardless of how Brock may have deceived Hull, Baby was satisfied witnessing Detroit return to British hands. Shortly after Hull first commandeered his home, Baby admonished the general and reminded him of their former friendship. Hull responded that "it was true enough but *circumstances were changed now.*" Seeing Hull as a captive in Brock's tent, Baby confidently said, "Well General, *circumstances are changed now indeed.*"[10] Baby's delight was short-lived once he realized the extent of his missing and damaged property. Brock's stay in Sandwich ended on August 18, but Baby's efforts to receive compensation for his wartime losses had just begun.[11]

According to Baby, upon viewing the depredations initially committed by Hull's men, Brock assured him that full reimbursement would be made: "Baby they have wacked you well, but you shall be rewarded to the full account, if not in money, in lands."[12] François overlooked any damage caused by Brock's men and consistently blamed the Americans for all his losses. Less than twenty-four hours after the surrender of Detroit, Baby wrote to Hull, who was being held in Detroit awaiting transfer as a prisoner to Montreal, for reimbursement of damages sustained to his property. Baby requested a total of £2,450, an immense sum, for two houses, ruined gardens and fences, stolen cattle, sixty acres of oats, seventy acres of wheat, forty acres of timothy grass, and one thousand young fruit trees.[13]

Hull responded by authorizing Taylor to "settle with Colonel Baby, in the same manner as he settles with others under similar circumstances."[14] Taylor denied payment, reasoning that Baby had incurred the normal costs of war, and the United States had no obligation to reimburse him.[15] This decision infuriated Baby, solidifying his opinion of the Americans as callous for leaving him and his family short of food and shelter. He went with his father-in-law, James Abbott, to raid Detroit homes in search of his missing goods. When Baby recognized one of his carpets on the floor at Richard Smyth's house, he retrieved it. Yet, given the large sum that he sought, Baby was unlikely to be satisfied no matter what he could salvage. In 1824, he finally received compensation of £444 and 800 acres of land from the British government. Baby considered his rank worthy of 1,200 acres and petitioned the government for several more years, to no avail.[16]

Hull's takeover of Baby's home was merely one instance from the War of 1812 era that reinforced the family's negative view of America. The triumvirate of James, François, and Jean-Baptiste would individually and collectively see action at the River Raisin, Battle of the Thames, and across the Niagara frontier. Like François's home, James's residence was also commandeered by a U.S. general and ravaged by American forces. Unlike François, James received recompense from the British in the form of the lucrative position of inspector general for Upper Canada at York (today Toronto), granted to him after the conflict. Additionally, both James and François became prisoners of war: James at the Battle of the Thames in 1813, after which he was taken to Sandwich and detained by General William Henry Harrison within his own home; and François at Delaware, Upper Canada, in 1814. Demonstrating the misinformation published during the period, François's capture led the *Providence Patriot* to propagandize, "Capt. Lee . . . made prisoners of a number of British officers; among whom is the famous Col. Baubee who, with his command of Indians, so gloriously displayed himself in ravaging, burning and laying waste the Niagara frontier, and murdering the unresisting and helpless women and children." In fact, François worked to ransom American prisoners from Indians just prior to the massacre at the River Raisin in January 1813, and there is no other evidence that he acted uncivilly in the Niagara region.[17]

During the war, other British Canadians went through a similar process of disaffection from the Americans. It resulted in a firmer sense of the international border between British Canada and the U.S. and the first inklings of a distinctly Canadian identity. After the Americans captured the Western District in October 1813, they ravaged many farms and homes in the region. The British decision to abandon the theater, in favor of Niagara and the Lower St. Lawrence River Valley, contributed to the difficulties experienced by residents of Sandwich, Amherstburg, and surrounding locales. As with François Baby, many people struggled to get compensation from the British or Americans for their property losses. Also like Baby, most of these victims blamed the Americans for their suffering. Since the mid-eighteenth century, inhabitants of the Detroit River region had largely resisted outside efforts to impose political or national conformity. If anything, individuals like Duperon Baby shifted as necessary with the changing political winds. In many ways, the War of 1812 accomplished in the region what earlier conflicts, particularly the American Revolutionary War (1775-1783), had not: bring significance to political divisions represented by the international border.[18]

Recent scholarship on Canadian identity suggests that the Babys were part of an emerging trend in the region. Inhabitants of the Western District could assimilate multiple cultural influences. Beginning with Duperon, the Babys had the ability to be anything to anyone. In equal parts because of their father's earlier loyalty to the British crown, the regional parliamentary positions they had filled for years, and their treatment at the hands of the Americans during war, the Baby sons' identification as British subjects was certain. Yet the brothers also never lost their French cultural affiliation. In 1792, James and François Baby were the sole members of French descent in the first parliamentary governments of British Canada.[19]

During the French Revolutionary and Napoleonic Wars (1793-1815), British imperial authorities might have looked upon the Baby family with suspicion. Instead, the Babys' cultural dexterity was treated as an asset. The family represented an extreme and early case of the duality, or "divided loyalties," that has come largely to define Canadian national identity. Culturally, the most dominant feature of the Canadian people is their bicultural, British-French, heritage. Another characteristic is their dual fascination with and repudiation of all things American. In their French ethnicity and British subjecthood, the Babys embodied the two dominant cultural influences in Canadian identity. Moreover, with their proximity to U.S. territory and their wartime experiences, they viewed Americans as both friends and enemies.[20]

The formation of a national identity is a gradual process, one that Canada grapples with to this day. Amidst the bicentennial of the War of 1812, it is tempting to attribute too much influence to the war. Still, for the Detroit River region, the war no doubt played a key role in defining what it means to be Canadian – then and now. For François Baby and others in the Western District, the ravages committed during the initial American invasion and later occupation went far in distinguishing a British-Canadian "us" versus an American "them." For later generations up to the present, hindsight has allowed Canadians to take pride that their forbearers survived American invasion attempts.[21] François Baby's residence, the headquarters for one of British Canada's greatest military achievements in the taking of Detroit, began the war as the shell of a house. After the war, the structure and its surrounding property, situated along the Detroit River, would help to mark the boundary of the modern Canadian homeland. Today, a rebuilt version of Baby's home, on the original site, is a Canadian National Historic Site and Windsor's Community Museum. The building provides a visible reminder of the multiple eras, nations, and peoples that have shaped the Detroit River region.

NOTES

1. William Hull, *Memoirs of the Campaign of the North Western Army of the United States* (Boston: True & Greene, 1824), 46. The French surname Baby is pronounced "BAW-BEE" and occasionally appears in written records as Baubie, Babee, or Babie. However, by the late eighteenth century, descendants on either side of the Detroit River used the Anglicized "Baby" spelling. François was also known as Francis, but, unlike his brother James (Jacques), did not indicate a clear preference for the Anglicized spelling of his name. Therefore, the original French spelling is used in this essay.

2. For the American invasion and occupation of Baby's house, see Lieut. Col. St. George to Maj. Gen. Brock, July 15, 1812, in *MPHC*, 15:103-4; William S. Hatch, *A Chapter in the History of the War of 1812 in the Northwest* (Cincinnati: Miami Printing and Publishing, 1872), 28-29; R. Alan Douglas, *Mansion to Museum: The Francois Baby House in Its Times* (Windsor: Herald Press, 1989); and Sandy Antal, *Invasions: Taking and Retaking Detroit and the Western District during the War of 1812 and Its Aftermath* (Windsor: Essex County Historical Society, 2011), 5.

3. This work builds on previous studies of the American-Canadian border and national identity in the Detroit River region. See R. Alan Douglas, *Uppermost Canada: The Western District and the Detroit Frontier, 1800-1850* (Detroit: Wayne State University Press, 2001), 3-19; Alan Taylor, *The Civil War of 1812: American Citizens, British Subjects, Irish Rebels, & Indian Allies* (New York: Knopf, 2010), 7-11, 106-10; Roger Gibbins, "Meaning and Significance of the Canadian-American Border" in *Borders and Border Politics in a Globalizing World*, ed. Paul Ganster and David E. Lorey (Lanham, MD: SR Books, 2005), 151-68; and John J. Bukowczyk et al., *Permeable Border: The Great Lakes Basin as Transnational Region, 1650-1990* (Pittsburgh: University of Pittsburgh Press, 2005), 10-77.

4. Royal Society of Canada, *Proceedings and Transactions of the Royal Society of Canada*, Second Series, 9 (1903): 168; Dale Miquelon, "Jacques Baby dit Duperont," in *Dictionary of Canadian Biography*, 15 vols. (Toronto: University of Toronto Press, 1966-2005), 9:38-40; John Clarke, "Baby, Francois (1733-1820)," in *Dictionary of Canadian Biography*, 5:41-46. For Baby family history and genealogy, see Christian Denissen, *Genealogy of the French Families of the Detroit River Region, 1701-1936* (Detroit: Detroit Society for Genealogical Research, 1987), 30-33; Sharon A. Kelly et al., eds. *Marriage Records, Ste. Anne Church, Detroit, 1701-1850* (Detroit: Detroit Society for Genealogical Research, 2001), 15; and Dale Miquelon, "The Baby Family in the Trade of Canada" (master's thesis, Carleton University, 1968). Duperon occasionally appears in written records as "Duperont."

5. Douglas, *Mansion to Museum*, 1-4, 10, 36 n13. The contract between François and Susanne is available in "Windsor's Community Museum Directory of Holdings" (unpublished), WCM.

6. Douglas, *Mansion to Museum*, 5-6.

7. Lydia B. Stetson Bacon, *Biography of Mrs. Lydia B. Bacon* (Boston: Massachusetts Sabbath School Society, 1856), 61. For Bacon, see the essay in this volume by Kerri Jansen.

8 Isaac Brock to George Prevost, August 17, 1812, in *Select British Documents of the Canadian War of 1812*, ed. William C.H. Wood, 3 vols. (Toronto: Chaplain Society, 1920-28), 1:465-70; 467 (quote). For the Dodemead family, see *Askin Papers*, 1:304 n21; and the essay in this volume by Kristen Harrell.

9 Isaac Brock to Thomas Evans, August 17, 1812, in *The Documentary History of the Campaign upon the Niagara Frontier*, ed. E.A. Cruikshank, 9 vols. (Welland, ON: Tribune Office, 1896-1907), 3:186.

10 Hull and Baby quoted in A.W. Cochran to his mother, September 13, 1812, in *Select British Documents*, 1:522.

11 "François Baby Timeline" (20-135:2039), George F. McDonald Papers, WCM; Taylor, 161.

12 Brock quoted in François Baby to William Rowan, December 15, 1838, RG8, Vol. 613, 200-1, Library and Archives Canada, Ottawa. A copy of the letter is also in "Windsor's Community Museum Directory of Holdings."

13 François Baby to William Hull, August 17, 1812, Baby Family Papers (20-11), Microfilm 3:92, WCM.

14 William Hull response to Baby request, [undated], Baby Family Papers (20-11), Microfilm 3:93.

15 For Taylor's decision, see Peter Audrain to [?], August 25, 1812, Baby Family Papers (20-11), Microfilm 3:93.

16 George B. Catlin, *The Story of Detroit* (Detroit: Detroit News, 1923), 207; Clarke, "Baby, Francois (1768-1852)," 8:33-35. See also Baby's later complaint of his reward in 1838 in "Windsor's Community Museum Directory of Holdings." For Smyth, see Harrell.

17 *Providence Patriot*, March 19, 1814. For James Baby, see Tom Davies, "Ontario Heritage Foundation – A Report for the Heritage Trust – The Duff-Baby House" (unpublished), 38, WCM. For François Baby's conduct at the River Raisin, see Anthony J. Yanik, *The Fall and Recapture of Detroit in the War of 1812: In Defense of William Hull* (Detroit: Wayne State University Press, 2011), 150; Silas Farmer, *The History of Detroit and Michigan: Or the Metropolis Illustrated* (Detroit: S. Farmer, 1884), 280; and James V. Campbell, *Outlines of the Political History of Michigan* (Detroit: Schober, 1876), 349.

18 Donald R. Hickey, *The War of 1812: A Forgotten Conflict*, Bicentennial Edition (Urbana: University of Illinois Press, 2012), 186; Miquelon, "Baby Family," 125. For tensions during the American occupation, see also the essay in this volume by Joshua Zimberg.

19 G.P. de T. Glazebrook, *Life in Ontario: A Social History* (Toronto: University of Toronto Press, 1968), 92; Davies, "Ontario Heritage Foundation," 4. For recent scholarship on Canadian identity, see Philip Resnick, *The European Roots of Canadian Identity* (Peterborough, ON: Broadview Press, 2005); Roy MacGregor, *Canadians: A Portrait of a Country and Its People* (Toronto: Viking Canada, 2007); Gary B. Madison et al., *Is There a Canadian Philosophy? Reflections on the*

Canadian Identity (Ottawa: University of Ottawa Press, 2000); and Andrew Cohen, *The Unfinished Canadian: The People We Are* (Toronto: McClelland & Stewart, 2007).

20 Resnick, 11. The Babys also had intimate knowledge of other sources of emerging Canadian identity, including British parliamentary political and legal systems, divergent French and British land policies during the late eighteenth and early nineteenth centuries, and geophysical and climatic features.

21 Robert Malcomson, *Historical Dictionary of the War of 1812* (Lanham, MD: Scarecrow Press, 2006), lxii.

Lydia Bacon: Army Wife, Intrepid Traveler

Kerri Jansen

During the week of her 25th birthday in May 1811, Lydia
Bacon left her Boston home and boarded a ship bound for
Philadelphia. Her husband of about four years, Lieutenant Josiah
Bacon, a quartermaster of the Fourth Regiment of the United
States Infantry, had been dispatched to Pittsburgh by way of
Philadelphia, and she had resolved to accompany him. Though
she never fought in battle, Bacon's place as an officer's wife kept
her close to defining moments in America's frontier conflict, from
the Battle of Tippecanoe in November 1811 to its declaration of
war on Britain in June 1812 to General William Hull's surrender
of Detroit in August of that same year. Though she was afforded
certain privileges that soldiers did not have, Bacon could not
entirely escape the harsh realities of war. During her seventeen-
month trip, she slept on the ground and on the hard deck of a
ship, slogged her way through the Black Swamp, came under
cannon fire at Fort Detroit, and was taken prisoner – twice.
She wrote about her incredible journey in letters to relatives,
which she combined into a journal more than twenty years later.
From taking in majestic mountain vistas to anxiously awaiting
post-battle news of her husband, Bacon's writing captures the
wonder and excitement, struggles and fear of a woman who chose
to experience hardships alongside her husband and other soldiers
on the frontier.[1]

Bacon was not the only army wife to accompany her husband

in a War of 1812 campaign. Women almost always traveled with armies. In addition to the wives and sometimes children of soldiers, civilians known as camp followers often trailed armies to provide support services like cooking, sewing, and cleaning. On rare occasions, they even took part in fighting. American Fanny Doyle, applauded for her bravery manning cannon in a battle at Fort Niagara on November 21, 1812, was the wife of a captured Canadian artillery officer. Bacon apparently never participated in a battle, but nonetheless stayed by her husband's side for nearly every step of his journey, from Fort Independence on Castle Island in Boston Harbor to Vincennes, Indiana Territory, and eventually back to Boston by way of Detroit.[2]

Bacon began her journey on a ship from Fort Independence toward Philadelphia to catch up with Josiah, who had traveled ahead by land to prepare for the troops' arrival. A bout of seasickness gave Lydia a taste of the difficulties she would experience following an army, but she adapted quickly and took delight in the lush scenery lining the Delaware River. In Philadelphia, the Bacons spent time with relatives and toured the Pennsylvania Hospital founded by William Penn, which impressed Lydia with its "beauty, Order, neatness & convenience."[3]

After spending a couple of weeks in Philadelphia, the regiment headed for Pittsburgh. Bacon and a couple of other women rode in a stage as the troops marched. In a letter dated June 1, 1811, Bacon described the journey: "the weather was serene, the roads good, all nature appeared in its richest dress." In fact, she so appreciated the scenery – "at once *grand, sublime, awful & sweet*" – that she was willing to endure constant jostling in the carriage in order to see it: "bounce would go my poor head, against the top of the Stage, till my brains were ready to fly. but all this, I could bear, for the sake of beholding, the scenery."[4]

Despite her discomfort, Bacon enjoyed the trek from Philadelphia to Pittsburgh. The soldiers in her husband's regiment had a much less pleasant experience. Adam Walker, one of the soldiers who marched in the regiment, wrote in his journal that the day they departed "was extremely warm, and we were almost suffocated with heat and dust." He made no mention of the hills and rivers that Bacon found so enthralling.[5]

Upon reaching Pittsburgh in mid-June 1811, the Bacons stayed in a hired house, with plenty of servants to help with housekeeping and meals. After a few weeks enjoying the hospitality, the regiment received orders to go to Newport, Kentucky, about three hundred miles away. The soldiers were needed to provide support for frontiersmen, who were in conflict with Indian groups in the Ohio River Valley. With regret, Lydia and Josiah left the friendly people and beautiful gardens they had enjoyed in Pittsburgh, and on August 2 again boarded a boat – this time headed up the Ohio River to Newport.[6]

Bacon was again overwhelmed by the beauty surrounding her, particularly the mountains, meadows, and farms lining the banks of the Ohio River. "The whole together reminds me of something I have read but never expected to realize," she wrote. And though she missed her family in Massachusetts dearly, the time spent alongside her husband made the arduous journey worthwhile. "I never have for a moment regretted accompanying him, It is a great source of happiness that we can be together," Lydia wrote.[7]

Soon after reaching Newport on August 9, 1811, Josiah's regiment was again ordered to move, this time to Vincennes in Indiana Territory, joining Governor William Henry Harrison's campaign against Indian groups along the Wabash River. A confederacy of tribes had formed in the area, led by the Shawnee brothers Tecumseh and Tenskwatawa. Tenskwatawa, a cunning spiritual leader also known as "the Prophet," denounced American influence and gained followers with his fiery condemnations of white settlers. Tecumseh, a respected war chief, built an alliance around his brother's spiritual movement and began putting together a pan-Indian resistance, supplied with British arms and ammunition. Harrison called on Josiah's regiment for support, as the Indians' conduct was becoming more and more threatening.[8]

The Bacons arrived at Vincennes under less-than-ideal circumstances. Lydia was sick with "fever-Ague," which left her very weak, and Josiah suffered from burns caused by gunpowder in a hunting accident. Due to his condition, Josiah stayed with Lydia at Fort Knox, a few miles north of Vincennes, when the troops joined Harrison in his plan to disperse hostile Indians who had gathered at Prophet's Town.[9]

As the Bacons recovered, Lydia took walks outside the fort, although she did not dare venture too far, for fear of "being scalped by our red Brethren." Although Bacon had never encountered an Indian, she, like many people during that time, thought of Native Americans as merciless savages, ready to butcher and scalp without provocation. Indians were feared and reviled throughout the frontier, especially during the tense standoff between the Americans and Tecumseh's Indian confederacy. Bacon had undoubtedly read or heard accounts of marauding Indians on the frontier from her home in Boston, which must have contributed to her fear. In early October 1811, Bacon had neither seen nor heard of Indians acting hostile toward her husband's regiment, but she described them as "deceitful in the extreme."[10]

Josiah soon healed and was dispatched to rejoin his men, who were near Terre Haute in western Indiana, about sixty miles away. They were building a fort on a bluff above the Wabash to serve as a stronghold against the Indians. When the fort was completed on October 28, 1811, they named it Fort Harrison in honor of their leader.[11]

Tension between the Americans and Tenskwatawa's followers continued to escalate. According to Walker, "many Indians came peaceably into camp, and held frequent Council, with the Governor; but all endeavors to effect an accommodation with the Prophet were [in] vain – they still continued stubborn and refractory, – and would not listen to any terms of peace made them by the Governor." Walker recorded that many men threatened desertion during this time, although Harrison was able to reduce their disillusionment with heartfelt speeches. "His eloquence calmed their passions, and hushed their discontented murmurings – and in a short time all became tranquil, and unanimity reigned throughout the army," Walker wrote.[12]

As the months passed at Vincennes, Bacon revealed that she felt restless and yearned for the people and familiar places of New England. Because the absence of the troops left Bacon and the other women without a guard, she slept with a loaded pistol next to her bed for protection. The separation from her husband wore on her, and she anxiously awaited any word on Josiah and the troops. When a message finally arrived, it carried news of a brutal battle. Just before 4 o'clock in the morning on November 7, 1811, the Indians had attacked Harrison's camp. Utterly surprised, the regiment experienced heavy losses. But the soldiers rallied quickly and managed to repulse the Indians, earning a victory near the confluence of the Tippecanoe and Wabash rivers. The Indians' loss at the Battle of Tippecanoe (as it became known) shook their faith in the Prophet, who had assured them of victory. Lydia wrote that "the event proved he was but a mere Man, & their confidence in him is shaken." But Tenskwatawa and especially his brother, Tecumseh, were far from defeated. They set to rebuilding their pan-Indian alliance, which would play a major role in the War of 1812.[13]

Bacon, who upon hearing news of the battle had feared the worst, was overjoyed to learn that her husband had survived. Josiah had two close calls with bullets – getting hit in the boot and in the hat – but escaped without injury. After the battle, Harrison retired to his base at Vincennes, and Josiah returned to his wife once again. The Bacons spent the winter in Vincennes, and in the spring of 1812, Josiah's regiment received orders to proceed to Detroit. Lydia made the four hundred-mile journey on horseback, with "a Bible, Homer[']s Iliad, and A huge Spunge cake" tucked into a bag slung from her saddle.[14]

On June 10, 1812, Josiah's regiment stopped in Urbana, Ohio, to join General William Hull and 1,500 Ohio militiamen. Word of the Fourth Regiment's success in Indiana Territory had reached Urbana; the soldiers were greeted with much celebration and led triumphantly through a decorated arch inscribed with the words, "*Heroes of Tippecanoe.*"[15]

A few days earlier, Ohio Governor Return Jonathan Meigs Jr. had met with Indian leaders to secure permission to create a military road through their lands, stretching from Urbana to Detroit. The route, although direct, would require hacking through the Black Swamp, a densely wooded marshland. Since the infantry had just trekked through two hundred miles of wilderness, the troops were allowed a few days' rest. Meanwhile, a regiment of militia led by Duncan McArthur got a head start on cutting a road through the Black Swamp.[16]

The Bacons rode on horseback along the road McArthur's men cleared, a privilege that spared them some of the struggles others in their company had to endure. Bacon wrote that she sometimes rested her feet on her horse's neck to avoid them dragging in the marsh; marching soldiers would have had no such luxury. Most soldiers' wives also had to march "on foot, some of the way mud up to their knees, & a little Child in their arms," she wrote. Slogging through the Black Swamp made travel tedious, even on horseback. But Bacon found amusement in small moments, such as the primitive way soldiers cooked their dinner: on sticks over a fire. She claimed to have slept well every night, despite camping on the ground and enduring frequent rains, because she stayed by her husband's side.[17]

Eventually, the army escaped the Black Swamp and approached Michigan Territory. On July 1, Hull hired the schooner *Cuyahoga* at the Maumee River to carry women, children, and heavy baggage, including his personal papers, to Fort Detroit by way of Lake Erie and the Detroit River. Josiah remained on land with the army, but Lydia elected to ride aboard the ship for the final leg of the journey.[18]

Within twenty miles of its destination, the *Cuyahoga* was fired upon by a British boat on the Detroit River near Fort Amherstburg. While other women fled to the ship's cabin, "*a love of novelty, spiced with curiosity*" kept Bacon on deck, watching the action. There she discovered that the U.S. had declared war on Britain. Hull, who had learned of the declaration hours before, tried to stop the *Cuyahoga* to avoid its capture, but his orders did not reach the schooner in time. Everyone on board became a prisoner of war, and the British confiscated the ship's cargo, including Hull's papers. The loss of these documents, among them correspondences relating to potential American war operations, gave British General Isaac Brock a distinct advantage in planning his later attack on Detroit.[19]

The night of July 2, 1812, Bacon slept aboard a prison ship on the Detroit River. As an officer's wife, she was treated politely, even allowed to dine in a tavern with British officers while the ship was anchored at Fort Amherstburg. At her request, she was released the next day to Detroit, in time to celebrate Independence Day. A British boat ferried her and the other female prisoners to land, with Bacon's white handkerchief as a flag of truce. While in Detroit, Bacon stayed in General Hull's home with his daughter and granddaughters.[20] The army arrived at Detroit a few days later. During the next month and a half, Lydia remained in the town while Josiah and the American army invaded Upper Canada before retreating to guard Detroit in mid-August. Lydia then watched as the British army built a battery on the opposite shore, mostly concealed behind a structure belonging to François Baby. [21]

On August 15, 1812, Brock sent Hull a demand of surrender, which "the general has not seen fit to comply with," Lydia wrote.[22] As messengers traveled to inform Brock of Hull's refusal, she left Hull's house in town and took his 3-year-old granddaughter into the fort for protection. The British began firing on the fort from across the river around 4 p.m. on August 15, their barrage answered by the Americans until around midnight, when the firing ceased. Bacon spent a sleepless night in the fort, listening to the cries of the women and children with whom she shared a refuge: "In vain I tried to court the drowsey God, Sleep was banished from my eyes, & many others found it as difficult as myself to get a moments rest – it was a night long to be remembered & a scene never to be forgotten."[23]

At dawn the next day, firing resumed. When cannon fire began to break into the walls of the fort, Bacon fled to a root cellar for safety. She described her rush to the bomb-proof cellar: "I felt as if my nerves would burst, my hair felt as if it was erect upon my head, which was not covered, & my eyes raised upward to catch a glimpse of the bombs shells & balls that were flying in all directions." When Bacon reached the cellar, she found it crowded with terrified women and children from town who had also taken refuge inside the fort: "What a scene here presented, such lamentation, & weeping, I never heard before, & I sincerely hope I never shall again." The refugees watched through the open door of the root cellar as enemy fire devastated the fort.[24]

Around 10 a.m. on August 16, Hull had seen enough. He flew a white flag over the fort and began negotiations to surrender. By noon, the surrender was official. As part of the terms, all American troops and supplies were surrendered to the British, including Josiah's regiment along with Lydia. As she watched the soldiers stack their arms and the dead being piled in a common grave, "a thousand emotions struggled in my breast, *too numerous for utterance, & too exquisitely painful to be described.*" Hull's young granddaughter, who apparently stayed with Lydia throughout the battle, was fascinated by the fine British uniforms. Too young to understand the gravity of the situation, the toddler called the uniforms "*pretty.*" When later compiling her journal, Bacon added, "poor Child she little thought or realized, the sorrow, the transactions of that day *might* bring upon her family,

& did *actually*, cloud their happiness for a long time afterwards."[25]

The girl's grandfather, General Hull, would later be court martialed and sentenced to death for what was judged to be a cowardly surrender. Though the sentence was commuted by President James Madison, Hull's reputation has never fully recovered from the accusations. Given the controversy surrounding Hull's conduct, it is noteworthy that Bacon never expressed disapproval of his actions, even though his surrender landed her on a prison ship for the second time in less than two months. Furthermore, she did not record criticisms from any of Hull's men. The omission could be the result of a personal relationship – the Bacon and Hull families shared a long, genial history – yet her narrative still merits consideration along with more "official" military accounts of Hull's surrender.[26]

Hull and the Bacons were put aboard the British ship *Queen Charlotte*. By that time, Bacon was determined to make the most of her situation, and she and the other prisoners did their best to remain in high spirits. It seems that they were successful: Bacon wrote that a British officer remarked that they were "a merry set of prisoners." She even made a large apple pudding to share, a welcome relief from the hard bread that the crew and prisoners typically received.[27]

Two weeks later, the *Queen Charlotte* landed at Fort Erie on the British side of the Niagara River. General Hull, being a prominent officer, was provided with a carriage, and he invited the Bacons to ride with him to Newark, New Jersey. At Newark, Hull requested that the Bacons be paroled, and they were released with the stipulation that Josiah would not participate in the rest of the war. Hull would not be paroled until September 16, 1812, after arriving in Quebec.[28]

The Bacons eagerly began their journey home to Boston. Although they had only twenty-five cents between them and more than two hundred miles to travel, the Bacons were in good spirits. Josiah was eventually able to obtain pay for his military service, which the distance and hazardous condition of Detroit had delayed. The Bacons hired a cart for their baggage, but were frequently stopped so Josiah could describe the recent battle and surrender for locals. Relying on the hospitality of people they came across on their route, the Bacons stayed in homes that were not always clean, comfortable, or quiet. But they endured these hardships, as they had endured countless others together, for the sake of returning home more quickly.[29]

The couple reached Boston at 10 o'clock on a Tuesday night in mid-September 1812. Though several members of Lydia's family had already retired for the night, all were roused for a joyous reunion. After a harrowing seventeenth-month journey, the Bacons were overwhelmed to once again be at home. Though Lydia was grateful for the experience, and especially glad to have been able to accompany her husband, nothing compared to embracing those whom she so dearly loved.[30]

Lydia never could have anticipated the scope of her journey. Her course wove through several of the defining conflicts in the early days of the War of 1812, seventeen months of watching the citizens of a young country struggle against their foreign and domestic enemies. Few women took on such an endeavor, and fewer still recorded their experiences. Though Bacon was subject to all the hazards and struggles that the war brought, she rarely complained about her circumstances. Her story, of an army wife determined to stay with her husband even through gloomy swamps and deadly cannon fire, demonstrates the bravery and loyalty of men and women who persevered on the frontier – without obligation, without recognition, without regret.

NOTES

1 Bacon's narrative was originally published as part of a larger biography by a family descendant (Lydia B. Stetson Bacon, *Biography of Mrs. Lydia B. Bacon* [Boston: Massachusetts Sabbath School Society, 1856]). The version used here is Mary M. Crawford, ed., "Mrs. Lydia B. Bacon's Journal, 1811-1812," *Indiana Magazine of History* 40 (1944): 367-86; 41 (1945): 59-79. The original manuscript is in the New York Historical Society. Little biographical information is available on Bacon, aside from the publications of her journal and brief references in secondary works. According to the 1856 family biography, Bacon grew up in Boston, the daughter of Levi and Mary Stetson. In 1807, she married Josiah, a childhood playmate. Sources disagree on the exact date of Lydia's birth. Crawford cites her birthday as May 13, 1786; the 1856 biography lists it as May 10, 1786. Bacon departed Boston on May 9, 1811.

2 For an overview of female experiences in the war, see Donald R. Hickey, *Don't Give Up the Ship! Myths of the War of 1812* (Urbana: University of Illinois Press, 2006), 191-200.

3 "Mrs. Lydia B. Bacon's Journal," 369-71.

4 "Mrs. Lydia B. Bacon's Journal," 371.

5 Adam Walker, *A Journal of Two Campaigns of the Fourth Regiment of the U.S. Infantry in the Michigan and Indiana Territories* (Keene, NH: Sentinel Press, 1816), 7.

6 "Mrs. Lydia B. Bacon's Journal," 372-73.

7 "Mrs. Lydia B. Bacon's Journal," 373 ("The whole"); 376-77 ("I never have").

8 Alan Taylor, *The Civil War of 1812: American Citizens, British Subjects, Irish Rebels, & Indian Allies* (New York: Knopf, 2010), 126-27; R. David Edmunds, "Tecumseh's Native Allies: Warriors Who Fought for the Crown," in *War on the Great Lakes: Essays Commemorating the 175th Anniversary of the Battle of Lake Erie*, ed. William J. Welsh and David C. Skaggs (Kent, OH: Kent State University Press, 1991), 59-60. For Tenskwatawa, see also Edmunds, *The Shawnee Prophet* (Lincoln: University of Nebraska Press, 1983).

9 "Mrs. Lydia B. Bacon's Journal," 379.

10 "Mrs. Lydia B. Bacon's Journal," 380 ("being scalped"); 381 ("deceitful").

11 "Mrs. Lydia B. Bacon's Journal," 381; Benson J. Lossing, *The Pictorial Field-Book of the War of 1812* (New York: Harper, 1869), 195.

12 Walker, 16.

13 "Mrs. Lydia B. Bacon's Journal," 381-84 (quote, 384); Walker 22-25; Taylor, 127. For Tecumseh's role in the War of 1812, see the essay in this volume by Tim Moran.

14 "Mrs. Lydia B. Bacon's Journal," 382-83; 61 (quote).

15 "Mrs. Lydia B. Bacon's Journal," 63; Walker, 45 (quote).

16 Anthony J. Yanik, *The Fall and Recapture of Detroit in the War of 1812: In Defense of William Hull* (Detroit: Wayne State University Press, 2011), 45.

17 "Mrs. Lydia B. Bacon's Journal," 61 (quote); 64-66.

18 Yanik, 5; "Mrs. Lydia B. Bacon's Journal," 66. Bacon never mentions the *Cuyahoga* by name, but describes it accurately as a "small unarmed Vessel" (66).

19 "Mrs. Lydia B. Bacon's Journal," 66; 67 (quote); Walker, 48; Yanik, 47-49.

20 "Mrs. Lydia B. Bacon's Journal," 68.

21 Yanik, 5-8; "Mrs. Lydia B. Bacon's Journal," 69. For François Baby's property, see the essay in this volume by Justin Wargo.

22 Yanik, 88; "Mrs. Lydia B. Bacon's Journal," 70.

23 "Mrs. Lydia B. Bacon's Journal," 71.

24 "Mrs. Lydia B. Bacon's Journal," 71-72.

25 "Mrs. Lydia B. Bacon's Journal," 72; Yanik, 9, 96.

26 "Mrs. Lydia B. Bacon's Journal," 74. For the debate over Hull's surrender, see Yanik, esp. 1-3.

27 "Mrs. Lydia B. Bacon's Journal," 73.

28 "Mrs. Lydia B. Bacon's Journal," 74; Yanik, 102.

29 "Mrs. Lydia B. Bacon's Journal," 75.

30 "Mrs. Lydia B. Bacon's Journal," 79. After returning home, Lydia and Josiah Bacon stayed in Boston until late 1815, when they moved to a small white cottage in Sackett's Harbor, New York (today Sackets Harbor), where Josiah worked as a commission merchant. Lydia would eventually become the head of the Sackett's Harbor Sabbath school. The Bacons moved a final time in 1829, to Sandwich, Massachusetts. Josiah died in 1852 at age 67. Lydia died the next year, while visiting her brother-in-law in Brookline, Massachusetts (Bacon, 85-348).

"They had won their battle, too":
An Odawa Narrative of the War of 1812
Daniel F. Harrison

Mii dash gaa-izhinaagadagobanen gichi-agindaasowin, gii-gichi-miigaadiwangobanen nitam.

This is an interpretation of what it must have been like, the first time we were involved in a great war.

– opening to War of 1812 narrative in the Odawa oral tradition

The historical reconstruction of Native American participation in the War of 1812 in the Great Lakes area has traditionally proven problematic. American accounts are dominated by sensational defeats at Frenchtown (today Monroe, Michigan) and Fort Dearborn (today Chicago), while British accounts tend to underplay the role of their native allies. This essay will consider a rare surviving narrative from the perspective of Odawa allies of the British. It appears to depict an American attack on Upper Canada and the role of Indians in defeating the invader. Collected in 1973 by linguists from the University of Toronto from an Odawa-speaking informant on Manitoulin Island, Ontario, the text, simply titled "A Battle in the War of 1812," was published in a report that enjoyed little circulation, and that among linguists. It was adopted as an instructional text by the Indigenous Languages Preservation and Promotion program (ILPP) at the University of Wisconsin, where, revised and re-translated, it is now available to a wider audience on the ILPP website.[1]

The text appears never to have been analyzed as a historical document. The present discussion will consist of a comparison of events depicted in the narrative with the available documentary record. Through a reading of the Odawa text in the context of British and American source material, it is possible to expand our view of this catastrophic period from the indigenous perspective. For while it is commonplace to declare the War of 1812 a stalemate from the British and American viewpoints, from that of the Native American, the Battle of the Thames in October 1813 represents the culminating disaster in a series of setbacks that began at Fallen Timbers in August 1794. This story presents one of the few intervening bright spots, where native allies joined the British in successfully defending their homeland against American expansion. We will almost certainly never know the "truth" of which actions are depicted in the Odawa narrative. Nevertheless, the text offers an entry point into a meaningful discussion of the Native American role in, and view of, the War of 1812 in the Great Lakes theater. It may be that the "truths" brought to light are, in fact, the higher ones.

The text poses problems: It is not simply a matter of matching up the incidents described with existing written histories, thereby expanding the overall narrative with an additional point of view. Narrative structures and conventions differ between Odawa and English. There is the factor of time: The narrative was conserved within an oral tradition for 160 years before it was committed to paper. Such narratives typically display dramatic compressions of time or space, where incidents that happen days or miles apart are represented as occurring at the same time or place. Nevertheless, in its broad strokes, the account exhibits remarkable consistency and integrity. The action is centered on the Odawa war chief Nibakom, whom we know details about chiefly from this source. In the translation used here, taken from the most recent ILPP version, each of the 189 sentences is numbered; in the following synopsis and discussion, these numbers will be referenced using square brackets.[2]

Synopsis: An American officer approaches an English officer, announcing his intention to take charge of the latter's Indians (*gidanishinaabemag*) [8-12]. The "white Canadian" officer tells Nibakom that all his people's lands will be taken by the Americans, if the Indians do not help, whereupon Nibakom agrees to aid the British [12-17]. After exchanging threats, the American and British leaders agree to fight (they declare war) [19-22]. The Indian and British forces assemble, and after a short march, encounter the Americans in battle [23-27]. While initially successful, the Indians are pushed back [28-31]. Nibakom looks around and realizes that the British have fallen back, and the Indians are fighting alone [32-34]. Nibakom orders his warriors to retreat, is wounded and left behind [35-44]. A passing British cavalry officer gives him a blanket and rides on, reporting Nibakom's situation to his superior [45-60]. Nibakom retreats slowly, taking medicinal herbs and gradually recovering, until he reaches the British camp, where his arrival is announced [61-75]. The commanding officer arrives, and Nibakom chastises him for retreating without notice [76-87]. Asked by the commander whether he will fight again, Nibakom declines to commit [88-91].

Again the American and British officers challenge each other, agreeing to meet in battle in two days' time; if the British general is defeated, Upper Canada will surely fall [92-94]. The general returns to Nibakom, asking his aid; the latter agrees, but will command his own troops in a separate group [95-103]. Nibakom confers with his troops, asking for volunteers; four braves respond [104-118]. They are told to count the enemy; that evening, appearing as bats, two braves count the enemy's tents, while the other two are liars and do nothing [119-134]. The two obedient braves report to Nibakom that the enemy has twelve rows of twelve tents each, with six men and their guns in each tent. The false braves are questioned separately, tell lies, and are chased away [135-147]. Nibakom knows that his men would not be adequate to the task of open battle. He tells his fellow chiefs that he will enter the fort at noon the next day [149-151]. That evening Nibakom leads his men stealthily to the American position, then orders them to sleep until dawn while he stands watch alone [152-158].

At dawn, Nibakom wakes his men, who run through the American camp, knocking down the tents and killing all the men as they emerge [159-163]. Nibakom then orders his men to stand close to the outer wall of the fort, making the soldiers inside lean over the wall to shoot [164-169]. The Indians shoot the soldiers until none lean over the wall, whereupon Nibakom orders his men to breach the wall [170-173]. Entering the fort, they find only a few American soldiers, who run away from their homes, leaving behind food and supplies [174-180]. It is noon; Nibakom lowers the American flag and raises the British flag over the fort [181-184]. Across the water, they see in the distance that their white allies have raised the British flag [185]. They are finished also, "they have won their battle, too" [186-187]. So the great battle which took place at that time was over [188]. "Good-day, my friends, those of you who are listening" (*Boozhoo nwiijkiwenydig giinwaa mnik bezndaageyeg*) [189].

Amid the wealth of detail in the text, several features stand out: the action occurs early in the war, on Canadian soil, in an area where the Odawa lived in substantial numbers; a series of challenges is exchanged between the American and British leaders; a skirmish occurs where the British fall back; the native allies first attack an American encampment, then a fortification; and the final attack occurs at approximately the same time as a successful attack nearby, "across the water," where the British flag is raised on both sides simultaneously. Of these five features, the first and last may be considered from a geographical as well as a historical standpoint. Among the early actions in the war, only William Hull's invasion and temporary occupation of Sandwich in July 1812 answers the description of occurring in Upper Canada, specifically, in a place where the Odawa lived.[3] Allowing for the dramatic compression of time, the defeat of the Americans on both sides of a narrow body of water (the Detroit River) would correspond to Hull's retreat from Canada, and his surrender of Detroit. These two events occurred over a brief span of time, between August 11 and 16. The other contender is along the Niagara, where the Battle of Queenston Heights on October 13, 1812, resulted in an invading American force being repulsed by British aided by Indians. But there was no corresponding victory against the Americans across the river.[4]

Taking as a working hypothesis that the narrative may refer to the actions along the Detroit River in July and August of 1812, we may attempt to interrelate the Odawa narrative with the historical record. The initial challenge posed by the American in the narrative [10] corresponds most closely with Hull's July 12 proclamation to the inhabitants of Canada upon his invasion at Sandwich. Amongst other bombastic rhetoric, Hull promised that "no white man, found fighting by the side of an Indian, will be taken prisoner – instant destruction will be his lot."[5] The British officer initially responding to this challenge by approaching the Odawa could well have been Lieutenant Colonel Thomas Bligh St. George, the aging commander at Fort Amherstburg. The fort, located about fourteen miles south of Detroit and thirty yards from the Detroit River, sat directly across a narrow channel from Bois Blanc Island, home to a band of Odawa.[6] St. George was given the task of recruiting Indians to the British side. At first he encountered resistance, particularly from the influential Wyandots, who lived in close proximity to Bois Blanc Island and had signed treaties with Hull.[7] The frustrated British officer's council with Wyandot, Shawnee, and Potowatomi leaders "became stormy as St. George angrily seized his sword hilt, threatening to cut off all supplies and presents," according to the historian Sandy Antal.[8] There is no mention of Odawa participation in these negotiations, but the narrative makes it clear that they were being pressured by the "white Canadian officer" who "did not tell Nibakom the truth. He concealed a little in telling him that, since they were Indians, they would be seized according to what the American had said" [12-13].

In the Odawa account, a second exchange of challenges ensues: "So the American leader (*gimaa*) said to that English leader: 'We will have a clash (*nkweshdaadwin*) unless you give me those Indians of yours.' 'No I won't! We will have a clash,' the English officer said to the American. So they declared war" [19-22]. A week after his initial proclamation, Hull wrote of his efforts to "detach the Indians from the British standard," including the "Ottawas, Chippewas, Pottawatomies, Delawares, Wyandots, Munsies, some Kickapoos, Si[ou?]x, and the Six Nations."[9] Hull did not trust natives as allies, wishing merely to secure their neutrality. The "English leader," meanwhile, now became Major General Sir Isaac Brock. Informed by St. George of the American invasion under Hull, Brock prepared to assume command at Fort Amherstburg. On July 22, 1812, prior to his departure from Fort George on Lake Ontario, Brock responded to Hull's grandiose proclamation in kind. He urged resistance by all Canadians and identified the native allies as "the brave bands of aborigines which inhabit this colony [who] were, like his majesty's other subjects, punished for their zeal and fidelity, by the loss of their possessions in the late colonies [the United States], and rewarded by his majesty with lands of superior value in this province. The faith of the British government has never yet been violated – the Indians feel that the soil they inherit is to them and their posterity protected from the base arts so frequently devised to over-reach their simplicity."[10] In the meantime, from the American headquarters at Sandwich, Hull's longstanding policy of seeking Indian treaties appeared to be working. The *New York Gazette* of August 5, 1812, printed a dispatch from Detroit that "the American flag waving on both sides of the river has astonished the natives and they are retiring to their villages and already holding councils to advise the natives to remain neutral."[11]

The next episode in the Odawa narrative, Nibakom's participation alongside the British in battle, seems to recount the skirmishes surrounding the Canard River near Fort Amherstburg between July 16 and 23, 1812. The skirmishes have been seen as an attempt by St. George to lure U.S. Colonel Lewis Cass into an ambush.[12] On this point, St. George's communiqué, written the day before Cass's July 16 foray, suggests a delaying tactic rather than a trap, for which St. George lacked the resources: "I hope the Enemy will move forward by land – The Canard is so strong a position that I think (with the assistance of the Indians) I can annoy them much before they can get to . . . [Fort Amherstburg] by that Road."[13] On July 17 and 18, the British brig *Queen Charlotte* and a gunboat completed flanking maneuvers on the Detroit River also aimed at forcing the Americans to use the slower land route to Amherstburg. The delaying tactic worked: The British and Indians checked American forces, allowing time for Colonel Henry Procter to relieve St. George at Amherstburg in advance of Brock.[14]

Although St. George accomplished his overall goal of slowing a possible American attack, the Odawa narrative hints at poor coordination between the British and their native allies. The account, when combined with American and British sources, helps to explain why the British fell back after Cass's initial attack on July 16. Cass wrote to Hull: "After the first discharge the British retreated – we continued advancing. Three times they formed, and as often retreated. We drove them about a half a mile, when it became so dark that we were obliged to relinquish the pursuit. . . . We could gain no precise information of the number opposed to us. It consisted of a considerable detachment from the 41st regiment, some militia, and a body of Indians."[15] On his arrival at Amherstburg, Procter informed Brock of Indian successes against the Americans: "There has been Skirmishing two or three times on the Canard which is about five miles from here, in which the Enemy have lost men – On the 25th they advanced to a Fork on the River, were attacked by the Indians and retreated with the loss of some killed; the Indians having one killed and another wounded."[16] In turn, Brock summarized the overall action to Canadian Governor-General Sir George Prevost as "some skirmishes . . . between the troops under Lieut.-Colonel St. George and the enemy, upon the river Canard, which uniformly terminated in his being repulsed with loss."[17] Unfortunately, these reports stop short of including precise details about the fate of Britain's Indian allies in the skirmishing. Only the Odawa narrative describes the injuries suffered by Nibakom.

After the skirmishes at the Canard River, the Odawa narrative departs further from American and British accounts. While the role played by native forces in the later siege and surrender of Detroit is well documented, Hull's retreat from Sandwich must be pieced together from fragmentary references. Upon first crossing from Detroit to Sandwich on July 12, the general had commandeered the unfinished home of militia officer François Baby as his headquarters, erecting a fortified camp that he called Fort Hope. Hull promptly wrote to Secretary of War William Eustis of his plans for "one or two batteries opposite to the batteries at Detroit."[18] At least one of the batteries appears to have been built; upon recrossing the river to Detroit on August 8 with the main body of the army, Hull ordered the small remaining force, commanded by Major James Denny, to relocate from Fort Hope to a position directly across from Detroit. Fort Gowie, as it has come to be known, was defended by 250 infantry and 30 artillerymen, the latter commanded by a Lieutenant Gowie. The position evidently included a commandeered private residence surrounded by a picket – a rudimentary stockade made of close-set poles, their upper ends sharpened so as to impale (in French, *piquer*) those attempting to climb over. Judging by accounts of Detroit's fortifications, the poles would have been a dozen to fifteen feet in height. Upon abandoning Fort Gowie on August 11, Denny's troops set fire to the picket, contrary to Hull's orders;

the fire spread and destroyed the house.[19] In his 1869 account, the historian Benson J. Lossing avers that upon its abandonment, "the American camp at Sandwich and vicinity was immediately taken possession of by British troops, under Captain Dixon, of the Royal Engineers."[20]

It is against this historical patchwork that the climactic final episode of the Odawa narrative must be set. The capture of the encampment [161-163] and the stockaded fort enclosing homes [164-179] may be construed as representing Fort Hope and Fort Gowie, respectively – although both, according to the American account, were abandoned without loss of life. Beyond that, one must speculate as to the source of the epic battle scenes in the Odawa narrative in which more than a thousand Americans are killed. Allowing for dramatic compression of space, this portion of the narrative could incorporate elements of the August 15, 1812 – the day preceding the surrender of Detroit – attack on Captain Nathan Heald's evacuees from Fort Dearborn by a band of Potawatomi, relatives and traditional allies of the Odawa. Led by Black Bird, the Potawatomi overtook a mixed group of regular American troops, militia, Miami Indians allied with the Americans, and civilians. In the ambush, some fifty-five were killed and others were captured. The attack was said to have been inspired by the recent British and Indian success in capturing Fort Mackinac on July 17, and by dissatisfaction with the quantity of the goods left at Fort Dearborn as a bribe against such a reprisal.[21] If we allow for both spatial and temporal compression, the capture of Fort Mackinac itself may have inspired elements of the Odawa narrative. Among the native allies of the British attackers were Odawa from Walpole Island, who lived some fifty miles northeast of the Bois Blanc band.[22] Details of the Detroit and Mackinac actions could have merged into a single oral tradition as the Odawa bands moved and mingled over the years.

We may have to accept that the ambiguities and contradictions surrounding the climax of the Odawa narrative underscore that the "truth" – that is, the relationship between the Odawa and the British and American accounts – remains a contested issue. The British and Native American alliance was not void of tension. Nibakom's disparaging assessment of the British performance in battle is of a piece with Tecumseh's characterization of Procter as "a fat animal, that carries its tail upon its back, but when affrighted, it drops it between its legs and runs off."[23] The same threat of dispossession that motivated Indian groups to aid the British against the Americans later claimed Canadian First Nations, including the Odawa. But in the early 1800s, the natives' overall perception of colonial European powers was as paternalistic trading partners, principally in the fur industry. The Americans, by contrast, were competitors, demanding land for agriculture, grazing, and urbanization.

To Nibakom, like Tecumseh, a British victory promised a return to *status quo ante bellum*: the way things were before the war. But time did not stand still, let alone run backward. Brock's assurances of July 22, 1812, notwithstanding, the straits of Detroit were far too important to British Canadian settlers, strategically and economically, to accommodate the Odawa. Like their counterparts in Michigan, the Odawa on the Canadian side of the Detroit River were displaced – some to nearby Walpole Island, others far to the north, where the story of Nibakom was kept alive on Manitoulin Island. An 1869 petition to the "Great Chief," Canadian Governor-General Sir John Young, included an Odawa claim to their ancestral home on Bois Blanc.[24] Such was the strategic importance of the Detroit River, however, that Young declined to honor the claim. Instead, Bois Blanc became home to the popular Detroit-area amusement park, Bob-Lo. The relationship in 1812 between Native American and British interests in this region can thus be seen as one of temporary convergence only. Nonetheless, when Nibakom and his Odawa warriors looked across the water and saw the British flag flying on both sides, on that day at least, they had won their battle, too.

NOTES

1 For the original 1973 translation, see Sam Osawamick, "A Battle in the War of 1812," in *Odawa Language Project: Second Report*, ed. Glyne L. Piggott and Jonathan Kaye (Toronto: Centre for Linguistic Studies, University of Toronto, 1973), 82-99. All references in this essay are to the newer translation: Osawamick, "A Battle in the War of 1812," trans. J. Randolph Valentine, in Indigenous Languages Preservation and Promotion (ILLP), Center for the Study of Upper Midwestern Cultures, University of Wisconsin, imp.lss.wisc.edu/~jrvalent/old_nlip/NLIP_ Institute_2006_bu/attachments/Osawamick-1812.pdf (accessed June 14, 2012). The tribal name "Odawa" will be used in place of "Ottawa," except when the latter is in direct quotations.

2 For additional brief references to Nibakom, see J. Randolph Valentine, *Nishnaabemwin Reference Grammar* (Toronto: University of Toronto Press, 2001), 546-50.

3 William N. Fisher, *Memorial of the Chippeway, Pottawatomy, and Ottawa Indians, of Walpole Island! Touching Their Claim of the Huron Reserve, Fighting, Bois Blanc, Turkey, and Point au Pelee Islands* (Sarnia, ON: Canadian Book & Job Office, 1869), 6-7.

4 For an overview of Hull's surrender, see Anthony J. Yanik, *The Fall and Recapture of Detroit in the War of 1812: In Defense of William Hull* (Detroit: Wayne State University Press, 2011), 68-85. For the Battle of Queenston Heights, see Alan Taylor, *The Civil War of 1812: American Citizens, British Subjects, Irish Rebels, & Indian Allies* (New York: Knopf, 2010), 187-90.

5 Hull quoted in *The Life and Correspondence of Major General Sir Isaac Brock*, ed. Ferdinand Brock Tupper (London: Simpkin, Marshall, 1845), 187. For Hull's relationship with Native Americans, see the essay in this volume by Steve Lyskawa.

6 For Fort Amherstburg's strategic location, see George Prevost to Lord Liverpool, May 18, 1812, in *Documents Relating to the Invasion of Canada and the Surrender of Detroit, 1812*, ed. E.A. Cruikshank (Ottawa: Government Printing Bureau, 1912), 26; Helen Hornbeck Tanner et al., eds. *Atlas of Great Lakes Indian History* (Norman: University of Oklahoma Press, 1986), 106-7; and Sandy Antal, *A Wampum Denied: Procter's War of 1812* (Ottawa: Carleton University Press, 1997), 37-38.

7 For the fragile American alliance with the Wyandots, see William Hull to William Eustis, July 15, 1812, in *Documents Relating to the Invasion of Canada*, 60; and Lyskawa.

8 Antal, 44.

9 William Hull to Henry Dearborn, July 21, 1812, in *Documents Relating to the Invasion of Canada*, 78.

10 Isaac Brock's Proclamation, July 22, 1812, in *Life and Correspondence of Major General Sir Isaac Brock*, 190.

11 *New York Gazette*, August 5, 1812, reprinted in *Documents Relating to the Invasion of Canada*, 75-76.

12 Alec R. Gilpin, *The War of 1812 in the Old Northwest* (East Lansing: Michigan State University Press, 1958), 81. See also Yanik, 59.

13 Thomas Bligh St. George to Isaac Brock, July 15, 1812, in *Documents Relating to the Invasion of Canada*, 62.

14 Yanik, 6-7.

15 Lewis Cass to William Hull, July 17, 1812, in *Documents Relating to the Invasion of Canada*, 71.

16 Henry Procter to Isaac Brock, July 26, 1812, in *Documents Relating to the Invasion of Canada*, 89-90.

17 Isaac Brock to George Prevost, August 17, 1812, in *Life and Correspondence of Major General Sir Isaac Brock*, 248.

18 William Hull to William Eustis, July 13, 1812, in *Documents Relating to the Invasion of Canada*, 57. For François Baby's house, see Antal, 43; and the essay in this volume by Justin Wargo.

19 William Hull to William Eustis, August 8, 1812, in *Documents Relating to the Invasion of Canada*, 126; Yanik, 75; Antal, 74; Silas Farmer, *The History of Detroit and Michigan: Or the Metropolis Illustrated* (Detroit: S. Farmer, 1884), 221-23. For Hull's explanation of the fire, see William Hull to Isaac Brock, August 15, 1812, in *Documents Relating to the Invasion of Canada*, 145.

20 Benson J. Lossing, *The Pictorial Field-Book of the War of 1812* (New York: Harper, 1869), 284.

21 Yanik, 86-87.

22 Charles Roberts to [unaddressed], August 16, 1812, in *Documents Relating to the Invasion of Canada*, 150-52.

23 Tecumseh quoted in John Richardson, *Richardson's War of 1812: With Notes and a Life of the Author*, ed. Alexander C. Casselman (Toronto: Historical Publishing, 1902), 206.

24 Fisher, 4.

The Askins of Sandwich: A Family Experiences the War
Timothy Marks

Historians study war on a regular basis. In fact, some might argue that scholars spend an inordinate amount of effort and intellectual capital on past wars. Traditionally, war was, and is, studied from the perspective of the belligerents and other interested governmental entities. Tactics, strategy, and outcomes are most important to these scholars. This essay takes a different approach by focusing on the War of 1812 through the eyes of one family, the Askins. The Askins were leaders in the Detroit River region, and the family was deeply involved in the war as both combatants and civilians on both sides of the border. How a single family viewed the war, participated in its battles, and was affected by it is valuable to scholars and the public alike. The War of 1812 is often characterized as a "forgotten war" or a conflict of limited geopolitical consequences. For the Askins, though, the war had profound consequences, both triumph and tragedy.[1]

John Askin, the patriarch of the family, immigrated to New York from the north of Ireland at the age of 20 in around 1757. During the Seven Years' War (1756-63), Askin served in the British army, possibly at Ticonderoga, and after the war established a trading business at Albany. In 1763, Askin carried supplies for the business to Detroit in the midst of Pontiac's War (1763-65). The following year, he relocated to Michilimackinac, where he started his family and a successful enterprise centered on the fur trade.[2]

Askin began his family with a Native American woman. Three children were born of that relationship, all of whom had roles in the War of 1812. In 1772, while on one of his regular visits to Detroit, Askin married Marie Archange Barthe, whose forbearers were early French settlers of the Detroit River region. The scholar Milo Quaife has noted that the marriage helped to solidify a relationship between the British, French, and Native American communities in the region. The match also advanced Askin's commercial and other public interests. The couple subsequently returned to Michilimackinac and began their own family. Askin never denied his children from the first relationship, treating them the same as his six surviving children with Marie Archange. The entire family maintained close and caring relations.[3]

In 1780, the Askins removed themselves from Michilimackinac and settled in Detroit. Askin proceeded to build another successful trading business, which he used to help purchase the rights to extensive landholdings from Native Americans. Like most Detroiters, Askin remained a loyal British subject during the American Revolution. Life continued as normal in the immediate years following American independence, until Jay's Treaty of 1794 required the British to turn over Detroit to the United States. Under the treaty, British subjects could declare their intention to remain subjects of the crown within a year. Without declaring their allegiance, they automatically became American citizens. More than one hundred Detroit residents declared their British loyalty, including Askin and his oldest son, John Jr.[4]

By July 1797, Detroit leaders became concerned about the influence of British loyalists on their side of the river. Over time, most British subjects responded to the pressure by moving to Upper Canada. In 1802, despite his election as a trustee of Detroit, Askin joined his countrymen and settled near Sandwich. He named his new estate Strabane, after a town in his home county in Ireland.[5]

The Askin family remained an important part of the Detroit River region for years to come. Family members ran a trading empire on both sides of the river and purchased large tracts of land in British Canada and in the Old Northwest. The War of 1812 thus had a significant impact on the family. John Askin's children and grandchildren were deeply involved with the war on multiple levels. According to Askin, family members who fought in the war included his four sons, three sons-in-law, and ten grandsons. All of his sons, and two of his three sons-in-law, served the British crown. His son-in-law Elijah Brush fought for the Americans and was twice exiled from Detroit during the war; he died shortly after returning home in the fall of 1813. All the Askin men served their countries honorably and several with distinction. Askin's daughters were also affected by the war. Adelaide, Brush's wife, had to care for her family while her husband was sent away. Eleanor Pattinson (also called Ellen), Askin's youngest daughter, died while fleeing a battle in Upper Canada; in a sense, she, like Elijah Brush, was a casualty of the war. The conflict touched the entire Askin family.[6]

Two of Askin's sons, John Jr. and Charles, corresponded regularly with their father and other family members about their experiences in various military operations. Their letters provide a chronicle of the tensions between Britain and the United States, starting with the fallout from the *Chesapeake-Leopard* Affair in June 1807 through the War of 1812. John Jr. was assigned as an Indian agent for the British army on St. Joseph Island at the northern edge of Lake Huron and was present at the fall of Fort Mackinac. He wrote often to his parents about goings-on at the strategic Straits of Mackinac. Askin's fourth child, Charles, served the British army throughout Upper Canada, from Sandwich to York (today Toronto). Charles kept a journal of many of the battles he participated in, sending word back to Sandwich of the heroism of family and friends.

John Jr.'s appointment as an interpreter and storekeeper at

St. Joseph in June 1807 coincided with the rising tensions between the U.S. and Britain. For the next several months, he and his father and brothers documented preparations for war in different parts of the Detroit River region and British Canada.[7] On August 18, James Askin wrote to his brother Charles from Strabane about escalated military activities by the Americans at Detroit and by the British at Sandwich. The Americans carried out frequent patrols and drilled their militia on a regular basis. In Upper Canada, on the other hand, the militia was less prepared. James lamented, "If there are not some Alterations made in the Militia Laws, I entertain little hopes of seeing them better Disciplined even in the course of Twenty Years."[8]

On August 24, 1807, Charles wrote to his father that the fear of war was not so pronounced at Queenston, on the British side of the Niagara River, as reports out of Detroit and Montreal suggested for those areas. Still, Charles requested that his commission as a captain in the militia be sent in case a conflict began.[9] In September, John Jr. wrote to his father at length about how the recent war scare interacted with Americans' exaggerated fears of Indians in the north: "The appearance of Rupture with America will blow over I hope shortly. the Americans generally make great noise & stick at triffles. they are constantly in Alarm either by an Indian War or at the least shadow of Bands of Indians they imagine their heads in danger of being scalped[.] No wonder poor Devils they have reason to fear the Indians in particular from the latters Cruelty to them." Although the U.S. and Britain avoided war in 1807, as John Jr. hoped, he foresaw the weaknesses in American-Indian relations that undermined U.S. military efforts five years later.[10]

At the start of the War of 1812, the Askin men remained in prime locales to observe and partake in the conflict. In July 1812, the Americans occupied Sandwich and attempted to advance toward Fort Amherstburg. A fervent loyalist who would have fought had his aging body allowed it, John Askin Sr. still looked upon U.S. General William Hull favorably. Askin was particularly impressed with how Hull kept his troops in control and protected the Canadians' property, crops, and livestock, noting, "However should it be our lot, to fall under any other Authority, I would not prefer any man, to the present General Hull."[11]

On July 17, 1812, the American fort at Mackinac Island fell to the British. A group of Indians, aided by a small number of British regulars and traders led by Captain Charles Roberts, trader Robert Dickerson, and John Askin Jr., forced the Americans to surrender the post without firing a shot. The loss had a deeply demoralizing effect on Hull's troops at Detroit and Sandwich. The most discouraging news for the Americans was the prominent role played by Britain's native allies.[12] In a letter to his father, John Jr. praised a group of Ojibwa and Odawa warriors whom he led in the operation: "I never saw so determined a set of people as the Chippawas and Ottawas were. Since the Capitulation, they have not tasted a single drop of liquor, nor even killed a fowl belonging to any person, a thing never known before, for they generally destroy everything they meet with."[13]

Two other Askin brothers, James and Alexander, also contributed to early British victories in the war. In August, the brothers, both militia officers, participated in the joint British-Indian force that turned back Hull's advance on Fort Amherstburg in skirmishes at the Canard River. Almost simultaneously, on August 5, the Shawnee warrior Tecumseh led an Indian ambush on a regiment of Ohio volunteers at Brownstown, south of Fort Detroit. The losses at Mackinac and Brownstown, resistance at the Canard, and news of forthcoming British and Indian reinforcements to the region all convinced Hull to retreat to Detroit on August 8. Days later, Askin's American son-in-law, Elijah Brush, asked John Sr. to take care of his family if events on the American side of the river went badly.[14]

Charles Askin participated in the outcome feared by Brush and other Americans: the fall of Detroit. At the time, Askin was assigned to the militia at Fort Amherstburg and joined the invading force that landed at Spring Wells, a few miles south of Fort Detroit. He described in his journal the experience of entering the fort and being surrounded by superior numbers of armed American troops. Of the Americans, Askin wrote, "they did not march with the honors of War," and he speculated that the "Am. Army were so mortified that they had to surrender without fighting that they were indifferent."[15] One of the American prisoners was Brush. He was sent to Fort George on the Niagara front for several weeks before being paroled. After returning to Detroit in the fall of 1812, he was exiled again in February 1813 with other residents who protested the British treatment of American prisoners following the battles at the River Raisin. Brush returned to Detroit for a final time after the Americans retook control of the town in the fall of 1813. He died from a disease a few months later, on December 14, 1813.[16]

Together, the failed occupation of Sandwich, the capitulation of Mackinac, and the surrender of Detroit signaled a depressing start to the war for the Americans. Askins contributed to each of the British triumphs. The same was true for the Americans' next major defeat, at the second battle at Frenchtown (today Monroe, Michigan) in January 1813. James Askin enthusiastically described to his father the battle, in which the invading Americans failed to retake Michigan Territory: "I have the happiness of informing you that the American Army was defeated so effectually that every man was either killed or taken prisoners, with the exception of two only who made their escape." The letter also included the disturbing news that John Askin Sr.'s grandson Robert Richardson Jr. was wounded in the leg during the action. Robert was the fifteen-year-old son of Madelaine Askin Richardson and Dr. Robert Richardson Sr. The boy volunteered for the expedition to the River Raisin.[17]

Following the battle, Dr. Richardson corresponded with John Askin Sr. about Robert's condition. "It gives me real Satisfaction to be able to Say I think poor Robert now out of danger," Richardson wrote. The proud father went on to state that his son fought with valor, "behaved like a little hero," and "has born[e] his wound like a man." Despite the encouraging report, Robert Jr. never fully recovered from his injury and died at the age of 20 in 1819.[18]

Dr. Richardson also addressed the devastating casualties suffered by both sides at Frenchtown. He blamed the high number of British losses on the poor tactics and incompetence of commanding officers: "The loss has been very severe, indeed ten times more than was necessary." Richardson cautioned Askin to not divulge his concerns for fear of reprisal. The doctor also denounced the massacre of Americans by Britain's Indian allies after the battle. "Had I been commanding officer," Richardson claimed, "I should have considered myself responsible for the lives of every one of them." He described the River Raisin massacre as a "shamefull transaction."[19]

Richardson's son John came to a different conclusion about what transpired at Frenchtown. In a letter to his uncle Charles Askin, John Richardson described the events at the River Raisin in detail. He complained about American atrocities in much the same way his father complained of Indian behavior: "I was a witness of a most barbarous act of inhumanity on the part of the Americans, who fired upon our poor wounded, helpless soldiers, who were endeavoring to crawl away on their hands and feet from the scene of action, and were thus tumbled over like so many hogs." Richardson also triumphantly added, "However, the deaths of those brave men were avenged by the slaughter of 300 of the flower of [U.S. General James] Winchester's army." He mentioned the wound sustained by his brother, Robert, but overlooked the massacre of Americans by natives.[20]

Askins also participated in the other major front along the Canadian-American border, at the Niagara River. Charles Askin wrote to his father of the family members who contributed to the British victory at the Battle of Queenston Heights on October 13,

1812. John Sr.'s grandsons John and William Robertson "were both in the Battle and distinguished themselves," according to Charles. William, in particular, "behaved as gallantly as anyone engaged that day." As at Detroit, the victory at Queenston stopped the Americans from gaining a foothold in Canada.[21]

Askin women were deeply affected by the war as well. Archange Askin, the daughter of John Sr. and Marie Archange, married British Colonel David Meredith, who was assigned to duty in England and Ireland early in the French Revolutionary and Napoleonic Wars (1793-1815). In 1797, Archange joined her husband in England and reported back to her family in Sandwich with vivid descriptions of the war against France. One memorable letter describes the Battle of Fishguard, in which an irregular force of soldiers and civilians repelled a French invasion on the coast of Wales in February 1797: "all the laborers, servants, gentlemen, everybody, in fact, gathered together, armed with pitchforks, shovels, and clubs, anything that could be used as a weapon. They did so well that the *frogs* surrendered as prisoners." Archange remained upbeat, despite enduring periods of separation from David while he participated in different operations.[22]

In 1807, the Merediths returned to North America when David was assigned to a post at Halifax. Their daughters, Anne and Elizabeth, accompanied them to Nova Scotia, while their son, David Jr., enrolled in the Royal Military Academy in Woolwich, England. In March 1809, David Sr. died, leaving his family in financial straits such that they required assistance from John Askin Sr. Archange ultimately returned to Europe and died at Bruges, Belgium, in 1866.[23]

Other tragedies befell Askin women during the war. Like Archange, Adelaide Askin Brush depended on her father during the periods when her husband, Elijah, was away during the war. She and the couple's three sons likely divided her time between the family of the Detroit merchant George Meldrum and her parents' home at Strabane in Sandwich. In March 1813, Adelaide gave birth to a daughter and chose the family name of Archange after her mother and sister. Elijah would only know his daughter for a short time, between his return to Detroit in the fall of 1813 and his death that December.[24]

John Askin Sr.'s youngest daughter, Eleanor (Ellen), also died during the war. During General Henry Procter's retreat into Upper Canada in September 1813, Ellen, her husband, Richard Pattinson, her sister Therese, and Therese's husband, Thomas McKee, fled with the British troops. During the journey, Ellen fell ill and died at the home of Upper Canadian militia captain George Jacobs on October 12. Ellen is not counted as a war casualty in the traditional sense, but the stress of the conflict played a clear role in her premature death at age 25.[25]

Ellen's sister accompanying her during the retreat, Therese Askin McKee, suffered under different circumstances in the war. Therese married Captain Thomas McKee on April 17, 1797; the marriage was championed by Thomas's father, Colonel Alexander McKee, a longtime agent of the British Indian Department, and John Askin Sr.'s friend Prideaux Selby. The endorsements by Selby and Colonel McKee won over Askin's support for the arrangement: "The goodness of his [Selby] Character added to the respect we have for his Friend [Thomas McKee] and the Colonel renders it pleasing to us."[26]

Askin's early hopes for the marriage were not realized. In Therese McKee's few surviving letters, she never referred to her husband in a tender way, and it turned out for good reason. Letters from family friends to Askin often mention, sometimes obliquely, Captain McKee's alcoholism. In October 1800, William Harffy wrote, "as to say not for Attention to the Community at large but to answer private Malevolence. Mr. McKee has been much out of order for this two or three days, is now getting better. As for Mrs. McKee she tells Me She is perfectly well, her looks certainly bespeak it."[27] In July 1804, Isaac Todd related to Askin: "I am extremely grieved to hear of the Conduct of Captain McKee on Account of his Good Wife her fate has not been such as she deserved. we must be resigned to meet with Trouble which God inable us to bear[.]"[28] In December 1812, Therese wrote to her father that "Captain McKee suffers dreadfully with Rheumatism in the Head, but otherwise much better."[29]

Finally, after McKee's death in October 1814, one family friend addressed McKee's drinking directly. Alexander Henry consoled Askin: "Poor Mrs. McKee sufferd much while she was here with her unfortunate Husband. he had no command over himself. Continualy deranged with Liquor. if he had lived, Government could have no ralyance on him. I wish she was with you." Thus ended a marriage doomed to unhappiness by liquor and war.[30]

As the war ended, the Askin family patriarch's health was failing. John Sr. alluded to the family's losses and his decline in a tender letter to his children following Ellen's death in the fall of 1813. He offered "thanks to Almighty God that we, Our Family and connections in this Quarter Enjoy good health though its a sickly time & many people have died." The misfortune of losing Ellen, Askin confided, "Added to Age bears heavy on us."[31] In April 1815, Askin died at Strabane, only weeks after learning of the peace settlement between Britain and the United States. A letter from John Askin Jr's wife, Madelaine, to the family matriarch, Marie Archange Askin, captured the family's sadness at the passing of John Sr.: "No one can appreciate the weight of your sorrow more than we. You have lost the most beloved of husbands and we the tenderest of fathers. Our tears will not bring him back to us, and we must then submit to the will of Almighty God. He gave him to us and it has pleased Him to take him back." Madelaine further wrote, "My dear John is almost inconsolable."[32]

The extended Askin family continued to serve Canada through the nineteenth century, leaving an impressive commercial, military, political, and literary legacy. Despite many hardships, the family cemented its status in the War of 1812. They worked together in business, confronted numerous challenges, and went on to become important actors within their communities. Each of the Askin men remained loyal to their country (in the case of Elijah Brush that meant the United States). The Askin women were brave and strong. Archange Meredith followed her husband to England and experienced war in two hemispheres. Ellen Pattison was, in a sense, a casualty of the war. A pregnant Adelaide Brush found support in loving households on both sides of the river, while her husband was exiled. Madelaine Richardson endured an injury to her son at the second battle of Frenchtown. And Therese McKee suffered a marriage to a military husband who abused alcohol.

This was a family not unlike others in the War of 1812, with friends and businesses on both sides of the border, with husbands, brothers, sons, and, sometimes, daughters in harm's way. At the same time, few families could boast so many or such far-reaching connections to the war. The Askins impart to us the experience of war at a human level, the pain, fear, happiness, sorrow, and love of family members for one another.

NOTES

1 General and specific studies of the War of 1812 abound. For an overview of major events, see Donald R. Hickey, *The War of 1812: A Forgotten Conflict* (Urbana: University of Illinois Press, 1989). For an exception to the trend of neglecting civilians in the war, see Alan Taylor, *The Civil War of 1812: American Citizens, British Subjects, Irish Rebels, & Indian Allies* (New York: Knopf, 2010). For the Great Lakes and Detroit River region, see David C. Skaggs and Larry L. Nelson, eds., *The Sixty Years' War for the Great Lakes, 1754-1814* (East Lansing: Michigan State University Press, 2001); Dennis Carter-Edwards, "The War of 1812 along the Detroit Frontier: A Canadian Perspective," *Michigan Historical Review* 13 (1987): 25-50; and Anthony J. Yanik, *The Fall and Recapture of Detroit in the War of 1812: In Defense of William Hull* (Detroit: Wayne State University Press, 2011). For Canada's experience far from its mother country and adjacent to a sometimes hostile neighbor, see Graeme Wynne, "On the Margins of Empire (1760-1840)," in *The Illustrated History of Canada*, ed. Craig Brown (Toronto: Key Porter Books, 1997), 189-278.

2 Limited information is available for Askin's early years in British North America.

See Milo M. Quaife's useful introduction to the *Askin Papers*, 1:1-21. For other profiles of the Askin family, see *City of Detroit*, 2:993-94; Alexander C. Casselman, "Biography of John Richardson," in John Richardson, *Richardson's War of 1812: With Notes and a Life of the Author*, ed. Casselman (Toronto: Historical Publishing, 1902), lxi-li; Louise Rau, "John Askin: Early Detroit Merchant," *Bulletin of the Business Historical Society* 10 (1936): 91-94; Agnes Haigh Widder, "The John Askin Family Library: A Fur-Trading Family's Books," *Michigan Historical Review* 33 (2007): 27-57; and Kimberly Steele, "'Will Diligently and Faithfully Serve': Mr. Askin's Indentured Servants," in *Revolutionary Detroit: Portraits in Political and Cultural Change, 1760-1805*, ed. Denver Brunsman and Joel Stone (Detroit: Detroit Historical Society, 2009), 140-46.

3 *Askin Papers*, 1:13-16.

4 *MPHC*, 8:410-11.

5 *City of Detroit*, 2:994. For the Askin family's experiences after the American Revolution, see Douglas D. Fisher, "Loyalty for Sale: British Detroiters and the New American Regime," in *Revolutionary Detroit*, 152-57.

6 *Askin Papers*, 1:11-16.

7 *Askin Papers*, 2:545, 550-51.

8 James Askin to Charles Askin, August 18, 1807, in *Askin Papers*, 2:566.

9 Charles Askin to John Askin Sr., August 24, 1807, in *Askin Papers*, 2:567-68.

10 John Askin Jr. to John Askin Sr., September 8, 1807, in *Askin Papers*, 2:572. For American fears of Indians, see also the essay in this volume by Steve Lyskawa.

11 John Askin Sr. to James McGill, July 17, 1812, in *Askin Papers*, 2:709. Askin notes at the end of his letter that since he started writing, Hull had claimed the private property of several British Canadians. For more on the American occupation of Sandwich, see the essay in this volume by Justin Wargo.

12 "Charles Askin's Journal of the Detroit Campaign, July 24-September 12, 1812," in *Askin Papers*, 2:713.

13 John Askin Jr. to John Askin Sr., July 18, 1812, in *Richardson's War of 1812*, 25.

14 "Charles Askin's Journal of the Detroit Campaign," 2:711-15; John Askin Jr. to John Askin Sr., September 16, 1812, in *Askin Papers*, 2:731; Yanik, 6-8, 68-74; Elijah Brush to John Askin Sr., August 11, 1812, in *Askin Papers*, 2:729. For the skirmishes at the Canard River, see the essay in this volume by Daniel F. Harrison.

15 "Charles Askin's Journal of the Detroit Campaign," 2:719. For events leading to the surrender of Detroit, see the essays in this volume by Wargo, Harrison, and Kerri Jansen.

16 For Brush's turbulent wartime experiences, see the essay in this volume by Sharon Tevis Finch.

17 James Askin to John Askin Sr., [after January 22, 1813], in *Askin Papers*, 2:748.

18 Robert Richardson Sr. to John Askin Sr., February 7, 1813, in *Askin Papers*: 2:749. For Robert Richardson Jr.'s death, see *Askin Papers*, 2:748 n2. For the treatment of casualties on the frontier, see the essay in this volume by Scott A. Jankowski.

19 Richardson Sr. to Askin Sr., February 7, 1813, 2:749 ("the loss"); 750 ("Had I" and "shamefull"). For the aftermath of the battles at Frenchtown, see also the essays in this volume by Jankowski and Carly Campbell.

20 John Richardson to Charles Askin, February 4, 1813, in *Richardson's War of 1812*, 303. Richardson went on to become the first Canadian-born novelist to gain widespread fame. See the essays in this volume by Tim Moran and Meghan McGowan.

21 Charles Askin to John Askin Sr., in *Askin Papers*, 2:735.

22 Archange Meredith to Marie Archange Askin, March 21, 1797, in *Askin Papers*, 2:95-98; 97 (quote).

23 Judy Jacobson, *Detroit River Connections: Historical and Biographical Sketches of the Eastern Great Lakes Border Region* (Baltimore: Clearfield, 1994), 40-41.

24 Jacobson, 58-63.

25 *Askin Papers*, 1:12, John Askin Sr. to his children, November 12, 1813, in *Askin Papers*, 2:773.

26 John Askin Sr. to D.W. Smith, April 3, 1797, in *Askin Papers*, 2:102.

27 William Harffy to John Askin Sr., October 17, 1800, in *Askin Papers*, 2:318.

28 Isaac Todd to John Askin Sr., July 20, 1804, in *Askin Papers*, 2:422.

29 Therese McKee to John Askin Sr., December 26, 1812, in *Askin Papers*, 2:743.

30 Alexander Henry to John Askin Sr., May 9, 1815, in *Askin Papers*, 2:783.

31 John Askin Sr. to his children, November 12, 1813, 2:772 ("thanks"); 773 ("Added"). For the epidemic in the Detroit River region at this time, see the essays in this volume by Finch and Joshua Zimberg.

32 Madelaine Askin to Marie Archange Askin, [no date], in *Askin Papers*, 2:784 ("No one"); 785 ("My dear").

Navarre-Anderson Trading Post, Monroe, Michigan
Photograph by Joel Stone, 2012. Digital image. Detroit Historical Society Collection.

Homestead Defense: The British Occupation from a Woman's Perspective

Carly Campbell

One evening early in the British occupation of Michigan
Territory, young Nancy Hubbard spotted a canoe filled with
Indian men rowing toward the beach near her family's property
on Lake St. Clair. Hubbard grew up in the Detroit River region
during a tumultuous time. In 1811, she moved with her parents
and seven siblings to Grosse Pointe, roughly nine miles from
Detroit, to establish a home. Her father died unexpectedly that
winter, leaving her mother to care for the eight children. The
family's struggles continued when her oldest brother, who acted as
a surrogate father to Nancy, left to help defend Michigan Territory
during the early stages of the War of 1812. After the surrender of
Detroit in August 1812, her mother planned to stay at the home
only until the crops could be gathered. However, the Hubbards'
string of bad luck continued; before they could depart, the Indians
spotted earlier by Nancy landed on shore.[1]

An Indian woman first approached the Hubbard home.
She then motioned to the men aboard the canoe, who quickly
"sprang ashore, ran up to the gate and leapt over it like so many
demons of the forest [and] ran up to the house," Nancy recalled.
Her oldest sister greeted them at the door and spoke kindly in
French. "Come in and warm, for it is cold today," she conveyed
as she guided them inside to the fire. They shouted at her in a mix
of confusion and anger, but still followed her in with "all their
implements of war, painted black and red. They were hideous

looking creatures. They had war clubs, scalping knives, and tomahawks," as they sat in the front room.[2]

While the painted warriors were distracted, the Hubbards snuck out the back door and fled to a neighbor's house. In the family's absence, the natives plundered the home and destroyed its few possessions, even smashing dishes to pieces. They only passed over the clothes belonging to the sister who had greeted them, identifying them by her size and shape. Later that night, the Indians spoke to other Grosse Pointe inhabitants, promising to kill the Hubbards if they proved to be Americans. The fearful townspeople told the Indians that the family was English but, knowing this would not appease them for long, sent a number of men to protect the family. Many nights afterward, the Indians returned to harass the family, even stealing a number of black horses. In her papers, Nancy recalls an important fact about the British occupation of Detroit: "When Hull surrendered the Fort to the British, we were left to the Indians."[3]

Events such as these became commonplace after the British seized Detroit on August 16, 1812. Along the Detroit River, according to United States Indian agent John Anderson, "the horror of that unexpected transaction was destrassing, officers braking their swords, soldiers their guns, wemen crying & wringing their hands."[4] Fearful responses to the occupation were not due to the invading British soldiers and Upper Canadian militias. Those who truly frightened the settlers were Britain's Indian allies. No longer restrained, they were free to harass settlements such as Grosse Pointe and Frenchtown (today Monroe, Michigan), far from Detroit's stockade. Local Indians had the freedom to do what they wished with the land and its inhabitants because the British were unwilling or unable to intervene. With most American men away fighting the enemy or exiled as prisoners, women were required to take up defense of their homes.

As soon as Michigan territorial Governor William Hull

relinquished power, the British made their presence known. On the day of the capitulation, General Isaac Brock issued a proclamation: "Officers of Militia will be held responsible that all Arms in possession of Militia Men, be immediately delivered up, and all Individuals whatever, who have in their possession, Arms of any kind, will deliver them up without delay."[5] Few settlers trusted that the British would provide adequate protection. The lack of weapons, combined with the narrow ribbon farms in the region, created a landscape in which the inhabitants had no security in numbers.[6] Brock soon assigned Colonel Henry Procter to supervise the territory before leaving for the Niagara front. The general gave explicit directions to use Indian raids to help keep the American inhabitants at bay. In his final letter to Procter before dying at the Battle of Queenston Heights in October 1812, Brock emphasized that "the enemy must be kept in a constant state of ferment."[7] Despite Brock's orders, Procter initially governed the region with a light hand, allowing inhabitants to go about their usual routines and trades. At one point during the early months of the British occupation, he mentioned to Judge Augustus B. Woodward that, if the territory were to be returned to the U.S., he would like to keep it in the same prosperous condition that he found it.[8]

Procter's early expressions of leniency toward Michigan Territory residents were ultimately undermined by Britain's native allies. The British never adequately restrained Indian groups from taking retribution against settlers – any settlers – in the decades-long struggle for frontier lands. The problems began at the start of the occupation. The natives ransacked farmhouses, stole cattle, and destroyed crops. They drove away families and slaughtered others. However, the British hesitated to criticize or disallow such practices because they needed the Indians to assist in their conflict with the Americans. Without native support, British forces would not have had the manpower necessary to control the entirety of Michigan Territory. The situation gave leverage to the Indians, and they took full advantage.[9]

From the native perspective, the British occupation offered an opportunity to reverse the tide of white settlement in the Old Northwest. Unfortunately for women living on the frontier, they were often the only ones left to confront Indian raids. One particular woman stands out above others in the region because of her bravery and poise. Elizabeth Knaggs Anderson of Frenchtown was remembered as being a "tall, handsome woman in her prime, with a fair complexion and dark auburn hair."[10] She was the wife of tradesman, Indian agent, and militia colonel John Anderson, who was a known adversary of the Indian population. From the beginning of the occupation, therefore, John's position created numerous troubles for the family. Eventually, he had to leave the region to avoid arrest, and Elizabeth became a heroine.[11]

Elizabeth Anderson came from a large family. All five of her brothers were active in the militia, known in the community, and at odds with the Indians. Her mother, Rachel Fry Knaggs, formerly of Philadelphia, was a defiant woman herself. She was singled out by Colonel Procter to be transported to Detroit from her home at the River Raisin. At 80 years old, robbed of nearly everything, including her clothing, Knaggs flirted with death on the journey. Despite the difficulty, she arrived safely. When asked how it was that she had survived, Knaggs replied, "My spunk kept me warm." Descending from such a line, Elizabeth's own boldness was not surprising.[12]

The Andersons endured Indian threats even before the British seized power in August. John was a popular man in society, receiving many accolades, including an appointment as justice of the peace. For several years, he served as captain of the militia and became a colonel at the onset of the war. Anderson's high profile made him a target for the British and their native allies. He took an especially active role in Frenchtown, helping to guard the River Raisin settlement against Indian raids. Around July 7, 1812, a rumor about a possible Indian attack began to circle the town. Panicked, the mostly French inhabitants buried their belongings for safekeeping, and the militia burned spare provisions, including more than one thousand barrels of flour and great quantities of pork. Later, upon learning of Hull's capitulation from British Indian agent Matthew Elliott, residents also received word of Brock's declaration that private property would be protected. The news lulled Frenchtown residents into a false sense of security. "All those who had hid their property in the ground, or in the woods brought it home," Anderson wrote in an autobiography shortly after the war. "But the promise, & writing was but of little consequence."[13]

On August 20, Elizabeth was alone with the couple's three children when the first assault of her homestead began. A group of Indians and British soldiers came to the River Raisin to harass her husband. In a matter of minutes, they destroyed the home and threatened Elizabeth and the children. According to Francis Gandon, a fellow resident of Frenchtown, "the burning of the stockades and the blockhouses, and the plundering and destruction of Col. John Anderson's property" followed shortly after Hull's surrender.[14] The acts, committed primarily by natives, were supervised by Elliott and Major Peter Chambers. British officials justified the action because they considered the Anderson home to be a public military storehouse; the men added that they could not be held responsible for the Indians' behavior. Elizabeth protected the children and escaped to a neighbor's house. When John discovered them, he recalled that the meeting was "soroful in deed. I found them all in teers and what shall we do was the question." Elizabeth pleaded with him to alter his behavior: "You will be killed said my wife in teers and what will become of those poor little children." The family came to a consensus that it should move to Detroit until the Americans returned.[15]

Shortly after this decision, John escaped imprisonment and moved to Ohio, where he joined the American army and did not see his family again for nearly thirteen months. He left knowing that he was likely conceding his property at the River Raisin to the mercy of the Indians. During his absence, however, Elizabeth rose to confront the British occupiers and defend the family's home from Indian attack.[16]

On January 22, 1813, the American army that had briefly regained control of the River Raisin was defeated by a group of Indians and British. The days that followed were catastrophic for residents, including Elizabeth Anderson. The Indians marched American prisoners, "nearly naked with feet bleeding," from home to home, offering them for sale. Elizabeth and other unharmed residents combined their resources to buy the prisoners' freedom. A group of Indians claimed to have captured a Colonel Anderson and scalped him. They proceeded to bring a "number of scalps, and some presoners" to Elizabeth's home, and "they danced at hir door, cauling on hir to come and pick out hir husbands scalp." Only later did her torment end, when she discovered that her husband had not died.[17]

Indians then began to ransack homes. They entered Elizabeth's, hoping to carry away her valuables and perhaps torch the house. She sat upon a chest that contained nearly $900 in gold and silver as the Indians surrounded her. Despite their threats, they could not force her off the chest. According to a family history, "One [Indian] upraised his tomahawk and bade her rise. 'I won't' said the plucky lady. 'If you don't get up, I kill you,' said the Indian." He then made an obscene gesture in reference to scalping her. Still, she stood her ground. As the history recounts, "the Knaggs blood showed itself in Mrs. Anderson. 'If you are a brave Indian you can tomahawk me now,' she said, sarcastically and defiantly," opening her dress wide to allow him an accurate shot. Her courage filled the man with unexpected admiration for the white woman, and he spared her life. Elizabeth watched as the warriors departed her house. She then gathered her children and some belongings and returned to Detroit, where she stayed until her husband returned with the liberating American army in the fall of 1813.[18]

The events at the River Raisin shocked the nation. Locally,

American respect for the British was lost. Procter attempted to protect his position in the territory by ordering a number of American men to leave Detroit under the pretense that they had broken an article of the capitulation. The twenty-nine men united in writing a petition of grievances that accused Procter of being in violation of the same article. Judge Woodward circulated a separate petition against the British-Indian atrocities at the River Raisin, which included demands such as the return of the inhabitants' weapons. Procter rejected the petition and exiled potential troublemakers from the territory. Problems in the region mounted. An epidemic ripped through the settlement, and many perished without proper care. In addition, Indian raids continued in unpredictable patterns. On February 4, 1813, Procter declared martial law and suspended the territory's civil and criminal laws.[19]

With Ohio troops, John Anderson returned to his home at the River Raisin on September 12, 1813, two days after Master Commandant Oliver Hazard Perry's triumph over the British in the Battle of Lake Erie. He and several others "went over to the river to exemin the battle ground, it was destrassing to see that flurishing and rich settlement abandoned, by man & beast." He was shocked when he "came to the fatal spot, whare those brave men was burned a live, every countaness was clothed in sorrow, to see the bones amongst the ashes." When Anderson reached his own property, he found that his deserted home was burned to the ground along with many others surrounding it. There were only a few signs of life left, orchards with their boughs hanging heavy with fruit and Anderson's trading post that he shared with François Navarre. Although marked with bullet holes from the disturbances at Frenchtown, the Navarre-Anderson Trading Post remains to this day the oldest surviving wooden structure in Michigan.[20]

During the last months of John's exile, Elizabeth and the children had lived in the home of prominent Detroiter Solomon Sibley. Sibley was part of the local group exiled by Procter for pressuring him to stop the mistreatment of American prisoners by Britain's Indian allies. John marveled at Elizabeth's courage in defending the Sibley home and later described her actions to Sibley. "Mrs. Anderson had it in contemplation two or three times last summer [1813] to leave the house on account of the Indians," John wrote, "you may think how it was for a woman alone, but when she thought of the house and property, how it would be destroyed, she was determined to hold out. A number of nights she never went to bed." Largely because of Elizabeth's heroic efforts, the Sibley home fared better than most structures in Detroit in the final weeks of the British occupation.[21]

Michigan Territory continued under martial law until late September 1813, when American forces regained control of the region. As the American troops pulled nearer, Procter ordered all public buildings in Detroit and Fort Amherstburg burned and began a hasty retreat. General William Henry Harrison found the territory in a state of desolation. Many of the homes still standing lacked fences, windows, and floorboards, and most people were without adequate clothing. For those who remained at the River Raisin – nearly all of French descent – the main source of sustenance was boiled, chopped hay.[22] It's no wonder that residents remembered the end of the occupation as a glorious occasion. One such witness was young Nancy Hubbard, who recorded her memory of the return of American forces in a short autobiography years later: "Then the army came back and took Detroit again. It was a day of great rejoicing. All the people went out to meet them. It was a splendid scene. Their guns glistened in the air. It was a splendid day."[23]

The British occupation of Michigan Territory placed inhabitants in great peril. Indian attacks were an ever-present threat, and, with many men gone, women were often left to protect frontier homesteads. Elizabeth Anderson stepped into the role of defender in protecting herself, her children, and her community. Without such acts of bravery, the territory could have experienced even greater devastation. Nancy Hubbard, Rachel

Fry Knaggs, and Anderson exemplified everything that a frontier woman needed to be: strong, independent, and resilient. Their actions helped to defend a land, define a territory, and shape the future of the state of Michigan.

NOTES

1 Nancy Hubbard Howard, "A Brief Life of Fifty-Four Years Spent in Michigan (1811-1865)," 2, Nancy Hubbard Howard Papers, BHC.

2 Howard, 3.

3 Howard, 4.

4 Richard C. Knopf, ed., *A Short History of the Life of John Anderson* (Columbus, OH: Anthony Wayne Parkway Board, 1956), 1.

5 "Brock's Proclamation Following the Surrender of Fort Detroit, 1812," in *Documents Relating to the Invasion of Canada and the Surrender of Detroit, 1812*, ed. E.A. Cruikshank (Ottawa: Government Printing Bureau, 1912), 155-56.

6 Alan Taylor, *The Civil War of 1812: American Citizens, British Subjects, Irish Rebels, & Indian Allies* (New York: Knopf, 2010), 154.

7 Brock quoted in Sandy Antal, *A Wampum Denied: Procter's War of 1812* (Ottawa: Carleton University Press, 1997), 129.

8 Nell Herndon, "Detroit under British Rule, 1812-13" (master's thesis, Wayne University, 1933), 12.

9 *City of Detroit*, 2:1018. For Indian grievances and motivations against the Americans, see the essays in this volume by Steve Lyskawa and Daniel F. Harrison.

10 B.R. Ross, "History of the Knaggs Family," in the *Evening News* (Detroit), January 18, 1902, Folder 2, John Anderson Papers, Bentley Historical Library, University of Michigan, Ann Arbor.

11 Little has been written about the Andersons outside of John's autobiography, which was published posthumously (*Short History of the Life of John Anderson*) and a series of articles in the *Evening News* in 1902. For a brief account of Elizabeth's experiences during the war, see also Talcott E. Wing, *History of Monroe County, Michigan* (New York: Munsell, 1890), 39-40.

12 Knaggs quoted in Wing, 109.

13 *Short History of the Life of John Anderson*, 26.

14 "Affidavit of Francis Gandon Concerning Massacres, Etc., Committed by Indians at Sandy Creek," in *MPHC*, 8:643.

15 *Short History of the Life of John Anderson*, 27.

16 *Short History of the Life of John Anderson*, 19, 29.

17 *Short History of the Life of John Anderson*, 32. For the treatment of American prisoners at the River Raisin, see also the essays in this volume by Timothy Marks and Scott A. Jankowski.

18 Ross.

19 Herndon, 53-58; *City of Detroit*, 2:1038-42. For the protest against Procter, see also the essay in this volume by Sharon Tevis Finch.

20 *Short History of the Life of John Anderson*, 41.

21 John Anderson to Solomon Sibley, December 6, 1813, in Clarence M. Burton, *History of Detroit, 1780 to 1850: Financial and Commercial* (Detroit: Burton, 1917), 63.

22 Herndon, 62-64. For conditions in the region following the British retreat, see also the essay in this volume by Joshua Zimberg.

23 Howard, 4.

"It was a hideous sight to see": Treatment of Casualties on the Frontier

Scott A. Jankowski

During the War of 1812 in the Detroit River region, the treatment of casualties was extremely inconsistent due to the frontier environment. Medical physicians had little involvement with the care of soldiers because of the distant clashes and turbulent circumstances. The absence of physicians left soldiers and settlers to struggle with diseases and battle wounds. Many illnesses were not understood, resulting in few treatment options. Moreover, the level of hostility between Americans and their British and Indian enemies exacerbated the problem. European rules of war carried to North America faded as troops, warriors, and pioneers fought brutal battles deep into the frontier. Therefore, the overall treatments for wounded soldiers depended greatly on individual circumstances and had unpredictable outcomes.[1]

The War of 1812 took place during a period of transition in the history of medicine. By the American Revolutionary War (1775-1783), the influence of archaic humeral theory was declining in European and American medicine. The theory regarded the distinct bodily fluids as the central aspect of health and observed only a single disease for all humans. Instead, physicians started to realize that several different diseases existed, including skin rashes and smallpox. These specific diseases did not change medical treatment; bleeding, purging, and blistering continued regardless of symptoms. Few physicians had the expertise to carry out surgeries, including amputations and removal of bodily stones. Hence, troops were especially limited in their treatment options in battle.[2]

From its founding, the United States Army aspired to follow the European model of warfare with its emphasis on international law. Works such as Hugo Grotius's *On the Law of War and Peace* (1625) and Emeriti Vattel's *Law of Nations* (1758) helped to define rules for declaring war, engaging the enemy, surrendering, and treating prisoners. These provisions dramatically improved conditions for prisoners, including the sick and wounded, by instituting prisoner exchanges. Enemy armies conducted person-for-person exchanges or made other arrangements. The early U.S. incorporated similar rules of warfare. However, as Americans advanced into the frontier, militias and even the regular army increasingly ignored European conventions.[3]

The frontier was exceptionally violent throughout early American history. Tumultuous conflicts between European colonists and Native Americans defined the colonial experience. During the Revolutionary War, American soldiers and civilians employed unlimited warfare in order to expand into Ohio Country. Native warriors fought back, killing numerous militiamen and settlers. Americans generally had superior forces and were not above razing entire native villages. In 1782, Pennsylvania militiamen slaughtered nearly one hundred unarmed Delaware Indian men, women, and children at the Moravian missionary village of Gnadenütten (today Gnadenhutten, Ohio).[4]

The Battle of Brownstown, on August 5, 1812, was the first battle in the War of 1812 on American soil in the Detroit area. It was also the first experience that many soldiers had with treating battle casualties. U.S. Major Thomas Van Horne was leading about 150 soldiers to gather supplies when they were ambushed by dozens of Indian warriors. The soldiers quickly retreated, leaving their supplies, the wounded, and the dead behind. Robert Lucas, who served as a scout during the war, later testified that there were hundreds of natives, roughly three times that of

American forces. His estimate was discredited by British officers, who noted that there were only twenty-five Indian warriors who fought against the Americans. The casualty figures were rough at best. Lucas stated that seventeen soldiers and officers were killed, approximately twelve men were wounded, and another seventy were missing.[5] Thomas Verchères de Boucherville, a merchant and British-Canadian soldier, found the Indians' treatment of the Americans appalling: "They [the native warriors] scalped everyone they could overtake and placed these trophies of their bravery on long poles which they stuck up in the ground by the roadside. They also drove long stakes through the bodies of the slain which were left lying thus exposed. It was a hideous sight to see and little calculated to encourage the enemy when passing it on the way to Detroit."[6] The natives allowed only their able-bodied American prisoners to live. When an American soldier was injured, a warrior went behind the prisoner and dealt him a tomahawk blow. The leader of the pan-Indian alliance, Shawnee chief Tecumseh, had ordered no torturing of soldiers or mutilation of corpses. Although sources disagree over whether Tecumseh was present at Brownstown, accounts by several British soldiers and Canadian militiamen affirmed Verchères's description of the horrific scene.[7]

Nevertheless, natives followed established procedures for taking care of their wounded. Days after the ambush at Brownstown, the British and their Indian allies clashed again with the Americans near the Wyandot village of Maguaga (today parts of Trenton and Wyandotte, Michigan). The limited American victory left numerous casualties on both sides. Verchères received a bullet in his leg that he attempted to mend by "applying a little earth after the manner of the Indians." Not surprisingly, rubbing dirt in his wound made it worse. A British surgeon at Amherstburg removed the bullet, but could not help with the shot still scattered in Verchères's thigh. Tecumseh directed him to visit a recognized native healer, who applied an herbal remedy.

Within ten days, the native treatment healed Verchères's remaining wounds, allowing him to return to duty.[8]

Violence was not restricted to the Detroit River region, yet the eastern theaters of the war had more trained physicians to treat casualties. In New York, American surgeons and their mates treated numerous diseases and impairments. They took care of troops with pneumonia, dysentery, typhus, rheumatism, chronic diarrhea, and other unknown fevers and undetermined diseases. The surgeons and their mates used ether, quinine, opium, and homeopathic remedies as well as the old methods of bleeding, purging, and blistering to care for the sick and injured. Doctors also tended to wounded combatants on or near battlefields. William Beaumont, an American surgeon's mate in the war who later became famous for his research on gastric physiology, helped more than two hundred wounded soldiers at the Battle of York (today Toronto) in April 1813. After the Americans won the battle, the retreating British blew up the fort's magazine. Beaumont described that those who "belong'd to our Regt [regiment] their wounds were of the worst kind, compd [compound] fractured of *legs, thighs & arms fractures* of *Sculls*, – on the night of the explosion, we were all night engaged in amputating & dressing the worst of them."[9] During the war, surgeons in the East also began to deduce certain reasons behind diseases and started to sanitize hospitals, tents, and other facilities by cleaning latrines, floors, and walls.[10]

By comparison, medical treatments were scarce in the Detroit River region. In July 1812, physicians at Fort Detroit prepared for casualties by requisitioning supplies for their new hospital, such as blankets, bedsteads, mutton, chicken, butter, and opium. However, most of the fort's American medical personnel did not stay after General William Hull surrendered Michigan Territory. Some fled to Ohio, others crossed the Detroit River to live with friends or relatives in Upper Canada, and a handful were taken prisoner. Many residents succumbed to pneumonia-like symptoms, which, at the time, they referred to as ague or brain fever. Once the Americans recovered Detroit in the early fall of 1813, the town was plagued with disease. The few available surgeons had difficulty with their mates, who were often more interested in consuming the alcohol intended for patients. Problems also mounted because of the scores of wounded soldiers who returned to the region.[11]

The battles at the River Raisin of January 1813 produced the largest number of casualties in the region during the war. As American General James Winchester's army camped at the Maumee River before invading the Detroit area, his men suffered from hunger, cold, and lack of clothing. In addition, fevers were rampant in the camp. Hundreds of troops fell sick, and many died due to the harsh conditions. One soldier wrote, "What we suffered at Defiance [the encampment] was but the beginning of affliction. We now saw nothing but hunger, and cold, and nakedness, staring us in the face."[12] Winchester's army then marched into the British-occupied territory. A detachment of one thousand Kentuckians established a position in Frenchtown (today Monroe, Michigan) along the River Raisin. But British Colonel Henry Procter reacted quickly. Early in the morning of January 22, Procter's six hundred British soldiers and one thousand native allies attacked the Kentuckians while they were still sleeping. As the left flank of the American army caved in, the natives converged upon them, ultimately forcing surrender.[13]

Procter took American prisoners and gathered wounded soldiers from both sides in the hopes of moving them across the Lake Erie ice to Fort Amherstburg, but he had difficulties transporting the casualties. Therefore, he ordered the severely wounded U.S. soldiers to remain in Frenchtown and wait for sleds to move them to the fort. The British placed the wounded Americans in Frenchtown homes, which were converted into hospitals, to care for their injuries. Dr. John Todd, an American surgeon, and his mate, Dr. Gustavus Bower, attempted to treat the casualties, but on the morning of January 23, nearly two hundred Indians returned to the town. Some survivors reported that the natives were looking for alcohol when they began to rob and pillage the American soldiers and the settlers' homes. The natives then set fire to the houses with the injured soldiers inside, as well as several barns. When the wounded tried to escape from the flames, they were tomahawked, killed, and scalped. Dr. Todd and his mate were taken hostage, and approximately sixty Americans were slaughtered. As the surgeons were escorted away from Frenchtown, Dr. Todd explained the dreadful incident to a British officer, but the British were more concerned with their own wounded. When the American public learned of the massacre, they were horrified, giving birth to the battle cry, "Remember the Raisin!"[14]

Other battles in the region had different and sometimes more positive outcomes for wounded soldiers. The Battle of Fort Stephenson on the Sandusky River (today Fremont, Ohio) was one such example. In July 1813, the British marched thirty miles to assault the fort with more than two thousand soldiers and Indian warriors. With only 160 American troops, Major George Croghan was advised by General William Henry Harrison to retreat. Croghan declined, and Harrison allowed him to maintain the fort. On August 2, 1813, the British attacked, but did not have scaling ladders to take the fort. While the Americans barraged the exposed British soldiers, the native warriors refused to attack. Finally, after a few brutal hours, the British called for a ceasefire. Soldiers taking cover outside the fort begged for water. Major John Richardson described the state of his fellow British troops as they pleaded for survival: "The first division were so near the enemy, that they could distinctly hear the various orders given in the fort, and the faint voices of the wounded and dying in the ditch, calling out for water, which the enemy had the humanity to lower to them on the instant."[15] The regard shown for wounded soldiers was a surprising outcome compared to the battles of Brownstown and the River Raisin. Many more British soldiers would have likely died without receiving water from the Americans. Croghan thanked his officers and soldiers "for their gallantry, and good conduct" throughout the battle.[16]

Despite their acts of kindness at Fort Stephenson, Americans were equally capable of mistreating the British and their native allies. In early October 1813, following the American victory on Lake Erie, Harrison's army pursued Procter's retreating forces in Upper Canada. The Americans caused turmoil in the rural areas along their march by burning homes and destroying farms. On October 5, the Americans defeated their enemies in the Battle of the Thames. The Americans first overran a line of British soldiers, forcing scores to surrender. Then the American cavalry charged through a swamp and broke hundreds of natives led by Tecumseh. The Shawnee chief's death caused his warriors to retreat to the forest. The American army took approximately six hundred British prisoners after killing twelve and wounding twenty-two. The Indians lost thirty-three warriors, while the Americans suffered sixteen deaths and around fifty wounded.[17]

After the battle, reports circulated that the Americans mutilated Tecumseh's body, dividing his flesh among the soldiers. Verchères had doubts: "According to some of our officers who were taken prisoners of war, that brave warrior [Tecumseh] was hacked into little pieces by the enraged Kentuckians and taken to Detroit, but I have never really believed this barbarous story."[18] There is little disagreement that the Americans mistreated their British prisoners. Richardson later wrote of the hunger and despair of his fellow soldiers, who were forced to march to Fort Stephenson. Medical treatment was sparse, and the Americans dealt harshly with the wounded. One British soldier was inflicted with a violent blow to his head and needed help. "When visited by the officer of the guard, a complaint was preferred by the injured man," according to Richardson. "But the liberal republican, with true patriotic feeling, justified the act of his countryman, and concluded by threatening a repetition of the punishment." By the following summer, when the Americans finally prepared to release the captives, many of them had contracted malaria. American physicians instructed a drummer boy to cut the troops, hoping that bloodletting would equalize the body and save their lives. Although well-intentioned, the aggressive medical treatment often did more harm than good, causing many to perish.[19]

During the War of 1812, the treatment of the sick and wounded on the Detroit frontier was at best inconsistent and at worst lethal. The region witnessed some of the fiercest fighting of the war, as the Americans, British Canadians, and Indians all contested the same terrain. While the battles were deadly, the aftermath was often worse. Medicine was almost nonexistent in the region. The distance from population centers resulted in a severe shortage of experienced surgeons and physicians. Diseases spread unchecked during and immediately after the war. Hungry and depleted troops and settlers suffered without medical help. Although some combatants made moral decisions to provide for their injured adversaries, most chose aggression over compassion. Far from realizing the civilized ideals of international law, the frontier was an unforgiving wartime environment.

NOTES

1 Aside from published journals, letters, and memoirs, there is little scholarly work on frontier medicine during the War of 1812. For a first-hand account by a surgeon on the Great Lakes, see John C. Fredriksen, ed., *Surgeon of the Lakes: The Diary of Dr. Usher Parsons, 1812-1814* (Erie, PA: Erie County Historical Society, 2000). For a broader survey of medicine in Detroit, see Larry W. Stephenson, *Detroit Surgeons: 300 Years* (Grosse Pointe Farms, MI: Dorian Naughton Publishing, 2011).

2 Mary C. Gillett, *The Army Medical Department, 1775-1818* (Washington, DC: Center of Military History, United States Army, 1981), 1-21.

3 Stephen C. Neff, *War and the Law of Nations: A General History* (New York: Cambridge University Press, 2005), 83-268; Charles M. Wiltse, "Thomas Jefferson on the Law of Nations," *American Journal of International Law* 29 (1935): 66-81; and Jeremy Rabkin, "Grotius, Vattel, and Locke: An Older View of Liberalism and Nationality," *Review of Politics* 59 (1997): 293-322.

4   John Grenier, *The First Way of War: American War Making on the Frontier, 1607-1814* (New York: Cambridge University Press, 2005); Peter Silver, *Our Savage Neighbors: How Indian War Transformed Early America* (New York: Norton, 2007); John Maisner, "Crawford's Defeat: Raids and Retaliation on the Frontier," in *Revolutionary Detroit: Portrait in Political and Cultural Change 1760-1805*, ed. Denver Brunsman and Joel Stone (Detroit: Detroit Historical Society, 2009), 86-91.

5   John C. Parish, ed., *The Robert Lucas Journal of the War of 1812 during the Campaign under General William Hull* (Iowa City: State Historical Society of Iowa, 1906), 47-52.

6   Milo M. Quaife, ed., *War on the Detroit: The Chronicles of Thomas Verchères de Boucherville and the Capitulation, by an Ohio Volunteer* (Chicago: Fireside Press, 1940), 90.

7   For primary and secondary accounts of the battle, see *War on the Detroit*, 88-93; James Dalliba, *A Narrative of the Battle of Brownstown* (New York: David Longworth, 1816); and Anthony J. Yanik, *The Fall and Recapture of Detroit in the War of 1812: In Defense of William Hull* (Detroit: Wayne State University Press, 2011), 72-73. For myths and realities surrounding Tecumseh, see the essay in this volume by Tim Moran.

8   *War on the Detroit*, 98-105; 100 (quote).

9   William Beaumont, *Wm. Beaumont's Formative Years: Two Early Notebooks, 1811-1821*, ed. Genevieve Miller (New York: Henry Schuman, 1946), 14-17; 16 (quote).

10 Gillett, 166-67.

11 Physicians & Surgeons, General Hospital, 1801-1812, Lawrence Reynolds Papers, BHC; Gillett, 162-65; Stephenson, 29.

12 William Atherton, *Narrative of the Suffering and Defeat of the North-Western Army under General Winchester* (Frankfort: A.G. Hodges, 1842), 19. See also Gillett, 164-71.

13 For the battles at the River Raisin, see Sandy Antal, *A Wampum Denied: Procter's War of 1812* (Ottawa: Carleton University Press, 1997), 161-216; Frank B. Woodford, *Mr. Jefferson's Disciple: A Life of Justice Woodward* (East Lansing: Michigan State College Press, 1953), 114-25; Ralph Naveaux, *Invaded on All Sides: The Story of Michigan's Greatest Battlefield Scene of the Engagements at Frenchtown and the River Raisin in the War of 1812* (Marceline, MO: Walsworth, 2008); and Dennis M. Au, *War on the Raisin: A Narrative Account of the War of 1812 in the River Raisin Settlement, Michigan Territory* (Monroe, MI: Monroe County Historical Commission, 1981).

14 United States Congress, *Barbarities of the Enemy, Exposed in a Report of the Committee of the House of Representatives* (Worcester, MA: Isaac Sturtevant, 1814), 139-41; Antal, 161-87. For the aftermath of the massacre, see the essay in this volume by Carly Campbell. Dr. Todd was the uncle of Mary Todd, wife of Abraham Lincoln. G. Glenn Clift, *Remember the Raisin! Kentucky and Kentuckians in the Battles and Massacre at Frenchtown, Michigan Territory, in the War of 1812* (Frankfort: Kentucky Historical Society, 1961), 130.

15 Richardson, 180; David D. Anderson, *Ohio: In Myth, Memory, and Imagination, Essays on the Ohio Experience* (East Lansing: Midwestern Press, 2004), 39-46. For Richardson, see the essays in this volume by Moran, Timothy Marks, and Meghan McGowan.

16 Croghan quoted in Richardson, 185.

17 Antal, 315-53. For casualty estimates, see Richardson, 234. For the Battle of the Thames, see also the essays in this volume by Moran and Joshua Zimberg.

18 *War on the Detroit*, 145. Antal also questions the mutilation story because it would have violated native burial procedures, and it is not supported by other accounts (346).

19 Richardson, 244-93, 258 (quote); Antal, 365-67.

The Outlaw Andrew Westbrook
Meghan McGowan

Regarded as a traitor by the British and a hero by the Americans, Andrew Westbrook defied any single category in the War of 1812. Whether burning his house to ashes, demanding to be called Baron von Steuben, kidnapping Upper Canadian officials, or assisting American General William Hull in invading British Canada, Westbrook did not follow the path laid by any of the parties in the war. Ultimately, he manipulated the border between Canada and the United States through his knowledge of both sides to champion the American cause. But Westbrook's actions were motivated by personal circumstances more than by political ideology. In supporting the U.S. in the war, he found a novel way to get revenge against his former neighbors turned enemies in Upper Canada.[1]

Not unlike the Shawnee Indian leader Tecumseh, it is difficult to separate fact from fiction regarding Andrew Westbrook. Our best physical depiction of Westbrook comes from U.S. Indian superintendent Thomas McKenney, who visited him in 1826: "Westbrook is about six feet two inches. His hair was once sandy, or rather fox colour; but the fierceness of the reddish cast is now softened by an intermixture of grey. He has a fine face – his features being moderate in size, and well proportioned. . . . His form is good, with broad shoulders and chest . . . and well finished limbs. He has no education, yet he talks well, and is precise, and graphic in his descriptions."[2] Westbrook's traitorous reputation was both reflected and furthered by John Richardson's 1851 serialized novel, *Westbrook, the Outlaw; or, the Avenging Wolf.* Richardson paints Westbrook as evil and pathetic. Although this perspective is understandable given Richardson's British-Canadian heritage, much of the book is fictionalized. Westbrook may have been an "avenging wolf," but not one completely devoid of principles.[3]

Westbrook descended from a line of border crossers. During the American Revolutionary War (1775-83), his father, Anthony Westbrook, was a loyalist in Massachusetts and fought on the British side under Mohawk political and military leader Joseph Brant. For his wartime service, Anthony received two tracts of land in British Canada along the Thames River in a community that became known as Delaware (later Delaware Township and today part of Middlesex Centre, Ontario). In the mid-1780s, the Westbrook family migrated to the area. Andrew later inherited the land and became a prominent member of the settlement, working as a blacksmith, merchant, and land speculator. His status was reflected by his appointment as town constable in 1805. By the outbreak of war in 1812, Westbrook had expanded his original landholdings to an estate covering more than four thousand acres that included a distillery, barn, storehouse, sawmill, and gristmill. Few signs indicated that this town leader with strong British loyalist roots would become a paragon of treachery.[4]

Westbrook's fortunes and loyalties turned in response to a financial dispute. In 1810, he and other local merchants suffered from a commercial depression in the Thames River Valley. The following year, Westbrook and his local business partner Simon Zelotes Watson attempted to speculate in new lands, but had their ambitions blocked by the government's chief representative in the area, Colonel Thomas Talbot. Talbot likely had designs on the land for his own expansive portfolio. His actions infuriated Westbrook and Watson. In March 1811, Watson angrily accused Talbot of shattering the men's plans to settle the land and declared, "I shall then turn to you the primary and ultimate cause of all my misfortunes." The fallout between Talbot and Westbrook likely served as the primary motivation behind Westbrook's decision to align with General Hull and the Americans when the opportunity presented itself.[5]

There was also an impulsive quality to Westbrook's actions. On July 10, 1812, his business partner Watson did not classify Westbrook as an American by birth or sentiment on a survey of Delaware residents that he sent to Detroit.[6] Two days later, Hull landed in Sandwich with his invading army and began distributing a proclamation promising to protect residents' property in exchange for support. Watson and another local resident, Ebenezer Allen, helped in circulating Hull's proclamation. The evidence is inconclusive if Westbrook joined them.[7]

However, Westbrook soon took the lead in gathering local support for Hull. On July 27, British Lieutenant-Colonel Henry Bostwick detained him based on a tip provided by Daniel Springer, a magistrate in Delaware Township appointed by Talbot. According to Springer's testimony, "Westbrook had been very officious in causing a Petition to be circulated, addressed to Gen Hull, requesting him to save them & their property, stating that they would not take up Arms against him." The following day, Springer wrote directly to General Isaac Brock, the British commander in the region, about Westbrook's traitorous activities. Westbrook defended his actions by declaring that he "had too much property to risk it, by opposing the Americans," which was likely true. Like many Upper Canadians, Westbrook probably had confidence in the success of Hull's invasion.[8]

The difference is that he continued supporting the Americans long after Hull's failure was apparent. After escaping his detainment, Westbrook served the Americans as a guide in Upper Canada in the area between Lake Erie and the Thames River. He continued providing help to Hull after the general withdrew from Sandwich in early August 1812. Westbrook delivered intelligence to Detroit about activities across the river. Later, Westbrook escalated his involvement from guiding and spying for the Americans to leading raids into his former province. For a year, between September 1813 and September 1814, Westbrook and his old business partner Simon Watson terrorized settlements along the Thames River and Lake Erie.[9]

Westbrook's first well-documented excursion took place in late January 1814, when he captured his old nemesis Daniel Springer and prominent British-Canadian militia Colonel François Baby in his former town of Delaware. Upon the group's arrival in Detroit, Baby at first denied participating in military activities. His escorts responded by pointing out that Westbrook had captured Baby in his military uniform! Baby subsequently acknowledged serving under General Henry Procter in the war and was eventually released. Springer was carried to Kentucky and later escaped. Westbrook captured neither man by accident: Both were associates of Colonel Talbot, who remained Westbrook's primary target.[10]

Westbrook's most eccentric act during the war was setting fire to his home and other buildings. Sources differ on the exact date of the torching, although most place it during his return to Delaware to capture Baby and Springer in early 1814. Few acts more dramatically represented a change in loyalty during the war. The blaze coincided with his family's permanent move across the border.[11] After the war, when Westbrook sought compensation from the U.S. Congress for the damage, he and his supporters claimed that he destroyed his property to prevent it from falling into the enemy's hands.[12] Still, as with most of Westbrook's wartime actions, personal vengeance played a role. On January 23, 1814, American Colonel Anthony Butler wrote that Westbrook burned his property "rather than that they should be enjoyed by his persecutors." Westbrook eliminated everything that he had worked for rather than let it wind up with Talbot or another of his "persecutors."[13]

Westbrook provided a variety of services to his new country.

In addition to conducting raids and kidnapping Upper Canadian officials, he also led a company of spies for American Colonel George Croghan. His leadership on spying missions was later used as another reason for Westbrook to receive compensation for his lost property in the war.[14]

In the spring of 1814, Westbrook led a mission to intercept mail in Upper Canada. Despite several attempts, his party did not succeed. Yet Westbrook was incapable of going on a mission and returning empty-handed. He announced to his comrades that if they could not obtain the mail, they would instead capture Major Sikes Tousley, the commander of the Canadian militia between Amherstburg and York (today Toronto). Tousley would have been Westbrook's commander if he had stayed in Upper Canada. The hatred between the two men was described as "mutual and violent." After acquiring the major's address in the village of Oxford (today Oxford Centre, Ontario), Westbrook broke into his home and snatched Tousley from his bed. From there, Westbrook carried his prisoner either to what remained of his property or to another home near Delaware to retrieve a supply of wheat. At the home, Tousley attacked Westbrook with a musket fixed with a bayonet. The two men tussled until Tousley pierced Westbrook in the thigh. With the help of a soldier on the mission, Westbrook subdued Tousley and still managed to deliver him to Detroit.[15]

Westbrook next targeted his foremost rival from his past life in Upper Canada, Colonel Talbot. Between May and August 1814, Westbrook launched three successive raids on Port Talbot (today west of Port Stanley, Ontario), the center of the colonel's commercial empire on Lake Erie. Despite Westbrook's efforts, Colonel Talbot escaped all three attacks. During the raid of August 16, 1814, the climax of Westbrook's pursuit of Talbot, the colonel slipped out a back window of his home. Westbrook's raiders, disguised as Indians, proceeded to pillage the nearby village. They took "every particle of wearing apparel and household furniture, leaving the sufferers naked, and in a most wretched state," according to a report at the time. Westbrook's three raids on Port Talbot wreaked havoc on the settlement, even if they failed in capturing its namesake.[16]

Not all of Westbrook's raids into Upper Canada went unopposed. In early September 1814, he led a small party from Detroit back to the village of Delaware, where the raiders captured three captains, one militia lieutenant, and about thirty inhabitants. On their return, the men had traveled about twenty-five miles from Delaware when they were attacked by a group of Canadians. The ambush allowed the prisoners to break free. Westbrook and other members of his party fled in the confusion before later reuniting. He led them into the woods far from the road to hide from the enemy. Westbrook's familiarly with the terrain allowed his party to escape the close call and return safely to the U.S.[17]

Westbrook also faced various attempts by officials in his former province to bring him to justice for treason. In 1814, the young attorney general of Upper Canada, John Beverley Robinson, compiled a list of sixty suspected defectors to prosecute. The list included Westbrook, but he had already moved to Michigan Territory and was therefore safe from Upper Canadian law. Westbrook was indicted for treason in that same year at Ancaster in the Niagara region. In 1816, the Court of Quarter Sessions of the Niagara District also declared him an outlaw. Again, Westbrook was able to escape any punishment by staying in the U.S., but he still suffered some final indignities by his "persecutors." A crown commission, which included Thomas Talbot, was charged with looking into the extent of Westbrook's land and other holdings in Upper Canada. Former neighbors then petitioned to buy the property. In 1823, a sale of Westbrook's "land, premises and appurtenances" in Delaware was made to none other than his former accuser and kidnap victim, Daniel Springer.[18]

After the War of 1812, Westbrook settled on the St. Clair River in Michigan Territory in an area that became part of St. Clair

County. He was treated there as a hero instead of a traitor. Westbrook served as a county commissioner and supervisor of roads and became one of the wealthiest taxpayers in the region. He remained as eccentric as ever, demanding to be called Baron von Steuben. The first Baron von Steuben, an immigrant to the United States from Germany during the Revolutionary War, also created a new identity in America in order to escape a past life. Like von Steuben, Westbrook was celebrated for his service to the American cause. In 1828, Congress recognized Westbrook's wartime service by awarding him two tracts of land, the larger in Clay Township, Michigan Territory. He lived in the territory until his death in 1835.[19]

Westbrook followed a path of revenge to becoming an American citizen. During the War of 1812, he advanced his personal interests and the American cause by leading raids on his former province, kidnapping high-ranking Upper Canadian officials, and torching his own home. Westbrook's easy navigation of the American-Canadian borderlands made him a valuable asset to U.S. officers. Although he never fully succeeded in his aim of capturing Talbot, Westbrook terrorized his former rival and destroyed much of his property. It is no wonder Westbrook's reputation for treachery lived on in Canada long after the war ended. A man of many titles and names – traitor, patriot, Baron von Steuben, outlaw, avenging wolf – Andrew Westbrook's legacy is a mix of both the facts and fictions that he helped create.

NOTES

1 This study builds on previous works on Andrew Westbrook and his raids into Upper Canada during the War of 1812. See Charles O. Ermatinger, *The Talbot Regime: or, the First Half Century of the Talbot Settlement* (St. Thomas, ON: Municipal World, 1904), 49-56; and George Sheppard, *Plunder, Profit, and Paroles: A Social History of the War of 1812 in Upper Canada* (Montreal: McGill-Queen's University Press, 1994). For earlier biographical portraits of Westbrook, see Thomas L. McKenney, *Sketches of a Tour to the Lakes* (Baltimore: F. Lucas, jun'r., 1827), 146-51; William L. Jenks, *St. Clair County, Michigan, Its History and Its People*, 2 vols. (Chicago: Lewis, 1912), 1:106-7; and "Andrew Westbrook," Dictionary of Canadian Biography Online, University of Toronto, www.biographi.ca (accessed March 24, 2012).

2 McKenney, 150. Westbrook was fifty-five years old at the time.

3 The most recent edition is John Richardson, *Westbrook, the Outlaw; or, the Avenging Wolf* (Simcoe, ON: Davis Publishing, 2004). For Richardson, see the essays in this volume by Timothy Marks, Tim Moran, and Scott A. Jankowski.

4 "Andrew Westbrook."

5 Simon Watson to Thomas Talbot, March 22, 1811, in *The Talbot Papers*, ed. James H. Coyne, 2 vols. (Ottawa: Royal Society of Canada, 1908-10), 1:112; Sheppard, 51-52.

6 Simon Watson to [?], July 10, 1812, Folder July-Dec 1812, Box 1, Benjamin F.H. Witherell Papers, BHC. Although the recipient of the letter is uncertain, it is clearly postmarked to Detroit.

7 "Andrew Westbrook."

8 Henry Bostwick to Peter Chambers, July 27, 1812, in *Documents Relating to the Invasion of Canada and the Surrender of Detroit, 1812*, ed. E.A. Cruikshank (Ottawa: Government Printing Bureau, 1912), 94-95 (quotes); Sheppard, 52.

9 "Andrew Westbrook"; Sheppard, 52; *Talbot Papers*, 41.

10 Ermatinger, 50-51, 74; Sheppard, 106-7; William Henry Harrison to General John Armstrong, March 5, 1814, Box 1, William Henry Harrison Papers, BHC.

11 Ermatinger, 74; Jenks, 1:107; "Andrew Westbrook."

12 In defense of Andrew Westbrook to William Woodbridge, November 24, 1819, Box 17, William Woodbridge Papers, BHC; Report on Andrew Westbrook to the Committee on Private Land Claims, December 19, 1827, 20th Congress, 1st sess., Report 20, in *Miscellaneous Documents of the Senate of the United States for the Third Session of the Forty-Fifth Congress, 1878-79*, 4 vols. (Washington, DC: Government Printing Office, 1879), 1:29-30.

13 Butler quoted in Alan Taylor, *The Civil War of 1812: American Citizens, British Subjects, Irish Rebels, & Indian Allies* (New York: Knopf, 2010), 263.

14 In defense of Andrew Westbrook to William Woodbridge, November 24, 1819; Report on Andrew Westbrook to the Committee on Private Land Claims, December 19, 1827.

15 McKenney, 147-48; "Andrew Westbrook."

16 "The Report of the Loyal and Patriotic Society," quoted in Sheppard, 106. Ermatinger provides a slightly different timeline for the raids and does not place Westbrook at the August incident (74-77).

17 William Rayburn to John Miller, September 4, 1814, vol. 2:371-72, Duncan McArthur Papers, BHC.

18 Sheppard, 165; "Andrew Westbrook."

19 Jenks, 1:106-7; A Bill for the Benefit of Andrew Westbrook, Committee on Private Land Claims, H.R. 16, 20th Congress, 1st sess., December 19, 1827. For von Steuben, see Thomas Fleming, "The Magnificent Fraud: How a Lying Poseur Gave America Its Army," *American Heritage* 57 (Feb/Mar 2006): 58-65.

The Battle of Lake Erie
Sketch by Charles W. Jeffreys, c. 1921. Photo reproduction. Library and Archives Canada, Ottawa.

Uncommon Sailors in the Battle of Lake Erie
Rebecca Russell

On the morning of September 10, 1813, the sound of
cannons echoed against the shores of Lake Erie. At odds were
fleets of the strongest navies in the Western Hemisphere, the
Americans under the command of Master Commandant Oliver
Hazard Perry and the British under the command of Lieutenant
Robert Heriot Barclay. The battle would determine the control
over supply lines crucial to sustaining posts in the Great Lakes
region. Barclay's fleet protected Fort Amherstburg and the British
occupation of Detroit. Without the flow of supplies through
British-controlled waters, the posts would not have held for long.
Perry knew this, and it was his mission to force the British fleet
into submission, reversing what had been a losing war
for America.[1]

As scholars have long recognized, the Americans and British
struggled in the months preceding the battle to build ships fit
for naval engagement on the Great Lakes. But both Perry and
Barclay also faced shortages of an equally precious resource:
sailors. The commanders resorted to procuring all types of men,
some experienced seamen but also large numbers of farmers and
frontiersmen. These men could handle a gun, but were foreign to
sailing vessels, particularly the brigs and schooners common to the
Great Lakes. Even those men who had sailed for years were more
accustomed to the high tides and long voyages of the Atlantic
Ocean than to the conditions on fresh water. The men who fought

in the Battle of Lake Erie were the definition of "motley crews."[2]

The commanders solved their respective manning problems in similar and different ways. Both fleets fought at half-capacity and used a large percentage of nonsailors, or landsmen. Perry mobilized approximately 490 men, while Barclay mustered about 470. Although his complement consisted of more seasoned officers, Barclay had fewer experienced seamen than Perry. More than half of the men in the British fleet, about 240, were soldiers and other landsmen. The sailors came from the Royal Navy and Canadian maritime trades. Perry's men consisted of seamen who had followed him from his native Rhode Island to his new command on the Great Lakes in March 1813. Boys, African Americans, and members of the Pennsylvania, Ohio, and Kentucky militias made up the balance of his force. Perry also had to deal with sickness throughout his fleet. On the eve of the battle, more than one hundred of his men were incapacitated. Perry and several of his officers and surgeons were also ill, having contracted "lake-fever." The fleet's junior surgeon was so sick that he could not scale the sides of the ships to treat others. "He was hoisted in and out like a barrel of flour or a cask of water," according to surgeon's mate Usher Parsons.[3]

In the summer of 1813, Perry was desperate for men. As he waited for his ships to be completed at Presque Isle (today Erie, Pennsylvania), at the eastern end of Lake Erie, his more pressing problem was manpower. With a battle on the lake appearing inevitable, Perry did not have enough men to fight. On July 19, he wrote to his superior, Commodore Isaac Chauncey, at Lake Champlain:

> Give me men, sir, and I will acquire both for *you* and myself honor and glory on this lake, or perish in the attempt. . . . I again ask you to think of my situation; the enemy in sight, the vessels under my command more than sufficient, and ready to make sail, and yet obliged to bite my fingers with vexation for want of men. I know, my dear sir, full well you will send me the crews for the vessels as soon as possible; yet a day appears an age.[4]

Perry's plea worked. Within a week, Chauncey sent a group of men to Presque Isle. Instead of being grateful, however, Perry wrote back to complain about the "motley set, blacks – soldiers, and boys." The only consolation was that he was "pleased to see anything in the shape of a man."[5] Chauncey took offense at Perry's comments, stating, "I have yet to learn that the Colour of the skin, or cut and trimmings of the coat, can effect a man's qualifications or usefulness. I have nearly 50 blacks on board of this Ship, and many of them are amongst my best men."[6] It is possible that Perry's words stemmed from frustration over the quality of the men – black and white – more than prejudice. In the words of Sailing Master William V. Taylor, many of the men sent from Lake Ontario "were barely able to assist themselves." Chauncey kept his best black seamen on his ship. Perry had brought African-American sailors with him from Rhode Island, and about one-fifth of his men on Lake Erie were black. Still, the exchange might have taught him a lesson. Perry still complained about shortages in his fleet, but he also started to make do with the men he had.[7]

On August 12, Perry sailed west with the ten vessels in his fleet still short of the men necessary to fill his gun crews. In his desperation, the captain requested soldiers from General William Henry Harrison. Harrison promised a force of forty to fifty men. Instead, on August 31, one hundred Kentucky volunteers arrived at Perry's new base at South Bass Island in Put-in-Bay harbor in western Lake Erie. They could not have been more welcome, as evidenced by Perry greeting the new arrivals from his sickbed. Some of the men had experience as boatmen in Kentucky, but most had never belonged to a ship's crew. Perry biographer Charles Dutton has described the clash of cultures at Put-in-Bay: "The Kentuckians were as much an astonishment to the fleet as was the fleet to them. Clad in their typical garb of fringed shirts and leggings, bearing over their shoulders long rifles, they spent their first two hours in going over the vessels from mast to keel.

They were a cause of amusement at first to the officers of the ships."[8] Though the Kentuckians have been portrayed as simple-minded backwoodsmen, their experience proved crucial during the battle. They were later praised for their sharpshooting, which allowed them to target several British officers. Volunteers from Pennsylvania were also brought in to fill the ranks from their station at Presque Isle. These men received minimal training, but proved useful in the battle as marines – seaborne infantry. Perry had just enough sailors to fill his vessels, while the different groups of landsmen concentrated on manning guns.[9]

Based on his surviving letters, Barclay worried even more than Perry about manpower. Barclay started asking for a larger force in June 1813, with each succeeding letter sounding less hopeful and more frantic than the last. He was the victim of circumstance, having to compete for sailors as Britain fought a global war against Napoleonic France. Barclay had served heroically in that struggle at the Battle of Trafalgar in 1805 – the battle that secured British control of the Atlantic – and later lost his arm in another engagement against the French. Now he was far from the Atlantic theater, as was clear by his letter to General Henry Procter at Sandwich on June 29:

> The *Detroit* may be launched in ten days, but there is no chance of her being ready for any active service until a large proportion of stores, and Guns are sent here – And even admitting that she could be equipped – there is not a seaman to put on board her. The absolute necessity of Seamen being immediately sent up is so obvious that I need hardly point it out to you – The Ships are manned with a crew, part of whom cannot even speak English – none of them seamen and very few even in numbers.[10]

Barclay ultimately supplemented his meager forces with British Canadians from the Provincial Marine (a naval auxiliary) and the Royal Newfoundland Regiment (soldiers). After much harassment, Procter also allowed Barclay to use the 41st Regiment of Foot stationed at Fort Amherstburg. Around a hundred men, they provided much the same help as the militiamen in Perry's fleet by serving as marines rather than as traditional sailors.[11]

The Americans entered the battle with a slight advantage. Perry's least experienced men received more training than Barclay's last-minute recruits. The Americans also surpassed the British in number of ships, ten to six. Moreover, Perry's ships were built for the shallow waters of the lakes, whereas Barclay had to use deep-water ships that were harder to maneuver. Barclay had more guns, sixty-three to fifty-four, with longer range, but Perry's ships likely had more effective firepower at shorter distances.[12] Therefore, the battle would be decided in large part by which side's irregular seamen performed better. Perry helped to build cohesion among his men by holding a ceremony before the battle in which he raised a flag of his own making emblazoned with the words, "Don't Give Up The Ship." These words were spoken by Perry's friend, Captain James Lawrence aboard the USS *Chesapeake* in its ill-fated engagement against the HMS *Shannon* in June 1813. Lawrence died shortly after the battle. The symbol of the flag waving over the frigate USS *Lawrence*, named for Perry's fallen comrade, left an impression on the men who were to wage war on Lake Erie.[13]

Common and uncommon sailors alike made enormous sacrifices in the battle. On the morning of September 10, Barclay's fleet was visible from Perry's position in Put-in-Bay. Perry advanced on the British, followed by an unnerving hour of silence as each commander waited to reach firing distance. The first shot flew from the deck of the HMS *Detroit* a mile away. Surgeon's mate Parsons was the last of the fleet's medical personnel well enough to stand and cared for every man wounded on the *Lawrence*. The maneuverability that the *Lawrence* gained as a shallow-water vessel meant that the berth where Parsons attended the wounded was above water level and vulnerable to cannon fire. His account describes the thunderous sound as artillery splintered the sides of the *Lawrence*:

> For more than two long hours, little could be heard but the
> deafening thunders of our broadsides, the crash of balls dashing
> through our timbers, and the shrieks of the wounded. These
> were brought down faster than I could attend to them, farther
> than to stay the bleeding, or support the shattered limbs with
> splints, and pass them forward upon the berth deck. Two or
> three were killed near me, after being wounded.[14]

Many of the men Parsons cared for were killed by cannon fire
before they left the berth. One midshipman by the name of Lamb
was blown across the hold just after Parsons had finished applying
a splint to his arm. The surgeon later recalled, "As he was leaving
me, and while my hand was still on him, a cannon-ball struck him
in the side . . . which instantly terminated his sufferings." With
the *Lawrence* decimated, Perry famously took the few uninjured
members of his crew and the flag and rowed to take command of
the barely damaged USS *Niagara*.[15]

The bold action propelled the Americans to a resounding
victory. Following the battle, Perry penned his famous message to
Harrison: "We have met the enemy and they are ours. Two Ships,
two Brigs, one Schooner and one Sloop. Yours, with greatest
respect and esteem O.H. Perry."[16] Perry then attended to Barclay,
who was wounded twice in the battle. The commanders had much
in common. Nearly the same age, they were both given throw-
away positions on the Great Lakes, rather than more prestigious
assignments on the Atlantic. They received little support, few
supplies, and their desperate requests for manpower often went
unheeded. After the battle, Barclay wrote to his brother that
"since the battle he [Perry] has been like a brother to me."[17]

The uncommon sailors in the Battle of Lake Erie have
never received the same acclaim as Perry, but they made crucial
contributions to the American victory. After the battle, U.S.
Lieutenant Jesse Elliott boarded the HMS *Detroit* to take
possession and was overwhelmed by the carnage: "Such was the
quantity of blood on the deck, that in crossing it, my feet slipped

from under me, and I fell; my clothing becoming completely saturated and covered with gore!"[18] Most of the destruction came from the cannons in Perry's fleet manned by militiamen and other landsmen. In addition, the Kentucky sharpshooters, some placed high in the masts of the American ships, had shaped the outcome. Not a single British officer escaped the battle without an injury. The willingness of the militia volunteers to serve under Perry, most without any previous marine experience, helped to cripple British naval supremacy on the Great Lakes.[19]

After the battle, Perry wrote to Chauncey praising the courage of the men he had sent, all but apologizing for his earlier remarks. Chauncey reported to another correspondent: "Perry speaks highly of the bravery and good conduct of the Negroes, who formed a considerable part of his crew."[20] Barclay's force also included blacks. After the battle, American Colonel Micah Taul witnessed the unloading of prisoners, whom he described as "a motely set of fellows. A large number of them were negroes who had run away from their masters in the United States."[21] Taul's condescension revealed the barriers that African Americans faced to winning respect for their service. But to their credit, the Kentuckians and other militiamen, like Perry, came to value the contributions made by the black seamen.[22]

The service of African Americans in Perry's fleet inspired later generations to advance the cause of freedom and equality. A speech at a convention to revise the New York state constitution in 1821 highlighted the recent sacrifices of black seamen on Lake Erie. An abolitionist pamphlet reprinted the speech in 1851:

> In your late War they contributed largely towards some of your most splendid victories. On Lakes Erie and Champlain, where your fleets triumphed over a foe superior in numbers and engines of death, they were manned in a large proportion with men of Color. . . . They were not compelled to go; they were not drafted. No, your pride had placed them beyond your compulsory power. But there was no necessity for its exercise; they were volunteers; yes, Sir, volunteers to defend that

very country from the inroads and ravages of a ruthless and vindictive foe, which had treated them with insult, degradation, and Slavery. Volunteers are the best of soldiers; give me the men, whatever be their complexion, that willingly volunteer, and not those who are compelled to turn out. Such men do not fight from necessity, nor from mercenary motives, but from principle.[23]

Black sailors fought for a country that did not recognize them as full citizens, let alone as equal soldiers and sailors. Without the contributions of these and other uncommon sailors, the U.S. would not have had the manpower to destroy an entire British naval squadron for the first time. The triumph on Lake Erie changed American fortunes in the Great Lakes region, leading British forces to evacuate forts Detroit and Amherstburg. Perry could not have accomplished such a feat alone.

NOTES

1   For multiple perspectives on the Battle of Lake Erie, see William J. Welsh and David C. Skaggs, eds. *War on the Great Lakes: Essays Commemorating the 175th Anniversary of the Battle of Lake Erie* (Kent, OH: Kent State University Press, 1991). For an overview of the battle, see Donald R. Hickey, *Don't Give Up The Ship! Myths of the War of 1812* (Urbana: University of Illinois Press, 2006), 124-36.

2   This study builds on the insights of Gerard T. Altoff, *Deep Water Sailors, Shallow Water Soldiers: Manning the United States Fleet on Lake Erie, 1813* (Put-in-Bay, OH: Perry Group, 1993), esp. 1-15; and Altoff, *Amongst My Best Men: African-Americans and the War of 1812* (Put-in-Bay, OH: Perry Group, 1996), 35-43.

3   Usher Parsons, *Battle of Lake Erie* (Providence: B.T. Albro, 1854), 7 ("lake-fever"), 8 ("He was hoisted"); Pierre Berton, *Flames across the Border: The Canadian-American Tragedy, 1813-1814* (Boston: Little, Brown, 1981), 129-73; Gerard T. Altoff, "The Battle of Lake Erie: A Narrative," in *War on the Great Lakes*, 5-16; Theodore Roosevelt, *The Naval War of 1812*, 2 vols. (New York: G.P. Putnam's Sons, 1900), 1:308-11.

4   Oliver Perry to Isaac Chauncey, July, 19, 1813, in Laura G. Sanford, *The History of Erie County, Pennsylvania* (Philadelphia: J.B. Lippincott, 1862), 251.

5   Oliver Perry to Isaac Chauncey, July 27, 1813, in Sanford, 253.

6   Chauncey quoted in Altoff, *Amongst My Best Men*, 37.

7   Altoff, *Amongst My Best Men*, 37-39; 39 (quote).

8 Charles J. Dutton, *Oliver Hazard Perry* (New York: Longmans, Green, 1935), 124.

9 Anderson C. Quisenberry, *Kentucky in the War of 1812* (Frankfort: Kentucky Historical Society, 1915), 73-82.

10 Robert Barclay to Henry Procter, June 29, 1813, in *Select British Documents of the Canadian War of 1812*, ed. William C.H. Wood, 3 vols. (Toronto: Chaplain Society, 1920-28), 2:248-49.

11 Robert Barclay to James Yeo, September 12, 1813, in *Select British Documents*, 2:274-77.

12 Roosevelt, *Naval War of 1812*, 311-13.

13 Parsons, 13.

14 Parsons, 11-12. For the treatment of casualties on land during the War of 1812, see the essay in this volume by Scott A. Jankowski.

15 Parsons, 12-13; Altoff, "Battle of Lake Erie," 13-16.

16 Hickey, 129.

17 Barclay quoted in Berton, 171.

18 Jesse D. Elliott, *Speech of Com. Jesse Duncan Elliot, U.S.N., Delivered in Hagerstown, Md. On 14th November, 1843* (Philadelphia: G.B. Zieber, 1844), 8.

19 Quisenberry, 73-82.

20 Chauncey quoted in Altoff, *Amongst My Best Men*, 40.

21 Quisenberry, 77.

22 Altoff, *Amongst My Best Men*, 37-40.

23 William C. Nell, *Services of Colored Americans in the Wars of 1776 and 1812* (Boston: Prentiss & Sawyer, 1851), 20.

View of Amherstburg
Painted by Margaret Reynolds, 1813. Watercolor on paper. Courtesy of the Fort Malden National Historic Site of Canada, Amherstburg, Ontario.

The Uneasy Occupation of Amherstburg
Joshua Zimberg

On August 12, 1812, the *Political and Commercial Register* of Philadelphia made a stunning announcement: "We stop the press to announce the following important news . . . general Hull attacked Malden on the first of Aug. and took it that night. . . . The information was said to be brought there by reputable gentlemen."[1] Of course, the report was false. After occupying Sandwich, General William Hull cowered away from attempting to take Fort Malden, or as the British called their Upper Canadian garrison, Fort Amherstburg. General Isaac Brock then used the fort to initiate the attack leading to Hull's defeat and the British takeover of Detroit. With its powerful cannons positioned over the Detroit River, Fort Amherstburg played an essential role for the British in controlling the passage of men, goods, and information in Michigan Territory, Upper Canada, and the western Great Lakes. Thus, while the British kept firm control of Fort Amherstburg and Lake Erie, American armies in the Detroit River region became increasingly familiar with defeat.[2]

More than a year later, on September 27, 1813, American troops finally captured Fort Amherstburg. They held it until July 1, 1815, more than six months after the War of 1812 ended, when they returned the fort to the British. The occupation was possible because of American successes at the battles of Lake Erie and the Thames, which gave them control of the Detroit River region and western Great Lakes. These triumphs represented some of the few real victories that Americans saw during the war. United States Sergeant Alfred Brunson was stationed in the area until the fall of 1814; he heard early reports of victory after the Battle of Lake Erie, participated in the Battle of the Thames, and manned the cannons during the American occupation of Fort Amherstburg. Years later, Brunson published his experiences in a book that not only told of the triumphs, but also of the uneasiness of the American stay in the Western District of Upper Canada. American soldiers faced a host of problems caused by their poor relations with the Upper Canadians, a lack of resources, and the constant fear of enemy attacks. As a result, though the takeover of Amherstburg began as one of the great American victories of the war, it ended as an uneasy occupation.[3]

Brunson was born in Danbury, Connecticut, on February 9, 1793. As a young man, he spent time in Pennsylvania, New Jersey, and New York, where he learned to sail on the Hudson River. A committed Methodist, he married Eunice Burr, a cousin of former U.S. Vice President Aaron Burr, in 1812. They resided in Trumbull County, Ohio, in the summer of 1813 when Brunson decided to enlist in the American army. Brunson felt threatened by the Indians nearby and decided to face them with an army instead of alone at his front door. At the age of 20, Brunson was made an Orderly Sergeant in the 27th Regiment, U.S. Infantry. From the start, Brunson found his fellow soldiers wanting in manners and sophistication and told himself, "this is not the company Providence designed for you." Brunson promised God that he would become a minister if he survived his one-year enlistment. His company marched to Cleveland and then on to Sandusky Bay. By the late summer of 1813, Brunson was stationed at a camp outside of Fort Stephenson along the Sandusky River (today Fremont, Ohio).[4]

Across Lake Erie, at Fort Amherstburg, the British supply of food was reported to be down to one day's rations. Master Commandant Oliver Hazard Perry assembled a powerful

American fleet on the lake that stood in the way of the British obtaining more supplies. The British were forced either to engage the American fleet or risk starvation. On September 10, 1813, Lieutenant Robert Barclay left the port of Amherstburg with six British ships. The Battle of Lake Erie ensued. News soon reached the people of Malden Township surrounding Fort Amherstburg that Perry's flagship the USS *Lawrence* had been destroyed by the British fleet. Yet Perry assumed command of an unscathed vessel, the USS *Niagara*, and led the Americans to victory.[5]

On September 11, 1813, Brunson had not yet heard the news of the Battle of Lake Erie. He had recently arrived in Lower Sandusky, where his regiment was preparing for an attack on Fort Amherstburg, when a soldier ran down the hill with news of the battle. Brunson wrote, "We heard a tremendous shout and hurrahing, and then the booming of cannon. All eyes were turned in that direction, knowing that something glorious had occurred." The Americans finally had "victory on the lake."[6] That same day, General Duncan McArthur received a letter from Perry declaring "the whole of the enemies force consisting of 2 Shafts. 2 Brigs. 1 Schoo. & 1 sloop . . . 500 prisoners have surrendered to us . . . and were probably superior to us." The victory, America's first over a full British squadron, immediately changed the balance of power in the Great Lakes region. McArthur and his fellow frontier commanders, generals Lewis Cass and William Henry Harrison, prepared an advance into Upper Canada.[7]

General Henry Procter recognized that the British could not defend the forts at Amherstburg and Detroit without control of Lake Erie. On September 13, he gave orders to evacuate the region. According to Harrison, the British "burned the fort, navy yard, barracks, and public store houses" at Amherstburg.[8] The soldiers asked the loyalists surrounding the fort to leave with them. One resident observed, "the ports of Detroit and Amherstburg for some days previous to our departure, presented a scene of cruel desolation."[9] Many of Britain's Native American allies viewed the evacuation as a cowardly surrender and left Fort Amherstburg for home. However, Adjutant General John O'Fallon wrote that Procter convinced Tecumseh, the great Shawnee leader, and some of his followers that "they intend making a stand" against the Americans "sixty miles from this." With that goal in mind, "Genl. Proctor left this [fort] . . . with about 500 regulars and considerable Indian force."[10]

Meanwhile, the Americans continued preparations to advance on Amherstburg. The American command sent prisoners from the Battle of Lake Erie to Chillicothe, Ohio, and embarked with their troops from Sandusky Bay across Lake Erie toward the fort. The expedition stopped along the way at Perry's base on South Bass Island in Put-in-Bay harbor. The journey was treacherous; according to Brunson, "to turn in the troughs of the seas would have been to founder, when most likely all would have been drowned." Luckily, he could draw on his experience sailing ships on the Hudson River. Brunson was given command of an "old Mackinaw trading-boat" and directed it to safety.[11] The troops viewed the remnants of the Battle of Lake Erie. Brunson remarked, "the *Detroit* had not a spar left standing," and "the *Lawrence* was bored through and through."[12]

The Americans landed three miles south of Fort Amherstburg on September 27. Samuel Brown, a soldier at the scene, was ready for battle. He expected to see British redcoats. Instead, he found "a group of well dressed ladies advanced to meet" the Americans. They were scared and asked for mercy. Kentucky Governor Isaac Shelby "quieted their fears" by declaring that "we came not to make war on women and children but to protect them." The soldiers soon learned from the townspeople that the British had burned the forts at Amherstburg and Detroit. With this news, the army marched toward Fort Amherstburg "to the thunder of 'Yankee Doodle.'" As the troops entered, Brown discovered "the ruins of the fort and the naval buildings were still smoking." The town was "as dark and as gloomy as Erubus . . . Very few men were to be found," and there was an "exhibition of scalps in the street." For Brown, the display represented "a well known horrid traffic" that "completely blunted the feeling of humanity." The Americans took control of the town and the empty fort. At the onset of the war, President James Madison had identified the Indian raids coming out of Amherstburg as a leading American grievance. Finally, Americans could look to the destroyed fort with hope instead of terror.[13]

During the troops' first night in Amherstburg, Brunson noted, "we camped in and about the ruins of the old fort, in the open air." The Americans' good fortunes quickly turned, as it rained. The men had no tents or blankets, and Brunson "awoke and found my right, or upper, ear full of water . . . and turned over to let the water drain out." The troops heard rumors of an impending Indian attack during the night, and the men slept with their weapons beneath them. Brunson's company soon established more comfortable quarters in an abandoned house in the town. They found wood for fire and were given flour and pork. The soldiers cooked the slices of pork on sticks in the fire, which "on bread, tasted good to hungry men."[14]

On September 29, the troops marched to Sandwich and split up. Brunson went with the regiments led by Harrison that followed Procter and Tecumseh into the interior of Upper Canada. The remaining troops stayed with McArthur to cross the river and recapture Detroit.[15] The British left Detroit in a condition similar to Amherstburg. Upon arrival, Adjutant General O'Fallon witnessed "inhabitants stripped of their all." The people welcomed the return of American troops to Detroit. "So soon as our boats touched their shore," according to O'Fallon, "[they] displayed an American Flag which had been kept concealed and hailed us with a burst of rejoicing perhaps never before equaled."[16]

A few thousand Indians still resided in the woods near Detroit. McArthur wrote to his superiors, "the Ottoways, Chippeways, Potowatomies, Miamies, and Kickapoos . . . have come in for peace." The general subsequently formed a truce with these Indians who had not followed Procter and Tecumseh. The terms stated that the Indians would fight alongside the Americans. As a guarantee against retaliation, the Americans would keep some Indian women and children as prisoners. Peace for the larger region did not come so easily. Procter, Tecumseh, and the 41st Regiment of Foot refused to surrender.[17]

General Harrison led Colonel Richard M. Johnson's mounted men, Governor Shelby's volunteers, and 160 regulars in pursuit of the British and Indians up the Thames River. On October 5, the Americans met the British and Indians at the Battle of the Thames. Brunson explained that the recklessness of the Kentucky cavalry was so frightening that the British lines broke after the first shot. When the Indians saw that the British troops had fled, they quickly followed suit, but not before their leader, Tecumseh, was killed. The Americans achieved a resounding victory against the British and their native allies on land to complement Perry's triumph at sea. Having completed their mission, the Americans started west with designs on returning to Fort Amherstburg.[18]

During travel to and from the battle, the American troops experienced conflicts with British subjects in Upper Canada. The locals resented the Americans camping on their farms. In turn, the Americans viewed the Canadians with great disdain as loyalists. Before the battle, Brunson and other troops stayed on a Canadian farm, where the woman of the house kept bees. The woman gave Harrison a hard time for the intrusion and threatened him with the 41st Regiment. She was concerned that the Americans were stealing and expected that all of her beehives would be gone by morning. According to Brunson, Harrison politely responded, "Madam, I will put a guard over the bees," and he did. However, the troops learned of the hard time that the woman had given their general and sought revenge. The hungry Americans stole all of the hives and consumed the honey. Afterward, the American quartermaster paid the woman for her loss.[19] This was but one example. By the end of the journey, Cass noted, "in the pursuit of the enemy up the river Trench and in the return of the troops, great injury was done to the property of the inhabitants."[20]

The Americans returned to Amherstburg by late October 1813. Harrison determined that Detroit, Amherstburg, and Sandwich would be governed together. Brunson and the rest of the 27th Regiment were given orders to guard the region. Harrison issued a proclamation that declared martial law for the region and, similar to Hull's proclamation when he occupied Sandwich in 1812, promised Upper Canadians protection of private property. Cass was appointed the governor of the region. He entered the position with an unfavorable opinion of the inhabitants, remarking, "It would be altogether impolite to extend to them the rights enjoyed by our citizens generally."[21]

By the late fall of 1813, American-Canadian relations witnessed some improvement. A man from Detroit and a young Canadian woman wed. Many of the soldiers moved into Malden homes and participated in the community.[22] O'Fallon stated that the Canadians "all seem to conceive the conquest of their country as a blessing to them."[23] At the same time, there were still tensions related to the military occupation. The Americans worried constantly that local loyalists communicated secretly with British officials. Cass ordered Captain William Puthuff to "be vigilant patrolling the country" and to "prevent the inhabitants from holding all communication with the enemy." So long as the occupation lasted, the Americans and Canadians could not enjoy entirely friendly relations.[24]

In December 1813, a sickness spread throughout the American camps. Brunson blamed polluted water that the dehydrated troops had consumed during the crossing from Sandusky Bay to Amherstburg. Like many Americans, Brunson fell ill. He recalled, "Its effects were such that I could neither stand nor sit up, but had to lie down on the floor helpless, and could only roll over and let the green bile run out of my mouth, as thick as jelly." At first, doctors treated the men for ordinary bilious fever and were careless in their work. The doctors finally determined the nature of the fever and how to stop it, but not before nearly eight hundred people died, a number that far exceeded the number of American deaths in battle in the Detroit River region.[25] British spies discovered the sorry state of Amherstburg and reported to their superiors: "The American troops at this place have died in numbers 700 and that the balance are in a starving condition and would be glad to surrender on any terms."[26] Following the epidemic, only 700 men remained stationed at Amherstburg, of whom 340 were "fit for duty."[27]

The remaining troops lived in constant fear of an attack by the British or their Indian allies. The fears were not unwarranted. In January 1814, British General Gordon Drummond planned an attack on Amherstburg in which his soldiers would arrive on sleds. The snow melted early, however, and the troops retired their sleds for the winter. In the spring, Brunson noted, "Reports were rife that General Drummond was coming to retake Detroit and Malden."[28] Around the same time, American scouts in the woods between Amherstburg and Sandwich heard gunshots. The scouts' report convinced the American command that the British and Indians were attacking. According to Brunson, "the little garrison was put in the best possible state of defense" only to discover later that the gunfire had come from Frenchmen out hunting. Americans continued to harbor fears for the duration of their occupation, but the British and Indians never attacked. Of the rumors, Brunson admitted, "among the real, there were some ludicrous."[29]

Fort Amherstburg was still vulnerable due to a lack of troops. Marshaling resources to more active fronts, American military commanders ignored McArthur's constant requests for more men.[30] In the spring of 1814, a British flag officer came to Amherstburg on business. During his stay, a Pennsylvania militia regiment completed its tour of duty and wanted to go home. Despite requests to stay to give the impression of a stable fort, the Pennsylvanians walked away unarmed, directly in front of the British officer's quarters. To fix any damage, Colonel Anthony Butler ordered the 17th Regiment to walk by the British officer in a line, looking worn out from a march, to pretend that they had arrived to replace the Pennsylvanians. Brunson stated that the ruse "had its desired and designed effect; for the enemy kept at a respectful distance."[31]

The fort's difficulties stemmed in part from poor leadership. Many American officers were disobedient. Brunson carried more responsibilities as a result. He wrote, "I not only did my own duty, but much that belonged to the Captain and other officers of the company to do." One notable failure was not building a proper fort to replace the one burned by the British. Brunson and other soldiers throughout the Detroit River region lived in tents, vacant houses, and any other shelter they could find.[32] In June 1814, McArthur noted the poor defenses at Amherstburg and ordered his officers to construct a new fort. He was in the process of becoming the commander of the Army of the Northwest following Harrison's resignation to enter politics. McArthur was concerned that if "the enemy [was] again to possess himself of that strait, he would at once cut off all communication by water, between Lake Erie and Detroit."[33] The general returned to Amherstburg in August to view the completed work, but was not impressed. He described the makeshift structure as "one side . . . composed of an old house, and another side of an old stable [that] could be reduced to ashes, any night by a party of Indians with them bows and arrows."[34] Therefore, McArthur ordered the officers at Amherstburg to "immediately commence erecting a Pickquet work in the South west corner of the old British fort at this place, and have it completed with the least possible delay."[35] The construction started, but this too had problems. Colonel John Miller, the commander at Amherstburg, wrote to McArthur: "The work at this place progresses but slowly for the want of hands."[36] On another occasion, Miller complained, "We have but few tools, and what we have, are of the worst quality."[37] Not until months later, in December 1814, were the new defenses at Amherstburg completed.[38]

The condition of the fort mattered because fears of an Indian attack never completely disappeared, even after concerns about the British diminished. Over the course of the occupation, relations between the American soldiers and surrounding Indian groups worsened. The uneasiness of the Americans grew as tales of Indian killings circulated among the troops. In September 1814, James Witherell, a Michigan territorial judge who was part of the occupation of Amherstburg, described a recent Indian attack on an American soldier. The soldier retaliated and "split ones head nearly into pieces."[39] That same month, Colonel Miller warned McArthur: "We shall have a general Indian war in the course of a very short time, and we shall once more see our whole frontier settlement laid waste." Despite the threats and rumors, the expected assault by natives never materialized.[40]

In the fall of 1814, Brunson's term of service expired, but war had not yet concluded. The sergeant's troops wanted their leader to stay and promised to send a recommendation to President Madison to promote Brunson to lieutenant. However, Brunson recalled his earlier vow: "I had promised God, if he would spare me to the end of my term, I would return home and give myself to the work to which he had called me." This he did. Brunson returned to his family in Ohio and became a prominent Methodist preacher and missionary in the Old Northwest.[41]

Conditions at Amherstburg did not improve after Brunson's departure. There was little food at the fort, and soldiers often starved or ate very small portions. Miller was therefore elated to discover that the residents of Malden were storing "large quantities of Surplus Grain." On September 26, 1814, he issued a proclamation ordering the people of the area to bring their extra grain to specified areas for purchase by the military. If soldiers discovered that a resident was withholding grain, it would be destroyed and the person "severely Punished."[42] As a result of the new policy, however, the Americans ended up with more grain than the Canadian civilians. By the fall, the occupying army was distributing daily rations of food to the populace.[43] In December, Miller reported to McArthur that "provisions were very scarce at Detroit," Amherstburg, and Fort Gratiot, a post erected earlier that year at the juncture of the St. Clair River and Lake Huron (today Port Huron, Michigan). Miller asked McArthur to send 1,100,000 rations to help feed 4,000 people in the region over the next six months.[44] McArthur denied the request, stating that the soldiers could take whatever food they needed from the inhabitants. The army's failure to provide for the areas that it now governed did not endear the Canadians to American rule.[45]

Even worse, McArthur's solution for the food shortage was to conduct mounted raids into Upper Canada. For several weeks, in October and November 1814, McArthur led six hundred Kentucky militiamen and two hundred regular soldiers on a series of raids that terrorized settlements in Upper Canada. The mounted raiders destroyed towns and homes that they passed for seemingly no reason. McArthur ordered his men to take all the grain that they could carry and burn what was left over. Clearly, McArthur no longer subscribed to the promises made by General Harrison at the start of the American occupation.[46]

The Americans and British signed the Treaty of Ghent on December 24, 1814, marking the official end of hostilities in the War of 1812. Yet, before the Senate ratified the treaty on February 17, 1815, the destruction in Amherstburg escalated. On February 15, Colonel Butler expressed to McArthur that "a little blood letting may do them [the Canadians] good and make the country tranquil."[47] The Western District of Upper Canada was the only significant British territory in North America that the Americans controlled in 1815. Although by the terms of the treaty it should have been "restored without delay," the Americans occupied Amherstburg for another five months.[48] The Americans were concerned what might result from a renewed British military presence in the region, particularly with armed vessels on the Great Lakes. As the Americans prepared for their departure in the spring and early summer of 1815, the devastation of the Western District slowed but did not fully stop. On July 1, 1815, the United States finally returned control of Fort Amherstburg to Britain.[49]

As for Alfred Brunson, he traveled all over the northwest region, ministering to frontier settlers and proselytizing to Native Americans. In 1861, he became a chaplain for Union soldiers in the Civil War, but had to retire due to old age. On August 3, 1882, Brunson died, but not before he recorded his thoughts and experiences. In an essay on human nature, the minister perhaps recalled his service in the War of 1812, writing that if "difficulties . . . impede our progress, I awfully fear . . . blood will be required at our hands."[50] At Amherstburg, this was certainly the case. From the Battle of Lake Erie to their takeover of the fort, the Americans experienced great triumph. But occupying Amherstburg presented seemingly endless challenges, from procuring enough food and other resources to preparing for attacks by the British and their native allies that never came. By the time the Americans left, there was "nothing but dirt . . . and everything reflects distress and poverty," according to one witness.[51] The relationship between Western District residents and their American neighbors eventually healed, but not overnight. As late as 1821, townspeople attempted to sue the U.S. government over unpaid debts and damages that violated Harrison's proclamation of October 1813. Like a cold breeze across the waters of the Detroit River, the American occupation of Amherstburg spread an icy chill in the region that did not easily thaw.[52]

NOTES

1 "Malden Taken," *Political and Commercial Register* (Philadelphia), August 12, 1812.

2 From its founding in 1796, the fort was officially named Fort Amherstburg. During the War of 1812, the Americans referred to the fort as Fort Malden, after the name of its surrounding township in Upper Canada. The name was formally changed to Fort Malden when a new fort was built in 1837. Meanwhile, the town became known as Amherstburg. See Charles C. James, "Notes on Early Amherstburg," in *Early History of the Town of Amherstburg: A Short, Concise, and Interesting Sketch, with Explanatory Notes* (Amherstburg, ON: Echo, 1902), 4; and Donald R. Hickey, *Don't Give Up the Ship! Myths of the War of 1812* (Urbana: University of Illinois Press, 2006), 252-53. For an overview of the fort in the War of 1812, see Dennis Carter-Edwards, "Defending the Straits: The Military Base at Amherstburg," in *The Western District: Papers from the Western District Conference*, ed. K.G. Pryke and L.L. Kulisek (Windsor, ON: Essex County Historical Society, 1983), 33-41; and Carter-Edwards, "The War of 1812 along the Detroit Frontier: A Canadian Perspective," *Michigan Historical Review* 13 (1987): 25-50.

3 Alfred Brunson, *A Western Pioneer* (Cincinnati: Hitchcock and Walden, 1872).

4 Brunson, *Western Pioneer*, 107. For overviews of Brunson's life and work, see Ella C. Brunson, "Alfred Brunson, Pioneer of Wisconsin Methodism," *Wisconsin Magazine of History* 2 (1918-19), 129-48; and J. Christian Bay, *Going West; the Pioneer Work of Alfred Brunson, Briefly Interpreted* (Cedar Rapids, IA: Torch Press, 1951).

5 For the Battle of Lake Erie, see Gerard T. Altoff, "The Battle of Lake Erie: A Narrative," in *War on the Great Lakes: Essays Commemorating the 175th Anniversary of the Battle of Lake Erie*, ed. William J. Welsh and David C. Skaggs (Kent, OH: Kent State University Press, 1991), 5-16; and the essay in this volume by Rebecca Russell. For the battle's impact on Fort Amherstburg, see Dennis Carter-Edwards, "The Battle of Lake Erie and Its Consequences: Denouement of the British Right Division and Abandonment of the Western District to American Troops, 1813-1815," in *War on the Great Lakes*, 41-55.

6 Brunson, *Western Pioneer*, 121.

7 Oliver Perry to Duncan McArthur, September 11, 1813, vol. 1:32, Duncan McArthur Papers, BHC; Hickey, 124-25.

8 William Henry Harrison to John Armstrong, September 27, 1813, *American State Papers: Documents, Legislative and Executive, of the Congress of the United States*. Military Affairs, vol. 1 (Washington, DC: Gales and Seaton, 1832), 455; Carter-Edwards, "Battle of Lake Erie," 46.

9 James, *Early History*, 17.

10 "US Occupation of Canada, October 1, 1813," American Occupation of Amherstburg Folder, R. Frajolah Collection, Fort Malden National Historic Site of Canada, Amherstburg.

11 Brunson, *Western Pioneer*, 129.

12 Brunson, *Western Pioneer*, 130.

13 Sheridan Alder, "The American Occupation of the Western District" (unpublished paper, 1988), 12-13, Fort Malden (quotes); Brunson, *Western Pioneer*, 134; Carter-Edwards, "Battle of Lake Erie," 42.

14 Brunson, *Western Pioneer*, 135.

15 Brunson, *Western Pioneer*, 135-36.

16 "US Occupation of Canada, October 1, 1813." For the liberation of Michigan Territory, see the essay in this volume by Carly Campbell.

17 Duncan McArthur to John Anderson, October 6, 1813, in *MPHC*, 40:535.

18 Brunson, *Western Pioneer*, 139-140; Carter-Edwards, "Battle of Lake Erie," 47; Alan Taylor, *The Civil War of 1812: American Citizens, British Subjects, Irish Rebels, & Indian Allies* (New York: Knopf, 2010), 244-46; Thomas H. Raddall, *The Path of Destiny: Canada From the British Conquest to Home Rule, 1763-1850* (Toronto: Doubleday, 1957), 230-39. For the Battle of the Thames, see also the essays in this volume by Scott A. Jankowski and Tim Moran.

19 Brunson, *Western Pioneer*, 136-37; 136 (quote). For ideological differences between Americans and Canadians, see Taylor, 15-43.

20 Lewis Cass to John Armstrong, October 21, 1813, U.S. War Department Papers, W195, XVIII, United States Archives Collection, BHC. "Trench" was another name for the Thames River.

21 Cass to Armstrong, October 21, 1813; Brunson, *Western Pioneer*, 144; Carter-Edwards, "Battle of Lake Erie," 47.

22 James Witherell to Amy Hawkins Witherell, September 4, 1814, Benjamin F.H. Witherell Papers, BHC.

23 "US Occupation of Canada, October 1, 1813."

24 Alder, 13-14.

25 Brunson, *Western Pioneer*, 145.

26 "Two Spies" quoted in Alder, 25 n72.

27 John Miller to Duncan McArthur, September 16, 1814, vol. 2:434-38, McArthur Papers.

28 Brunson, *Western Pioneer*, 147; Carter-Edwards, "Battle of Lake Erie," 49-50.

29 Brunson, *Western Pioneer*, 147-51; 149 ("little garrison"); 147 ("among the real").

30 Duncan McArthur to John Armstrong, August 18, 1814, vol. 2:325-26, McArthur Papers.

31 Brunson, *Western Pioneer*, 147-48; 148 (quote).

32 Brunson, *Western Pioneer*, 144-46; 146 (quote).

33 Duncan McArthur to George Croghan, June 6, 1814, vol. 1:178-80, McArthur Papers.

34 McArthur to Armstrong, August 18, 1814.

35 McArthur General Order, August 22, 1814, vol. 2:334, McArthur Papers.

36 Miller to McArthur, September 16, 1814.

37 John Miller to Duncan McArthur, September 2, 1814, vol. 2:370, McArthur Papers.

38 Charles Gratiot to Duncan McArthur, December 17, 1814, vol. 3:681-84, McArthur Papers.

39 James Witherell to Amy Hawkins Witherell, September 4, 1814.

40 Miller to McArthur, September 16, 1814.

41 Brunson, *Western Pioneer*, 152; Brunson, "Alfred Brunson."

42 Declaration by John Miller, September 26, 1814, Oversized Photostats, McArthur Papers.

43 James Witherell to Amy Hawkins Witherell, September 4, 1814; Charles Gratiot to Duncan McArthur, November 24, 1814, vol. 3:633-36, McArthur Papers.

44 John Miller to Duncan McArthur, December 31, 1814, vol. 3:687-91, McArthur Papers. Fort Gratiot was named for the officer who supervised its construction, U.S. Captain Charles Gratiot.

45 Alder, 8.

46 Duncan McArthur to Jacob Brown, August 18, 1814, vol. 2:323-24, McArthur Papers; Alder, 18; Carter-Edwards, "Battle of Lake Erie," 49-54; Taylor, 265-67.

47 Butler quoted in Carter-Edwards, "War of 1812," 50. For other American raids, see the essay in this volume by Meghan McGowan.

48 "Treaty of Ghent; 1814," Yale Law School, "The Avalon Project: Documents in Law, History, and Diplomacy," http://avalon.law.yale.edu/19th_century/ghent.asp (accessed April 30, 2012).

49 Carter-Edwards, "Defending the Straits," 36; Raddall, 322-23.

50 Alfred Brunson, "Upper Mississippi Missions," *Western Christian Advocate*, November 9, 1838; Brunson, "Alfred Brunson," 146-48.

51 Milo M. Quaife, ed., *War on the Detroit: The Chronicles of Thomas Verchères de Boucherville and the Capitulation, by an Ohio Volunteer* (Chicago: Fireside Press, 1940), 171.

52 Martial Law in Western District under Procter and Harrison, October 20, 1821, Folder 1821, Box 1, Charles Larned Papers, BHC. For reconciliation efforts after the war, see the essays in this volume by Merry Ellen Scofield and James M. Shuryan.

Part Three:

Legacies

Battle of the Thames
Etching by John Dorival, c. 1833. Lithograph. Courtesy of the Library of Congress.

A Most Convenient Indian: The Making of Tecumseh
Tim Moran

In September 1813, British General Henry Procter penned
the news to his superiors that an American fleet had defeated
the British on Lake Erie and that he was abandoning Fort
Amherstburg to retreat to the Thames River. Preparing to
withdraw, he conceded, "I feel myself much at a loss with Respect
to the Indians." Procter's words proved prophetic, as his hastily-
organized march resulted in disaster for Britain's confederated
Indian allies under the leadership of the Shawnee warrior
Tecumseh. At the Thames, the American army under General
William Henry Harrison defeated the retreating British and
killed a number of Indians – including Tecumseh. As the majority
population on the northwestern frontier, Native Americans were
necessary allies of the inadequately supplied armies of the region,
particularly the British. For most white settlers, however, Native
Americans were feared, hated, or only reluctantly accepted.[1]

Tecumseh was an exception, a constructed hero whose
reputation glossed over an ugly and terrifying wartime reality that
included mass killings, plunder, and treachery between Indian
and white communities. He personified the romantic notion of a
perfect Indian leader that mushroomed in the decades following
the War of 1812. Literary scholars characterize this general
process as the creation of Indian metaphor, practiced by authors
of such repute as Cooper, Longfellow, Hawthorne, Thoreau,
Melville, and Twain.[2]

The Shawnee leader was no straw man. Tecumseh possessed unusual qualities of leadership, charisma, and thoughtfulness. The record is replete with admiring firsthand comments from contemporaries, including generals Harrison and Isaac Brock. The Indian coalition, which greatly expanded Britain's military strength on the frontier, testifies to Tecumseh's effectiveness. "He did us good service, and died bravely fighting for our cause," observed the Canadian historian John Charles Dent in 1880.[3]

By the late nineteenth century, as the last of the frontier residents and expeditionary participants wrapped up their memoirs and disappeared from history, the Tecumseh legend assumed messianic proportions. Romantic biographers portrayed him dressing down the British high command with preternatural battle wisdom, experiencing and sharing a premonition of his own death, discussing Alexander the Great, and, in his last moments, safeguarding children, delivering a supply of flour to a starving family, and saving Canadians' homesteads from harm.[4] Even while praising Tecumseh, Dent cautioned: "He has deserved well at our hands; but those enthusiastic hero-worshippers who have so persistently held him up to our admiration as the warm and affectionate friend of British ascendancy on this continent know little of the man and his motives."[5]

Despite Dent's warning, most Tecumseh literature remains celebratory and heroic, following a pattern established by writers in the mid-nineteenth century. John Richardson, who was less than seventeen years old when he served as an aide in Procter's army, described Tecumseh thirty years later as muscular with "a singularly wild and terrific expression to his features. It was evident that he could be terrible."[6] In 1857, a speech by "Judge Law," printed in the *Vincennes Western Sun*, stated:

> For all those qualities which elevate man far above his race, for talent, tact, skill, bravery as a warrior; for high-minded, honorable and chivalrous bearing as a man; in fine, for all those elements of greatness which place him a long way above his

fellows in savage life, the name and fame of Tecumseh will go down of posterity in the West, as one of the most celebrated of the Aborigines of this continent.

Law went on to describe Tecumseh as "Tall, athletic and manly, dignified, but graceful, he seemed the beau ideal of an Indian Chieftain." We now know that Tecumseh may have stood about 5-foot-9, but also had difficulty walking because one of his legs was significantly shorter than the other from a youthful hunting accident.[7]

Tecumseh's reputation as a pan-tribal leader developed in the years leading up to the War of 1812 by negotiations carried out in Ohio and in Indiana Territory beginning in 1806. Prior to that time, his status among Indians had primarily been as the leader of a small band of people who moved from western Ohio into Indiana Territory to avoid conflict with Americans. Tecumseh's brother, Tenskwatawa, brought the group to prominence when a series of his religious visions caused a Native American spiritual revival movement. Tecumseh became the public face of this new Indian confederation. In June 1808, British Indian Department deputy superintendent William Claus recorded a speech by Tecumseh to British officials at Fort Amherstburg: "their [the Indians'] intention at the moment is not to take part in the quarrels of white people; that if the Americans encroach upon them they are resolved to strike – but [Tecumseh] added that if their father the King should be in earnest and appear in sufficient force they would hold fast by him."[8]

Whites did not see the subtleties involved in Tecumseh's evolution. A single individual who appeared adept at communicating with Indian agents and native chiefs was a godsend to them. In July 1811, Harrison wrote to the United States War Department about Tecumseh:

If it were not for the vicinity of the United States, he would perhaps be the founder of an empire that would rival in glory

Mexico or Peru. No difficulties deter him. For four years he has
been in constant motion. You see him today on the Wabash,
and in a short time hear of him on the shores of Lake Erie or
Michigan, or on the banks of the Mississippi, and wherever he
goes he makes an impression favorable to his purpose.[9]

Indians, Americans, and British subjects in the northwestern
theater of the War of 1812 all needed a figure such as Tecumseh,
but for very different reasons. For Native Americans, Tecumseh
stood as a sign that the Indian way of life, including self-
determination, might yet be rescued from the onslaught of
white settlement and acculturation. For the British, Tecumseh
represented Indian progress along the path to European social
ideals and fulfilled the role of imperial subordinate, like native
intermediaries in other areas of Britain's empire. The British
capitalized on his coalition-building efforts to create the buffer
zone they wanted against American expansion.

Americans celebrated the native leader only after his power
was broken. Tecumseh's legendary strength amplified national
victories in a war otherwise remarkable for American mistakes and
poltroonery. The heroic defeat of an Indian warrior-leader countered
embarrassments that included General William Hull's surrender of
Detroit in 1812, General James Winchester's debacle at the River
Raisin in 1813, and the burning of Washington City in 1814.[10]

Creation of an Indian strongman was nothing new to either
Anglo-American or native interests. Tecumseh's identity as an
Indian of power and influence was much more solidly based than
most. Harrison's admiration for him was not unique. Mohawk
leader John Norton, of mixed Indian and British parentage,
viewed Tecumseh as a remarkable man and gifted in motivating
Indians in British service. Praise from Norton was praise indeed,
as the Mohawk was a confidant of British generals, served as
tribal war chief for the Iroquois confederacy in alliance with
the British on the Niagara frontier, and was the friend of British
aristocrats and antislavery leaders.[11]

General Procter initially had a similar high regard for Tecumseh. At Amherstburg, British commissary officer Robert Gilmor wrote that he would "promote the forwarding of Provisions to Tecumseth the Indian Warrior – well knowing that the General [Procter] would sanction any thing done for that essential service."[12] Some Americans believed the Shawnee had been commissioned a brigadier general by his British allies. A report to that effect heralding from Frankfort, Kentucky, was printed in the *Maryland Gazette* in October 1812. The most famous portrait of Tecumseh, produced in the mid-nineteenth century from a composite of earlier drawings, shows him wearing a British general's coat. Yet there is no British record of a general's commission. Some British officials may have called him "General," but at best he fit the military chain of command as an irregular leader of auxiliary forces.[13]

For a war leader, Tecumseh's career was remarkable for a reputation of bravery despite a lack of success in battle. Among Native Americans, this may have been because they remembered his individual behavior in intertribal skirmishes that were unimportant to either Americans or the British in assessing leadership. He was absent in November 1811, when Indians attacked Harrison's encamped troops in what the Americans named the Battle of Tippecanoe. At Detroit's surrender in August 1812, his Indian forces were not engaged, instead forming the threat that convinced Hull to capitulate. Tecumseh was also absent from the British and Indian victory at the River Raisin in January 1813, though he had been wounded in earlier skirmishes nearby.[14]

At the unsuccessful British siege of Fort Meigs in May 1813, Tecumseh admitted that Indian forces had disappointed: "Listen! When we last went to the Rapids, it is true we gave you little assistance. It is hard to fight people who live like groundhogs." Tecumseh's last major combat action was the unsuccessful Battle of the Thames that ended British control of the northwest in October 1813.[15]

His fame among whites grew mostly from what they interpreted as "civilized" behavior. For example, Tecumseh was credited with abstaining from – and even preventing – typical Indian violence against prisoners and settlers, as when he stopped the killing of prisoners at the first siege of Fort Meigs. Norton, who was not present, claimed later that the violence was caused by a "worthless Chippewa of Detroit having with him a number of wretches like himself," who wanted the reputation of having killed white soldiers but did not have the courage to meet them in battle. Tecumseh hurried to the scene and shamed the Indians to stop the killing.[16] From a Western point of view, this action made perfect sense. "Never did Tecumseh shine more truly himself than on this occasion; and nought of the savage could be distinguished save the color and the garb," wrote Richardson in 1842.[17]

But from an Indian point of view, Tecumseh's conduct violated tribal customs. War prisoners were legitimate prizes for them, meant to be shared for purposes ranging from ritual torture and execution to tribal adoption.[18] The humane impulse celebrated by Western chroniclers was a feature of Tecumseh's character that alienated him from Indian norms and was unlikely to advance his stature as a war leader. Tecumseh's interventions did not change fundamental Indian behavior or American perceptions. American artillery Lieutenant Joseph Larwill, at the second siege of Fort Meigs in July 1813, wrote that Indians were most feared for their violence to captives: "The bodies of three have since been found, some mangled in a most horrid manner. The hands cut off. The belly ripped open and powder horn placed therein & then scalped."[19] Americans considered Indian forces as under the sway of the British, not an intelligent native commander. Larwill's journal never specifically names Tecumseh. "This day the Indians assembled in the woods in rear of our Camp . . . They keep up a continual yell and fire with rifles and musketry for 1 hour. Finding that all did not go out to meet them they returned disappointed," Larwill noted on July 27, 1813. Tecumseh had planned the diversion.[20]

Tecumseh's later reputation for masterful control of u.
allies did not prove true during the war. Raiding, pillaging, and
terrorizing behavior continued in and around Detroit long after
Tecumseh's return to the area following the River Raisin battles.
British commanders found the Indian threat useful to prevent
any possible American uprising. Procter, meanwhile, attempted
to declare Michigan an Indian territory and to deny it to the
United States. Any attempt to claim that Indians behaved badly
only when Tecumseh was away falters in the face of evidence that
southern Michigan Territory, particularly along the Lake Erie
shoreline, was in almost continuous turmoil until the British and
Indian defeat at the Thames.[21]

At Fort Amherstburg, where Tecumseh's leadership ability
was most in evidence, contemporary accounts show that the
Shawnee leader was primarily viewed as an intermediary to deal
with growing Indian discontent. By 1813, supply lines along the
north shore of Lake Erie were disrupted by American forces,
leaving the Right Division of the British army dependent on Indian
allies but unable to get adequate provisions to sustain the mixed
force based at Amherstburg. Worse still, the supply of customary
bribes that sustained Indian loyalty had been cut off. Procter
had nothing to say about Tecumseh when he reported on Indian
loyalty. Instead, he urgently requested reinforcements to keep the
Indians in check and harped on the unreliability of native allies:

> Tho' I have purchased Indian Goods, the Issue of Presents to
> the Indians has been so inadequate, as to give some advantage
> to our Enemy whose Emissaries here are neither few, nor
> inactive. Major General De Rottenburg says that 'He knows by
> Experience that no Reliance can be placed upon Indians, that
> they move off at the Moment they are most wanted.'[22]

In late August 1813, Procter warned Canadian Governor-
General Sir George Prevost that he was unable to secure enough
presents to ensure Indian loyalty. "If the Indian Goods, in very

considerable Quantities, do not arrive here, within a Month," Procter wrote, "the Most serious Consequences may be apprehended."[23] Tecumseh had brought more than 3,000 Indian warriors to Canada and the Detroit River islands, but for Procter's scant 850 men this force was a problem. The Indians proved a fickle ally for Procter, one that was hard to wield especially after commander Oliver Hazard Perry's September 10 victory over the British fleet that secured control of Lake Erie. Tecumseh's influence did not extend to ordering Indians to behave as the British wanted them to. As a coalition-builder, Tecumseh was the channel for a council of senior Indian leaders, each of whom had a voice in establishing policy. Procter could only cajole, rather than order, his Indian allies to do things. He wrote to Prevost that, "Your Excellency is aware that the Indian Body is seldom disposable, never so, contrary to their Opinion, or Inclination. . . . no Influence will or can prevail on them, or any Part of them, to leave their Families; especially whilst the Enemy can choose his Points of Attack."[24]

For the British, the later construct of Tecumseh as Indian commander was particularly useful when the noble behavior of the martyred Indian "chief" could be played off against the apparent incompetence and alleged cowardice of Procter during the British defeat. Authors such as Richardson could use Tecumseh's challenges to Procter, basically speeches translated by interpreters, as evidence of a voice speaking truth to power. At the abandonment of Fort Amherstburg, Richardson's recounting has Tecumseh say to Procter:

> You always told us you would never draw your foot off British ground; but now, father, we see you are drawing back, and we are sorry to see our father doing so without seeing the enemy. We must compare our father's conduct to a fat animal, that carries its tail upon its back, but when affrighted, it drops it between its legs and runs off. . . . You have got the arms and ammunition which our great father sent for his red children. If you have any idea of going away, give them to us.[25]

Thomas Verchères de Boucherville, a British-Canadian soldier during the war, also claimed that Tecumseh harangued Procter at a public dinner by comparing the general to a "crawfish that does not know how to walk straight ahead," and insisting, "Every word you say evaporates like the smoke from our pipes."[26] These speeches were later introduced as evidence in the records of Procter's career-ending court martial in Britain in 1815. Prosecutors elevated Tecumseh as "that brave and superior man."[27] But were the speeches genuine? Tecumseh made many orations, but unlike other documents of the time, they read smoothly, glibly, and with a poetic consistency. In 1836, author James French wrote that he never heard Indians speak in the "highly wrought or figurative" manner in the translations of Indian speeches.[28]

The British retreat from Amherstburg into the interior of Upper Canada is a revealing indictment of Tecumseh's purported leadership. In July 1813, the Indian allies numbered more than 3,000; during the retreat, they dwindled to some 1,200; by the final battle, only 500 were present.[29] This desertion meant that the Indian forces barely outnumbered the British, though more than 1,000 Indian noncombatants also choked the mucky road and trails that the army was retreating along. Many of these Indian women and children were killed or wounded by the pursuing Americans.[30] Deluded British officials, far from the action, reassured one another that "Tecumseth at the Head of Twelve hundred Indian Warriors . . . were of the most essential service in preserving [the army] from Annihilation and in arresting the further advance of the Americans." By that time, the Indian leader was twenty-five days dead and the question of positive identification of his body was already contentious.[31]

While American troops scalped, took souvenirs, and even cut away strips of thigh skin to use as razor strops from a body thought to be Tecumseh, Harrison did not include the Indian's death in his official report of the battle. Some British prisoners stated that they recognized the corpse, but may have been telling aggressive Kentuckians what they thought the militiamen wanted to hear. Some Indians claimed that the Americans chose the wrong body, and that Tecumseh's remains were buried in a secret place on the swampy battlefield or spirited away and hidden elsewhere.[32]

Defeating Procter and a tired force of British troops held little luster for American participants. Neutralizing a confederacy of hated savage Indians, especially by killing its able leader in personal combat, was a much better story. As years went by, the importance of Tecumseh's body grew crucial to supporters of Richard M. Johnson, the Kentucky officer whose reputation as Tecumseh's killer fueled a political career. Johnson, a Democrat, campaigned as Martin Van Buren's vice presidential running mate in 1836, and his supporters made much of the slogan "Rumpsey Dumpsey, Rumpsy Dumpsey, Colonel Johnson killed Tecumseh." Elaborate paintings depicting the event showed Johnson on horseback, in full cockaded uniform, shooting a charging Tecumseh. Other accounts held that a wounded Johnson killed Tecumseh with his last pistol shot. Johnson's campaign heightened Tecumseh's legend and created a set of popular "facts" that made the Indian a national historical figure. As an elderly man, he admitted that the truth was hazy. "They say I killed him; how could I tell? I was in too much of a hurry . . . I fired as quick as convenient, and he fell. If it had been TECUMSEH or the PROPHET, it would have been all the same," Johnson said.[33]

Tecumseh also came ready-made to serve as Harrison's doughty foe. Harrison's "Log Cabin-Hard Cider" Whig presidential campaign of 1840 relied on his image as an Indian fighter and frontier leader. Political supporter Thomas Moores traveled to the site of the Battle of the Thames in June 1840, dug up several battlefield graves, and returned with bones that he displayed as the remains of Tecumseh. The bones joined the campaign song refrain, "Tippecanoe and Tyler Too," in firmly associating the Shawnee leader and his brother the Prophet with Harrison's successful presidential election.[34] During the same period, dramatized treatments of Tecumseh blossomed, with at least three plays written between 1836 and 1844. Recurring themes included Tecumseh guarding virtuous women, Tecumseh evoking virile American values against the treacherous British, and Tecumseh as noble savage. Authors like James French engaged in nostalgia for Indian culture that no longer posed a threat: "the more I found my feelings aroused, and my sympathies enlisted on their behalf . . . I was carried back, by a natural train of thought, to reflect upon what they once had been."[35]

Others used a more bombastic and nationalistic approach. Playwright Richard Emmons showed Tecumseh and Johnson grappling on stage in a death-fight while watched by the fair "Lucinda," an invented white captive. Defeated and dying, Tecumseh soliloquizes that "The Red man's course is run; I die – the last of all my race," a convenient gift to America despite the thousands of Shawnees still living at the time. Lest the audience have any doubt, stage instructions tell the band to strike up "Hail, Columbia" and "The GODDESS OF LIBERTY descends from the clouds in a car, enveloped in the Revolving Star of Columbia, accompanied by Freedom's anthem, bearing in her hand the Star Spangled Banner, the glorious mantle of her NATION'S GLORY!"[36]

The irony is that today Tecumseh's real accomplishments stand on their merits. He brought Indians into a coalition that was vital for British opposition to American interests in frontier territories. Had he avoided the British retreat and fought Harrison as vigorously as he proposed, it is possible that Indian interests might have created a buffer zone in the Northwest Territory. The Indians had less need of a martyr acceptable to whites than they did of a coalition-builder flexible enough to maintain their interests against American aggression and British convenience.

Perhaps it was foreordained that after the war, the Americans, British, Indians, and later, Canadians, would each need to amplify the Tecumseh character to a scarcely believable superman. Tecumseh was too convenient a subject for each group to resist. As a result, Tecumseh has become a magnet for folktales and folkways deprecating the shortcomings of ineffective leaders. In turn, his towering stature had the strange effect of diminishing the value of killing any other Indian in battle. Joseph Larwill and countless others obtained no special recognition from having done so – but to have killed the great Tecumseh in battle was a feather in the cap of an American vice-presidential aspirant and his coterie. Accordingly, Tecumseh became greater with every telling of the tale.

NOTES

1 Henry Procter to Francis de Rottenburg, September 12, 1813, in *Select British Documents of the Canadian War of 1812*, ed. William C.H. Wood, 3 vols. (1920-28; reprint, New York: Greenwood Press, 1968), 2:273. A note in Judge Augustus B. Woodward's handwriting totaled 4,174 "persons" in Michigan Territory, according to census figures cited for December 17, 1813. The number clearly did not take Native Americans into account. Folder 4 ("Surrender of Detroit, 1812-13"), Box 5, Augustus Brevoort Woodward Papers, BHC.

2 Elizabeth I. Hanson, *The American Indian in American Literature: A Study in Metaphor* (Lewiston, NY: E. Mellen Press, 1988), 118-19.

3 Dent quoted in *Tecumseh: Fact and Fiction in Early Records*, ed. Carl F. Klinck (Englewood Cliffs, NJ: Prentice-Hall, 1961), 136-39.

4 Glenn Tucker, *Tecumseh: Vision of Glory* (Indianapolis: Bobbs-Merrill, 1956), 296-318. Tucker's most-cited sources include the works of British-Canadian author John Richardson and the Lyman C. Draper collection, which encompasses early casuistic biographical work by Benjamin Drake whose self-declared task in 1821 was to "rescue the chief from oblivion" (Tucker, 366).

5 Dent quoted in *Tecumseh: Fact and Fiction*, 139.

6 John Richardson, *Richardson's War of 1812: With Notes and a Life of the Author*, ed. Alexander C. Casselman (Toronto: Historical Publishing, 1902), 207. Richardson fictionalized the war and Tecumseh in a poem, *Tecumseh: A Poem in Four Cantos* (1828), and in florid novels, such as *Wacousta* (1832) and *The Canadian Brothers* (1840). For Richardson, see also the essays in this volume by Timothy Marks, Scott A. Jankowski, and Meghan McGowan.

7 "Extract from work of Judge Law's, now in process of publication," *Vincennes Western Sun* (IN), December 11, 1857, Tecumseh Papers, BHC. For additional nineteenth-century works that helped to create the romantic legend of Tecumseh, see the plays Richard Emmons, *Tecumseh; or, The Battle of the Thames, a National*

Drama (1836); and George Jones, *Tecumseh and the Prophet of the West, An Original Historical Israel-Indian Tragedy, in Five Acts* (1844); the poems G.H. Colton, *Tecumseh: or, The West Thirty Years Since* (1842); Emmons, *The Fredoniad; or, Independence Preserved: An Epic Poem of the Late War of 1812* (1827); and George Longmore, *Tecumthe* (1824); and the novel James S. French, *Elskwatawa; or, The Prophet of the West* (1836). Later authors and biographers continued to build the Tecumseh legend, including Tucker; and John M. Oskison, *Tecumseh and His Times: The Story of a Great Indian* (New York: G.P. Putnam's Sons, 1938). For a modern romanticized portrayal of Tecumseh, see Allan W. Eckert, *A Sorrow in Our Heart: The Life of Tecumseh* (New York: Bantam, 1992). More scholarly works have also appeared in recent decades. See R. David Edmunds, *Tecumseh and the Quest for Indian Leadership* (Boston: Little, Brown, 1984); John Sugden, *Tecumseh's Last Stand* (Norman: University of Oklahoma Press, 1985); and Sugden, *Tecumseh: A Life* (New York: Henry Holt and Co., 1998). Other illuminating perspectives include Gordon M. Sayre, *The Indian Chief as Tragic Hero: Native Resistance and the Literatures of America, from Moctezuma to Tecumseh* (Chapel Hill: University of North Carolina Press, 2005); and Guy St. Denis, *Tecumseh's Bones* (Montreal: McGill-Queen's University Press, 2005), which traces the multiple attempts to locate authentic remains of the Indian leader.

8   R. David Edmunds, *The Shawnee Prophet* (Lincoln: University of Nebraska Press, 1983), 69-71; 71 (quote). For the partnership between the Shawnee brothers, see also Edmunds, *Tecumseh*, 96-97; and the essays in this volume by Steve Lyskawa and Kerri Jansen.

9   Harrison quoted in Reed Beard, *The Battle of Tippecanoe*, 2d ed. (Lafayette, IN: Tippecanoe Publishing, 1889), 44.

10 Sayre, 275.

11 Carl F. Klinck et al., eds., *The Journal of Major John Norton, 1809-1816* (Toronto: Champlain Society, 1970), 300, 321, 341. For the creation of mythic Indian leaders, see Joshua Piker, "Lying Together: The Imperial Implications of Cross-Cultural Untruths," *American Historical Review* 116 (2011): 964-86.

12 Robert Gilmor to Brigade Major McLean, March 27, 1813, Folder March 1813, Box 10, William Woodbridge Papers, BHC.

13 *Maryland Gazette*, Oct. 8, 1812; *Journal of Major John Norton*, lxxx, lxxxii-lxxiv.

14 For examples of Indian recollections of battle leadership, see *Journal of Major John Norton*, 113, 115, 185-87, 268.

15 Tecumseh quoted in Sugden, *Tecumseh's Last Stand*, 54. According to Sayre, Tecumseh spoke only in Shawnee, leaving interpretation of his words subject both to the interpolation of contemporary translators and the aims of those such as Harrison who were recording remembered translations for posterity (278). Thomas Verchères de Boucherville reported that Tecumseh understood some English, but needed a translator in order to fully understand military reports and messages. Milo M. Quaife, ed., *War on the Detroit: The Chronicles of Thomas Verchères de Boucherville and the Capitulation, by an Ohio Volunteer* (Chicago: Fireside Press, 1940), 141-42.

16 *Journal of Major John Norton*, 321.

17 Richardson, *Richardson's War of 1812*, 154.

18 Daniel K. Richter, "War and Culture: The Iroquois Experience," *William and Mary Quarterly* 40 (1983): 528-59.

19 Joseph H. Larwill Journal, July 21, 1813, Joseph H. Larwill Papers, BHC.

20 Larwill Journal, July 27, 1813.

21 Alan Taylor, *The Civil War of 1812: American Citizens, British Subjects, Irish Rebels, & Indian Allies* (New York: Knopf, 2010), 242. For Procter's ambitions for Michigan Territory, see Sandy Antal, *A Wampum Denied: Procter's War of 1812* (Ottawa: Carleton University Press, 1997).

22 Henry Procter to Edward Baynes, August 19, 1813, in *Select British Documents*, 2:262-63.

23 Henry Procter to George Prevost, August 29, 1813, in *Select British Documents*, 2:266-67.

24 Henry Procter to George Prevost, August 26, 1813, in *Select British Documents*, 2:264-65. For the lack of coordination between the British and their Indian allies, see also Taylor, 242-46; and Procter to Prevost, August 9, 1813, in *Tecumseh: Fact and Fiction*, 181-82.

25 Richardson, *Richardson's War of 1812*, 206.

26 *War on the Detroit*, 142.

27 Sugden, *Tecumseh's Last Stand*, 58.

28 French quoted in *Tecumseh: Fact and Fiction*, 224-25.

29 Sugden, *Tecumseh's Last Stand*, 108. Sugden writes that the Indians were each given a stick as the British battle lines were formed and that the sticks were collected and counted before combat began. For the Battle of the Thames, see also the essays in this volume by Jankowski and Joshua Zimberg.

30 Henry Procter to Francis de Rottenberg, October 23, 1813, in *Select British Documents*, 2:327.

31 George Prevost to Henry Bathurst, October 30, 1813, in *Select British Documents*, 2:327-29.

32 St. Denis, 9.

33 Johnson quoted in St. Denis, 11.

34 St. Denis, 10-11. For the Battle of Tippecanoe, see Jansen.

35 French quoted in *Tecumseh: Fact and Fiction*, 223-25.

36 Emmons quoted in *Tecumseh: Fact and Fiction*, 227.

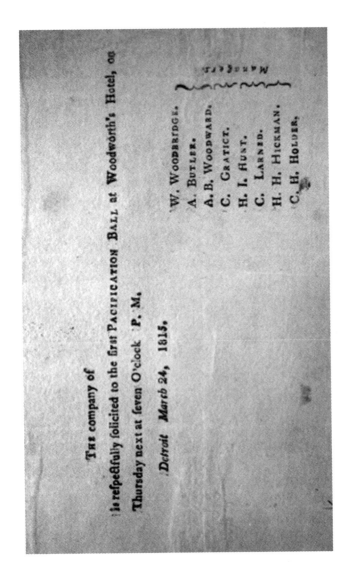

Invitation to the Pacification Ball
Printer unknown, 1815. Ink on paper. Courtesy of the Burton Historical Collection, Detroit Public Library.

Celebrating Peace on the Detroit Frontier
Merry Ellen Scofield

Every good peace treaty deserves a celebration, and none more so than the Treaty of Ghent, which ended the War of 1812. It was cause for a party that started in New York and spread with the news across a thankful nation. Few cities had more reason to celebrate than Detroit or more reason to tread diplomatically in its merriment. At stake were the feelings and attitudes of their British friends across the river. How to party appropriately would be a challenge for Detroit, although not to party at all was unthinkable.[1]

The Treaty of Ghent arrived in New York City on Saturday evening, February 11, 1815.[2] Within twenty minutes of the ship's landing, crowds of New Yorkers illuminated the streets with their candles, "the city resound[ing] in all parts with the joyful cry of a peace! a peace!"[3] Three days later, President James Madison had the document in hand.

Washington City was ready. As Madison and his advisors pored over treaty details on the second floor of the Octagon House, the first lady held an impromptu celebration in the rooms below. The president's enslaved manservant recalled the occasion years later: "The butler . . . served wine liberally . . . I played the President's March on the violin . . . others were drunk for two days . . . such a joyful time was never seen in Washington."[4] The next night, an exuberant crowd of well-wishers filled Dolley Madison's popular Wednesday night reception, and the gaieties continued well after the United States Congress adjourned on March 3.[5]

Rumors of peace spread rapidly along the coast.[6] Word of the treaty reached Hartford, Connecticut, while American envoy Henry Carroll was still en route to Washington, prompting spontaneous "merry music of bells," firing of artillery, and the "huzzaing of gathered crowds."[7] President Madison had yet to sit down with the document when the Court of Common Pleas in Amherst, New Hampshire, announced peace, "adjourned the Court, and the joy of the people burst forth."[8] More organized festivities followed. Philadelphia and Baltimore "were illuminated Wednesday evening," February 15.[9] Boston held a day of prayers, a "public thanksgiving," and fireworks on George Washington's birthday, February 22.[10] New York did the same, but topped it off a few weeks later with an elaborate peace ball "in the first style of elegance and fashion."[11] There, approximately six hundred fashionable New Yorkers mingled among live orange trees and laurel-entwined pillars, while a glittering mechanical sun twirled above them, diffusing "from its dazzling surface, the radiance reflected by 800 lights."[12]

On February 20, 1815, word of peace reached Detroit via a letter from the postmaster general. William Woodbridge, the new territorial secretary and a recent arrival to the region, wrote his wife on February 25: "The face of things is quite changed – instead of gloomy anticipations of ruined cornfields – burning houses – of scalped women & children – & all the horrors of war and desolation – we have the cheering news of peace, plenty and prosperity!"[13]

The town that received the "cheering news" was not a metropolis in 1815, even by frontier standards.[14] Louisville had at least double Detroit's thousand or so residents; Cincinnati had six times its population.[15] The entire population of Michigan Territory was less than eight thousand, and even those, according to one historian, were mainly "French and halfbreeds."[16] The town itself got mixed reviews. A local garrison commander wrote Woodbridge that the region was not worth defending and suggested that the government "remove every inhabitant," pay them for their troubles, and then reduce the whole territory "to ashes."[17] Based on that negativity, the new territorial secretary was surprised to discover an energetic community and beautiful scenery. He also found a town that loved to party.

"One would think," Woodbridge mused, "that the lives of this people consist in one constant succession of amusements."[18] A month into his arrival, he had already attended two private balls and two lavish winter picnics on the Rouge River, each picnic complete with a sleigh ride, fiddlers, card playing, and plenty of drink.[19] "What can I tell you?" he wrote his wife, " – dances, rides, dinners, card parties, and all the *et cetera* of dissipation, follow in one long train, treading each on the heels of the other!"[20] In such a town, not celebrating the peace was inconceivable, and within a week of receiving the news, a committee had formed to plan the appropriate festivities.

The committee of twenty-eight military and civic leaders was headed by Augustus B. Woodward and included, among others, Charles Larned, Charles Gratiot, Solomon Sibley, Antoine Dequindre, and Benjamin Woodworth. In a short draft, the men drew up a schedule of events, offered a possible start date, and proposed to invite special guests. On the surface, these plans for "dinners, balls, illuminations, [and] orations" appear to duplicate those happening elsewhere in the country. A closer look, though, reveals that Detroit celebrated in a way uniquely its own.[21]

For one thing, it would take more than an official letter from the postmaster general to convince Detroiters that an honorable peace had reached the western frontier; they made seeing the treaty a condition to party. "The undersigned," wrote Woodward in drawing up the celebration plans, "will promote public dinners, balls, illuminations, orations, etc., in such a manner as shall be found generally agreeable within three, or at most four weeks, *after the reception, here, of the treaty of peace [and] if the terms thereof shall appear to be honorable.*"[22] On February 26, 1815, the town had still not received the evidence it needed. Both

Woodward and Woodbridge wrote letters that day expressing their frustration – Woodward to the president, Woodbridge to his wife. "We were disappointed," Woodbridge remarked, "in the total failure of the Washington City mail this week, & of course we have not the pleasure of any corroboration of the news of peace."[23] Mail service to Detroit was notably unreliable. Although other copies of the treaty may have arrived earlier, at the latest, a transcript sent to Colonel Anthony Butler on March 21 from Chillicothe, Ohio, would have been available for scrutiny by the planning committee.[24]

The second consideration was timing. Detroit would not only wait for peace-treaty details to arrive before it celebrated, it would also wait for the end of Lent. Woodward's draft outlining the proposed celebration suggested a start date of "Wednesday, the twenty-ninth day of March."[25] That was not a random decision. In 1815, Easter fell on March 26. For Detroit's large Catholic community, the six-week period before Easter was a time of abstention, including the avoidance of secular entertainments.[26] Woodbridge had been surprised to see at least "49. ladies" at a February ball "although it was Lent," and noted at a winter picnic that, it being Lent, the "few French ladies" in attendance "only looked on" while others danced.[27] He also commented later that "the ending of Lent" had added to the peace celebration gaiety.[28]

Thus, with an acceptable treaty and a date that respected the local Catholic population, the planning committee set about determining the guest list. And here is where Detroit differed the most from other American communities. The town invited its former enemy, specifically directing that "gentlemen on the other side . . . be invited to our public dinners, and ladies on the other side . . . be invited to our balls."[29] Moreover, in order to facilitate the delicacy needed in such a situation, the planners used different language. Detroit would not celebrate peace; it would celebrate *pacification*. It was to be a *pacification* ball and a *pacification* dinner.

The term was not used by other American cities in speaking

of their celebrations. Neither was it used by Madison or Congress. The expression may have originated with Woodward, since he referred to the rumored peace as "a pacification" in his letter to President Madison on February 26, 1815.[30] He and others on the planning committee might have been aware that Europeans sometimes used the word when speaking of the recent British-American peace treaty, or they may have been delightfully referencing another treaty signed in Ghent, the 1576 Pacification that ended provincial hostilities in what is now the Netherlands.[31] Whatever its origin, pacification, and not peace, accurately bespoke of Detroit's conciliatory approach to its celebration, and residents readily adopted its use.[32]

The planners understood the tension along the borderlands and respected the need to step cautiously. A peace celebration, by any name, had the potential of being a politically charged event. Inviting the former enemy showed a determination for reconciliation, at least on the part of town leaders. However, the inclusion of British neighbors in Detroit's frontier social life had begun even before the March event was scheduled. Woodbridge casually mentioned the presence of ladies "from the British side" at a February ball held a good month before the pacification festivities.[33] Sandwich resident John Askin, an elderly Scots-Irish immigrant with roots in Detroit and Sandwich, declined his invitation to the pacification dinner. He did so, though, with an easy grace that came from a long connection with Detroit society, only regretting that "his advanced time of life and weak state of health" deprived him of joining in the festivities.[34] There was certainly resentment and residual anger on both sides of the river, but the property damage, the lives lost, and the general horrors of war were mainly the result of military and government actions. Local residents on both sides were victims of international circumstances beyond their control and sought to reestablish prewar economic and social conditions.[35]

The celebrations began on March 29, 1815. "Military salutes

were occasionally fired during the day," followed by a "sumptuous dinner" for invited gentlemen at five o'clock.[36] Later that evening, and in keeping with the international flavor of the celebration, guests walked down to the riverfront where they were treated to a stretch of "brilliant" illuminations running "on both sides [of the water] from the River Miamie . . . to the Lake Sinclair."[37] The next evening, beginning at 7 o'clock, "the first PACIFICATION BALL" was held at Woodworth's Hotel, and for two nights following, the merriment continued "in different houses in town and just out of it."[38] For that week in early spring, 1815, Detroiters and their friends from across the river drank too much, ate too much, danced too much, and, in general, celebrated the end of British-American hostilities with spirit and "universal hilarity."[39]

Although community leaders used plurals in drafting the proposed "dinners, balls [and] illuminations," there is no indication that further pacification activities occurred after the one week of festivities. Detroit continued to party, though, throwing an extensive celebration for President James Monroe in 1817. Meanwhile, the relative peace along the border would continue to require careful diplomacy for decades after the War of 1812.[40]

Two hundred years later, Detroit and Windsor consider themselves old friends. The two cities share a tunnel, a bridge, and mutual economic interests. However, nothing better symbolizes their friendship than the party they throw for themselves each June. For more than fifty years, citizens on both sides of the river have come together to celebrate the Fourth of July and Canada Day. They do so with festivities and fireworks that are, perhaps, today's version of the pacification celebration of 1815. The crowds are a little bigger, the flavor a little less French, the "illumination" a bit grander, and the food more ballpark than "sumptuous." But even with all the changes, it might be possible, in a quiet moment, to look across the darkened waters of the Detroit River and see, for just an instant, the ghost of lighted candles flickering along its banks in celebration of peace on the Detroit frontier.[41]

NOTES

1 The Detroit peace celebration has not been a topic of much interest to historians. See Frank B. and Arthur M. Woodford, *All Our Yesterdays: A Brief History of Detroit* (Detroit: Wayne State University Press, 1969), 125, for a romantic account of the celebration; Sandy Antal, *A Wampum Denied: Procter's War of 1812* (Ottawa: Carleton University Press, 1997), 391, for a brief and misdated depiction based on Frank Woodford's *Mr. Jefferson's Disciple: A Life of Justice Woodward* (East Lansing: Michigan State College Press, 1953), 123; R. Alan Douglas, *Uppermost Canada: The Western District and the Detroit Frontier, 1800-1850* (Detroit: Wayne State University Press, 2001), 87, which mentions the event in passing; and Harlan Henthorne Hatcher, *Lake Erie* (Indianapolis: Bobbs-Merrill, 1945), 176, which gives Lewis Cass credit for the planning, although Cass did not return to Detroit until months after the celebration was held.

2 Charles Jared Ingersoll, *Historical Sketch of the Second War between the United States of America and Great Britain*, 3 vols. (Philadelphia: Lea and Blanchard, 1849), 2:311; Rocellus Sheridan Guernsey, *New York City and Vicinity during the War of 1812-15*, 2 vols. (New York: Charles L. Woodward, 1889-95), 2:508. The treaty arrived on the HMS *Favorite* under the care of Henry Carroll, secretary of the American delegation at Ghent. Also on board was Britain's interim *chargé d'affaires*, Anthony St. John Baker. Charles Oscar Paulin and Frederic Logan Paxson, *Guide to the Material in London Archives for the History of the United States since 1783* (Washington, DC: Carnegie Institution of Washington, 1914), 40.

3 "Peace," *New York Evening Post*, February 13, 1815.

4 Paul Jennings, *A Colored Man's Reminiscences of James Madison* (1865; reprint, Orange County, VA: The Montpelier Foundation, 2010), 13-14. See also Charles Jared Ingersoll, *History of the Second War between the United States of America and Great Britain*, 2 vols. (Philadelphia: Lippincott, Grambo & Company, 1852), 2:64-65. The Madisons temporarily resided at the Octagon House after British forces burned the White House on August 24, 1814.

5 "Ball in Celebration of Peace," *National Intelligencer* (Washington, DC), April 28, 1815, announcing a public ball being held on May 1.

6 Word came to Savannah, Georgia, "on the 10th inst. and Charleston on the 12th," by way of a British fleet out of Bermuda. *New York Evening Post*, February 23, 1815.

7 "The Rejoicings," *American Mercury* (Hartford, CT), February 21, 1815. Citizens of Washington City were also aware of the treaty before the document reached President Madison. On the morning of February 13, a number of expresses brought news of the treaty's arrival in New York, at which point an "elated Congress" adjourned early. Jacob Barker, *Incidents in the Life of Jacob Barker: Of New Orleans, Louisiana . . . from 1800 to 1855* (Washington, DC: n.p., 1855), 123. See also "Peace," *Federal Republican* (Georgetown, DC), February 14, 1815.

8 "Peace," *Farmer's Cabinet* (Amherst, NH), February 20, 1815.

9 [Illuminations], *Albany Argus*, February 21, 1815.

10 "Peace," *Farmer's Cabinet*.

11 [The Peace Ball], *The Columbian* (New York City), March 20, 1815.

12 "Peace Ball in New York," *Independent Chronicle* (Boston), March 30, 1815.

13 William Woodbridge to Juliana Woodbridge, February 25, 1815, in a letter started on February 17, 1815, Folder Feb. 1815, Box 11, William Woodbridge Papers, BHC. See also Paul Leake, *History of Detroit: Chronicle of Its Progress, Its Industries, Its Institutions, and the People of the Fair City of the Straits*, 3 vols. (Chicago: Lewis, 1912), 1:108-9.

14 William Woodbridge to Juliana Woodbridge, February 25, 1815.

15 Isaac Smith Homans, "Commercial and Industrial Cities of the United States: Number LXXIV. Detroit Michigan," *Hunt's Merchants' Magazine and Commercial Review* 42 (January-June 1860): 422; "Population of the 61 Urban Places: 1820," U.S. Bureau of Census, www.census.gov/population/www/documentation/twps0027/tab05.txt (accessed April 29, 2012).

16 David Richard Moore, *Canada and the United States, 1815-1830* (Chicago: Jennings & Graham, 1910), 58. In 1820, Michigan Territory's population was 8,896 compared to 55,211 in Illinois, 147,178 in Indiana, and 581,434 in Ohio. See "Table 1: Growth of Population, 1790-1820," in Curtis Putnam Nettels, *Emergence of a National Economy, 1775-1815* (New York: Harper & Row, 1969), 383.

17 Duncan McArthur to William Woodbridge, late 1814, quoted in David Lee Poremba, *Michigan* (Northampton, MA: Interlink Books, 2006), 57.

18 William Woodbridge to Juliana Woodbridge, March 5, 1815, quoted in Charles Lanman, *Life of William Woodbridge* (Washington, DC: Blanchard & Mohun, 1867), 14.

19 William Woodbridge to Juliana Woodbridge, February 17, 1815 ("winter picnics"), and February 25, 1815 ("balls"), both referenced in a letter started on February 17, 1815, Woodbridge Papers. The winter picnics were called "beefstake" parties; the balls were weekly. On March 19, 1815, William Woodbridge wrote, "There was a ball last night, as there has been every week I believe since the 22nd." Woodbridge to Juliana Woodbridge, March 19, 1815, in a letter started on March 16, 1815, Folder March 1815, Box 11, Woodbridge Papers.

20 William Woodbridge to Juliana Woodbridge, March 5, 1815, quoted in Lanman, 14.

21 Augustus B. Woodward, draft of plans for peace events signed by Woodward and accompanied by twenty-seven other signatures (undated), Folder MS/Woodward, Augustus B. Jan.-Mar. 1815, Box 7, Augustus Brevoort Woodward Papers, BHC.

22 Woodward, draft of plans for peace events. Emphasis mine.

23 In his letter to the president, Woodward mildly questioned the authenticity of the peace news. Augustus B. Woodward to James Madison, February 26, 1815, James Madison Papers, Library of Congress, http://memory.loc.gov/ammem/collections/madison_papers/index.html (accessed April 29, 2012); William Woodbridge to Juliana Woodbridge, February 26, 1815, in a letter started February 17, 1815, Woodbridge Papers.

24 Charles S. Todd to Anthony Butler, March 21, 1815, in *MPHC*, 16:66-67. What Woodward and the other town leaders considered an honorable peace treaty is beyond the scope of this paper, although they may have been concerned that details of the treaty would incite, rather than mollify, animosities between Detroiters and their Canadian neighbors. As the area's legal authority, Woodward was aware of the complications, and historians have confirmed the uneven peace that continued between the sides, including conflicts over naval rights on the Great Lakes and the back-and-forth of military deserters and runaway slaves. See Alan Taylor, *The Civil War of 1812: American Citizens, British Subjects, Irish Rebels, & Indian Allies* (New York: Knopf, 2010), 430-35; Gregory Wigmore, "Before the Railroad: From Slavery to Freedom in the Canadian-American Borderland," *Journal of American History* 98 (2011): 437-54; and the essays in this volume by Joshua Zimberg and James M. Shuryan.

25 Woodward, draft of plans for peace events.

26 In 1815, Ash Wednesday fell on February 8. Detroit's population was largely of French-Catholic heritage. It also had a small population of Irish Catholics, which would grow large enough by the 1830s to support its own church, Holy Trinity, the second "English-speaking Catholic church in the territory." Willis Frederick Dunbar and George S. May, *Michigan: A History of the Wolverine State* (Grand Rapids: W.B. Eerdmans, 1995), 192.

27 William Woodbridge to Juliana Woodbridge, February 25, 1815 ("49. ladies"); William Woodbridge to Juliana Woodbridge, February 17, 1815 ("few French ladies").

28 William Woodbridge to Juliana Woodbridge, April 7, 1815, Folder Apr. 1815, Box 12, Woodbridge Papers.

29 Woodward, draft of plans for peace events.

30 Woodward began his letter to Madison with "The intelligence of a pacification, if authentic," from which point he fruitlessly asked for a position as secretary to the London legation, which he presumed Madison would be assembling. Woodward to Madison, February 26, 1815, Madison Papers.

31 A painting of John Quincy Adams by the Flemish artist Pieter van Huffel, completed at Ghent in 1815, depicts Adams holding a document that reads "Pacification of Ghent, December 24, 1814." Andrew Oliver, *Portraits of John Quincy Adams and His Wife* (Cambridge: Belknap Press of Harvard University Press, 1970), 53, 55. For the 1576 treaty, see "Pacification of Ghent," Encyclopedia Britannica, www.britannica.com/EBchecked/ topic/232634/Pacification-of-Ghent (accessed April 29, 2012).

32 The word "pacification" did not appear in Woodward's planning draft. However, invitations went out to a "PACIFICATION BALL" and a "Pacification Dinner," and Woodbridge referred to the celebration as a "pacification fête." Printed template of pacification ball invitation, Folder Jan.-Mar. 1815, Box 7, Woodward Papers. For other examples, see John Askin to Gentlemen Managers to the Pacification Dinner at Detroit, March 25, 1815, Folder MS/Woodward Augustus B. Jan.-Mar. 1815, Box 7, Woodward Papers; and William Woodbridge to Juliana Woodbridge, April 7, 1815.

33 William Woodbridge to Juliana Woodbridge, February 25, 1815.

34 John Askin to Gentlemen Managers, March 25, 1815. For Askin, see the essays in this volume by Sharon Tevis Finch and Timothy Marks.

35 For damages in the region during the war, see the essays in Part Two of this volume.

36 William Woodbridge to Juliana Woodbridge, April 7, 1815.

37 William Woodbridge to Juliana Woodbridge, April 7, 1815 ("brilliant"); Woodward, draft of plans for peace events ("from the River Miamie"). A typical 1800s illumination was the lighting of candles or gas lamps in all the windows of homes and businesses at night. Woodbridge called Detroit's attempt "nothing extraordinary," in part because participants only used "waxed candles." William Woodbridge to Juliana Woodbridge, April 7, 1815.

38 Printed template of pacification ball invitation ("the first PACIFICATION"); William Woodbridge to Juliana Woodbridge, April 7, 1815 ("in different houses"). In 1837, Benjamin Woodworth's hotel, by then renamed the Steamboat Hotel, was listed as being at the intersection of Randolph and Woodbridge streets. See Julius P. Bolivar MacCabe, *Directory of the City of Detroit . . . for the Year 1837* (Detroit: William Harsha, 1837), 74; and the essay in this volume by Kristen Harrell.

39 William Woodbridge to Juliana Woodbridge, April 7, 1815.

40 See "James Monroe, President of the United States, Tour in 1817," Clarke Historical Library, Central Michigan University, http://clarke.cmich.edu/resource_tab/information_and_exhibits/i_arrived_at_detroit/james_monroe.html (accessed April 29, 2012); and the essay in this volume by Kaitlin Cooper.

41 Woodward, draft of plans for peace events.

A Peaceful Border: The Rush-Bagot Agreement of 1817

James M. Shuryan

At 5,525 miles, Canada and the United States share the world's longest undefended border. Officially known as the International Boundary, the foundations for this peaceful border were laid out in a diplomatic "exchange of notes" – the Rush-Bagot Agreement of 1817 – later ratified by the U.S. Senate as the Rush-Bagot Treaty of 1818. The agreement attempted to settle disputes left unresolved by the Treaty of Ghent that had officially ended the War of 1812 in late December 1814. The U.S. renewed diplomatic talks after the war largely out of a concern for British naval armaments on the Great Lakes. John Quincy Adams, the American minister to Britain, initially made the request for discussions near the end of the Madison presidency (1809-17). Negotiations were started by Secretary of State James Monroe and finalized by acting Secretary of State Richard Rush after Monroe became president. Sir Charles Bagot represented the British in negotiations as minister to Washington. The agreement, while relatively unknown today and among the shortest treaties ever signed by the United States – roughly a page – has had an outsized influence by allowing the American-Canadian border to become among the most stable and peaceful in the world.[1]

The Treaty of Ghent did not resolve the major causes of the War of 1812. Instead, the treaty returned relations between the U.S. and Britain to *status quo ante bellum* (the state before the war). This agreement was acceptable to both sides because, with the defeat of Napoleonic France, Britain no longer had reason to seize America's trading vessels or impress (force into service) its merchant seamen on the high seas. Yet both countries still had merchant and naval ships on the Great Lakes. Moreover, the American-Canadian border lacked a clear line of demarcation. The Treaty of Ghent recognized that outstanding issues remained between the U.S. and Britain; its fourth article proposed a solution:

> In order therefore finally to decide upon these claims it is agreed that they shall be referred to two Commissioners to be appointed in the following manner: viz: One Commissioner shall be appointed by His Britannic Majesty and one by the President of the United States, by and with the advice and consent of the Senate thereof, and the said two Commissioners so appointed shall be sworn impartially to examine and decide upon the said claims according to such evidence as shall be laid before them on the part of His Britannic Majesty and of the United States respectively.[2]

The commissioners alluded to in the article resulted in the diplomatic process that produced the Rush-Bagot Treaty and a separate agreement, the Convention of 1818. Whereas Rush-Bagot focused on naval force reductions, the Convention of 1818 concentrated on the boundary line and related issues. The two treaties in 1818 stabilized the border, but they did not settle all boundary problems. The two countries and later a third, Canada, addressed various issues seven more times between 1818 and 1906 before reaching a final border agreement in the Treaty of 1908.[3]

Events in the Detroit River region following the War of 1812 illustrated the necessity of border and naval disarmament agreements between the U.S. and Britain. Americans were outraged at the ongoing harassment of merchant vessels by the British navy on the Great Lakes and the Detroit River. Under the guise of looking for military deserters, the British continued to stop and inspect the crews and cargoes of American ships. In the summer of 1816, Michigan territorial Governor Lewis Cass expressed indignation for several incidents involving the British schooner *Tecumseh*, which routinely stopped American ships that passed through the Bois Blanc channel off of Fort Amherstburg. In late May and early June, the British boarded and searched four American ships, all traveling to Detroit by Lake Erie. One of the vessels carried the Michigan territorial attorney general, Charles Larned. He and four other passengers and crewmembers on the vessels gave sworn depositions on the British actions, which were later printed in the *Niles' Weekly Register* of Baltimore. The newspaper also printed a letter from Cass to the commanding officer of the *Tecumseh* in response to the incidents. "In an aggression like this, the government of the United States can alone determine what course the honor and interest of the nation requires should be taken," Cass stated. But he still felt compelled to denounce "a practice for which the laws of nations afford no pretence; which is inconsistent with the relations existing between our respective governments; and, the continuance of which must be attended with serious and important consequences."[4] The British acknowledged the complaint, but considered it hypocritical since an American ship had recently followed a British vessel from the Niagara region and inspected it for deserters.[5]

The *Tecumseh* continued to harass American merchant ships at the mouth of the Detroit River. In July 1816, John R. Williams, the first mayor of the rechartered city of Detroit and one of Cass's business partners, was on a ship bound from Buffalo to Detroit. When the ship approached Fort Amherstburg, it was boarded by an officer and six men from the *Tecumseh* who searched the ship from stem to stern. Williams questioned the officer by "what authority he did these things?" The man replied, "by the order of his superior officer." Williams told him that his government would have to answer for the intrusion. "The officer replied his name was Henry Brooks and was not ashamed to own it," according to Williams. After the boarding party left, having found no deserters, Williams noticed a manned artillery piece at the fort aimed squarely at the ship. Astonished at the British arrogance, he wrote to Cass that he had "never felt more indignation at anything I ever witnessed before."[6] The incident marked the second time that Williams had major difficulties traveling between Detroit and Buffalo. In the early days of the War of 1812, his goods were lost when the U.S. Navy captured the British vessel that ferried his family to Buffalo.[7]

For Cass, this latest example of egregious conduct by the *Tecumseh* was the final straw. He considered the British actions a violation of American sovereignty that could not be ignored. The governor wrote an angry letter to Secretary of State Monroe describing the intolerable situation on the Detroit River. Cass emphasized the detail from Williams's description that the offending officer was acting at the behest of senior British officials. Cass warned Monroe that "from the tone and temper of public sentiment, if this practice is continued, I am confident it will terminate in blood."[8]

The British disagreed with Cass's assessment. William Baumgardt, the commanding naval officer at Amherstburg, suspected that Americans had designs on the island of Bois Blanc directly across from the fort. He faulted American ships for navigating the channel east of the island rather than sticking closer to the U.S. shoreline. Baumgardt considered the entire eastern part of the channel British territorial waters, which allowed Royal Navy vessels to board any and all ships. If the Americans insisted on forcing these provocations, the British would have no choice but to continue patrolling their waters. Despite this tough talk, neither Britain's naval officers nor its civilian authorities were eager for conflict with the U.S. on the lakes. The controversies in the summer of 1816 ultimately helped to propel both sides toward an acceptable accommodation.[9]

Disarmament of the lakes had been a recurring American desire. As early as 1794, President George Washington's administration had sought neutrality for the lakes. Secretary of State Edmund Randolph emphasized to American diplomat

John Jay in Britain: "In peace no troops to be kept within a limited distance to the lakes."[10] Leaders on both sides realized the potential danger and expense of keeping large military establishments in the border region. U.S. Secretary of State John W. Foster noted in 1892 that the framers of the 1817 agreement understood that maintaining naval forces on the lakes would be useless, dangerous, and expensive. "But upon the lakes only by disarmament could the menace of fresh conflicts on trivial occasion be averted from that quarter," Foster wrote. Without such an agreement, war was likely to reoccur.[11]

Once Adams initiated the discussion in 1816, the bulk of the work toward an agreement was completed by Monroe and Bagot. Indeed, if Monroe had not been elected president in November 1816, the final convention likely would have been known as the "Monroe-Bagot Treaty." On July 26, Bagot informed Monroe "that His Royal Highness the Prince Regent will cheerfully adopt, in the spirit of Mr. Adam's suggestion, any reasonable system which may contribute to the attainment of objects so desirable to both states."[12] On August 2, Monroe responded quickly with a detailed proposal for restricting naval vessels on the Great Lakes:

> I have the honor now to State that The President is willing, in the spirit of the peace which so happily exists between the two nations, and until the proposed arrangement shall be cancelled, in the manner herein after suggested, to confine the naval force to be maintained on the Lakes on each side, to the following vessels, that is, on Lake Ontario, to One Vessel not exceeding One Hundred Tons burthen and One Eighteen Pound Cannon, and on the Upper lakes to Two Vessels of like burthen and force, and on the Waters of Lake Champlain to One Vessel not exceeding the like burthen and force; and that all other armed vessels on those Lakes, shall be forthwith dismantled, and likewise that neither party shall build or arm any other vessel on the Shores of those Lakes.
>
> That the Naval Force thus retained by each party on the Lakes, shall be restricted in its duty, to the protection of its Revenue Laws, the transportation of troops, and goods, and to such other Services, as will in no respect interfere with the armed vessels of the other party.

Monroe's proposal established the framework and much of the exact language eventually adopted in the Rush-Bagot Agreement.[13]

Upon Monroe's election to the presidency, he turned the treaty negotiations over to his acting Secretary of State Richard Rush. (Rush held the position until Adams returned from Britain to become secretary of state in October 1817.) Rush's career in Washington was long and storied. He served as the attorney general of the U.S. under President James Madison, minister to Britain under President Monroe (after serving as the acting secretary of state), and secretary of the treasury under President John Quincy Adams; later, Rush finished his career as minister to France under President James K. Polk. Rush's counterpart, Charles Bagot, was slightly less experienced but no less capable. After serving as the British minister to Washington, he became an ambassador to the Netherlands and to Russia, and then the governor-general of Canada.

In 1817, Rush and Bagot quickly picked up the negotiations where Monroe and Bagot had left off. Diplomacy continued to center on the demilitarization of the Great Lakes and Lake Champlain. The two sides figured that fewer armed vessels would lessen the likelihood of an altercation. The final exchange of notes, signed on April 28 and 29, adopted Monroe's original proposal of limiting each country to one armed ship on lakes Ontario and Champlain and two armed ships on the rest of the Great Lakes combined.[14] Both sides recognized the agreement as instantly binding and began reducing their warships on the lakes. Monroe did not see a need to submit the treaty to the Senate for ratification and only did so the following year with prodding by Adams (who had become secretary of state). After waiting nearly a year, Monroe finally submitted the Rush-Bagot Agreement to the Senate for ratification on April 6, 1818. The Senate approved the treaty ten days later.[15]

The Rush-Bagot Agreement improved the overall security of the Detroit River region. With disarmament of the Great Lakes, there was much less chance that the British navy would interfere with American merchant ships. Although technically possible, since the agreement only barred interference "with the proper duties of the armed vessels of the other party," harassing unarmed vessels would have broken the spirit of the agreement.[16] The treaty also had an impact on British forts and outposts along the American-Canadian border. Indian groups in the Old Northwest had long viewed British military strength as a hedge against American expansion into the region. The reduction of British naval forces, however, illuminated the necessity for natives to reach some sort of accommodation with the Americans.[17]

In October 1818, the U.S. and Great Britain agreed to the Convention of 1818. The treaty resolved disputes regarding fisheries, boundaries, islands, and compensation for escaped slaves. The agreements on islands and boundaries were particularly important to preventing violations of the Rush-Bagot Treaty and reinforced harmonious relations with the British. The two agreements combined to address issues that the Treaty of Ghent left unresolved. Over time, there have been various tensions and issues that have necessitated further action and agreement from both countries. During the American Civil War, officials within the U.S. government, frustrated with Confederate raiders infiltrating the Union from Canada, pushed to rescind the Rush-Bagot Treaty. The problem reinforced the perception that the British government sympathized with the Confederacy, but the treaty survived the controversy. In 1908, Canada (now an independent country) and the U.S. decided to use modern surveying techniques to define a more accurate border. For borders along waterways, the two sides agreed to use buoys, monuments, and markers instead of the previous method of drawing lines on a chart. The formalized treaty created the International Boundary Commission with two commissioners from each country.[18]

The Rush-Bagot Treaty has had a profound effect on the shared histories of Canada and the United States. It laid a foundation for peace between the two nations, which subsequent agreements have helped to ensure. On April 13, 1967, the U.S. Senate designated April 28-29 as the "Rush-Bagot Agreement Days" in recognition of 150 years of peace along the border. Canadian Ambassador Albert Edgar Ritchie expressed his pleasure in a letter to New York Senator Jacob Javits, the bill's sponsor. The ambassador noted that during Cold War uncertainty, the world's oldest arms limitation treaty stood as an example to the rest of the world. Even with a myriad of new challenges, the same spirit of peace inaugurated in 1817 and commemorated in 1967 persists to this day.[19]

NOTES

1   For earlier treatments of diplomatic efforts over the Great Lakes after the War of 1812, see Alfred L. Burt, *The United States, Great Britain and British North America: From the Revolution to the Establishment of Peace after the War of 1812* (New Haven: Yale University Press, 1940), 373-98; Kenneth Bourne, *Britain and the Balance of Power in North America, 1815-1908* (Berkley: University of California Press, 1967), 3-32; and James M. Callahan, "Agreement of 1817 – Reduction of Naval Forces upon the American Lakes," in *Annual Report of the American Historical Association for the Year 1895* (Washington, DC: Government Printing Office, 1896), 367-92. For the Rush-Bagot Agreement, see "Exchange of Notes Relative to Naval Forces on the American Lakes," Yale Law School, "The Avalon Project: Documents in Law, History, and Diplomacy," http://avalon.law.yale.edu/19th_century/conv1817.asp (accessed April 16, 2012).

2   "Treaty of Ghent; 1814," "Avalon Project," http://avalon.law.yale.edu/19th_century/ghent.asp (accessed April 16, 2012). For the failure of the Treaty of Ghent to address issues in the Detroit River region, see Alan Taylor, *The Civil War of 1812: American Citizens, British Subjects, Irish Rebels, & Indian Allies* (New York: Knopf, 2010), 430-35.

3   "Convention of 1818 between the United States and Britain," "Avalon Project," http://avalon.law.yale.edu/19th_century/conv1818.asp (accessed April 16, 2012); "The Historic Treaties of the Boundary Commission," International Boundary Commission, www.internationalboundarycommission.org/history.html (accessed April 16, 2012).

4 Lewis Cass to the commanding officer of the British schooner *Tecumseh*, June 16, 1816, in *Niles' Weekly Register* (Baltimore), July 6, 1816. See also Burt, 378; Taylor, 433-35; and Willard C. Klunder, *Lewis Cass and the Politics of Moderation* (Kent, OH: Kent State University Press, 1996), 31.

5 David R. Moore, "Canada and the United States 1815-1830" (PhD diss., University of Chicago, 1910), 31.

6 John R. Williams to Lewis Cass, July 24, 1816, Folder 1816, Box 4, John R. Williams Papers, BHC. The letter is reprinted in *MPHC*, 32:521-22.

7 "War of 1812 – Williams Papers," in *MPHC*, 32:518-20. For Williams's attempt to get compensated for his losses, see the essay in this volume by Matthew R. Thick.

8 Lewis Cass to James Monroe, July 26, 1816, in *MPHC*, 16:502.

9 Moore, 31.

10 Randolph quoted in Callahan, 371.

11 John W. Foster, "Limitation of Armament on the Great Lakes," *Carnegie Endowment for International Peace*, pamphlet no. 2 (Washington, DC: Carnegie Endowment, 1914), 52.

12 Charles Bagot to James Monroe, July 26, 1816, "Avalon Project," http://avalon.law.yale.edu/19th_century/br1817l1.asp (accessed April 16, 2012).

13 James Monroe to Charles Bagot, August 2, 1816, "Avalon Project," http://avalon.law.yale.edu/19th_century/br1817l2.asp (accessed April 16, 2012).

14 "Exchange of Notes Relative to Naval Forces on the American Lakes."

15 Daniel Rice, "The Rush-Bagot Treaty (1818)," Rice on History, http://riceonhistory.wordpress.com/2011/09/30/the-rush-bagot-treaty-1818/ (accessed April 16, 2012).

16 "Exchange of Notes Relative to Naval Forces on the American Lakes."

17 Colin G. Calloway, "The End of an Era: British-Indian Relations in the Great Lakes Region after the War of 1812," *Michigan Historical Review* 12 (1986): 1-20.

18 Robin W. Winks, *The Civil War Years: Canada and the United States*, 4th ed. (Montreal: McGill-Queen's University Press, 1998); "Historic Treaties of the Boundary Commission."

19 *Rush-Bagot Agreement Days*, Public Law 90 PL 12, 90th Cong., 1st sess., Senate Report no. 185 (April 13, 1967), 1-3.

Frontier Nationalism: President Monroe Visits Detroit

Kaitlin Cooper

The inauguration of James Monroe as the fifth president of the United States on March 4, 1817, ushered in the "Era of Good Feelings," a period of growing American unity and national confidence. Monroe's tour of northeastern and northwestern states and territories between May and September 1817 marked the peak of those "good feelings." The phrase itself was coined during the tour by Boston's *Columbian Centinel*, after Monroe's visit to the city.[1] With the War of 1812 still a fresh memory, Monroe made strengthening military bases a priority in his inaugural address. His subsequent tour made good on the promise, for he reviewed troops at every post he visited. The tour also sought to unify America politically, as the Federalist party slowly collapsed in opposition to Monroe's Democratic-Republicans. The president's tour concentrated on New England, home to the last pockets of Federalist strength, as an act of both conciliation and assertiveness. Scholars often ignore that Detroit was also a stop on the tour: a surprising choice given that as a territory, Michigan could not directly improve Monroe's political fortunes. Yet, as a well-known frontier outpost, Detroit provided an ideal opportunity for Monroe to link his presidency with America's expanding territorial domain. Monroe's visit to Michigan Territory exemplified the deeper themes of nationalism and unification stressed in his early presidency. In return, the presidential visit allowed Detroit, a town on the fringes of American life, to feel part of the growing nation.[2]

Monroe began his tour on May 31, 1817, when he left Washington for Baltimore. He spent the early months of the tour traveling the northeastern states. Michigan Territory was one of his last stops, but it was there, on the western frontier, that Monroe's tour gained a significance that it could nowhere else. Unlike the eastern states, where the Federalist-Republican divide dominated politics, Michigan Territory had minimal party conflict. Monroe could thus focus his visit on broader nationalistic and unifying themes. The War of 1812 had given Detroit a certain prominence and occasional infamy for events ranging from General William Hull's surrender to Master Commandant Oliver Hazard Perry's epic victory in the Battle of Lake Erie. Monroe's visit could reaffirm that the exotic northwest region, founded by the French and recently occupied by the British, was a critical part of the United States.

Before 1817, no president had gone on an extended tour of the country since George Washington, and none had visited Detroit. For most residents, Monroe's tour would be their first contact with a president. It was fitting that Monroe was the first president to visit the region. As the acting secretary of war for much of the War of 1812, he understood Michigan Territory's plight. Monroe was the recipient of pleas from the Detroit River region, particularly from local leaders Lewis Cass and Augustus B. Woodward, seeking aid for the devastated area of Frenchtown. The battles at the River Raisin in January 1813 had left the local population destitute. Without so much as a nonvoting delegate in Congress, which territories received upon reaching a population of 5,000 free male inhabitants, Monroe was in many respects Michigan's closest thing to a representative. The presidential visit answered local demands for support after the tumultuous war years. The visit also deepened nationalist sentiment within the territory, which was lacking at times in the past due to its remoteness and heterogeneous population.[3]

On August 13, 1817, the president arrived in Detroit

by ship from Buffalo. He was met at the *Rivière aux Écorces* (Ecorse River) by a cavalcade, a procession of people on foot and horseback.[4] Because of its distance from urban centers, Detroit received news slowly. Aside from a notice in the *Detroit Gazette* on July 25 that the president would be visiting Detroit sometime in the next few weeks, there was no knowledge of his exact arrival date. With some expectation of his visit, local leaders and military officers made advance preparations to host Monroe. Yet the town waited to put together a formal committee to handle the event-planning until Monroe was only hours away. Major A. Edwards, Colonel Stephen Mack, Captain Antoine Dequindre, Captain James McCloskey, Solomon Sibley, Austin E. Wing, Charles Larned, and Oliver W. Miller were "appointed to make suitable arrangements for the President of the United States," according to the *Detroit Gazette*.[5]

The committee's preparations included writing an address to the president to read upon his arrival. The address conveyed local goals for the presidential visit:

> The local advantages of our country, the richness and almost inexhaustible fishery, an extensive fur trade, and other increasing inland commerce, were well calculated to attract the eye of enquiry, and invite emigration. . . . But, accustomed to the exercise of their elective franchise, the American People will rarely select a country as their residence, in the government of which they have neither voice or participation – in the form of which they have neither will or control. A government resulting not from common will but common necessity. A law of Congress, empowering the citizens of our territory to enter upon the representative grade of government, contemplated by the ordinance of '87, the establishment of permanent national roads, and an exposure of our valuable public lands in the market would be productive of immediate and beneficial results to our territory. Our country would then become a welcome resort for Eastern enterprise and industry, and a permanent barrier against savage rapacity and foreign intrigue.[6]

The address betrayed the insecurity that Detroiters felt about their place in the nation. The town's position would be secured only if it could become a viable settlement option for easterners. Despite abundant resources, Detroit, and Michigan Territory as a whole, was not seen as an attractive destination because of its distance from eastern population centers, lack of representative government, and reputation as a corrupt and war-torn outpost. Therefore, locals wanted Michigan to progress in the stages toward statehood. Residents also viewed the lack of roads and available lands for sale as deterrents for potential settlers. Detroit might have welcomed Monroe as a hero, but the town also sought action on a number of issues inhibiting its growth.

The day after he arrived, Monroe attended to reviewing the troops at Fort Detroit. The presidential visit offered the fort a chance for redemption. In August 1812, Monroe had referred to Hull's surrender as "the disaster at Detroit," which "has fix'd an impression on the national character which must be removed."[7] Territorial Governor Lewis Cass, in a letter to Solomon Sibley, expressed hopes that the presidential review of the troops would be highly publicized.[8] The event offered the chance to erase memories of the war – not only locally, but nationally. Based on reports of the presidential review, it seems to have lived up to the expectations of Cass and other territorial leaders. According to the *Detroit Gazette*, "The appearance of the troops and the manner in which they performed several handsome manoeuvres reflect much honor upon Col. Smith and the officers of his command."[9]

The pomp and circumstance of the military review was followed by a ceremony for a local hero, General Alexander Macomb. The event offered another opportunity for Detroit to demonstrate its contributions to the larger nation. Born in Detroit in 1782, Macomb lived in the town until leaving at age 16 to join the New York militia. He served as a general in the War of 1812 and became a national celebrity for repulsing a much larger British army – by some estimates more than 10,000 strong, the largest ever to invade the U.S. – at the Battle of Plattsburg in September 1814. By 1828, Macomb would become the commanding general of the U.S. Army. The ceremony for him included the presentation of an engraved sword by Governor Cass, as voted by the New York legislature. President Monroe's attendance added to the prestige of the event and allowed local leaders to further recast Detroit's image: no longer the site of national humiliation, but the hometown of one of America's great military leaders.[10]

Monroe's visit included multiple balls and formal evening events. The most notable took place on the third day, August 15. The evening began with a dinner at Governor Cass's home and then continued with a ball at the Steamboat Hotel, owned by Benjamin Woodworth. At the ball, Detroit's Board of Trustees and President Monroe exchanged speeches, which celebrated Detroit's prominent future role in the Union. The president put Detroit's growth into a larger context:

> Your [Detroit's] establishment was of necessity, in its origin, colonial; but on a new principle . . . the national government promotes your growth, and in so doing, from the peculiar felicity of our system, promotes the growth and strength of the nation. At a period . . . you will become a member of the union. . . . In the interim, the legislative body, composed of the representatives of a free people, your brethren, will always be ready to extend a just and proper remedy to any inconvenience to which you may be exposed.[11]

A few days earlier, the welcoming committee had expressed frustration with the obstacles, particularly the lack of representation and adequate transportation, which kept Michigan Territory isolated from the rest of the nation. Either intentionally or by coincidence, Monroe responded by emphasizing the importance of the territory and reassuring inhabitants that it shared in the nation's growth and vice-versa. For a frontier town, particularly with Detroit's recent past, Monroe's message was significant. The president spoke the words that his hosts wanted to hear.

Monroe reinforced his words with action. Fulfilling his

promise to make the national government more responsive to local needs, Monroe allowed time to meet directly with residents. They eagerly took him up on the offer. Two concerns dominated the personal meetings: the need for a road connecting Detroit to Ohio through the area then known as the Black Swamp and the opening of more land for sale in the region. Each of the issues was related to development and offered Monroe the most direct opportunity for solving local problems. In eastern cities, there were multiple levels of representation and well-established connections to the national government. Michigan Territory was still forging such connections, which meant that Monroe embodied the government as a whole.[12]

There is limited information indicating whether Monroe had the same positive reaction to the townspeople as they had to him. On the fourth day of his stay, the president penned a short letter, which states little about Detroit. Instead, the note describes Monroe's plans for leaving and moving onward to Ohio:

> I arrived here three days since after a very favorable passage over the Lake. I shall set out for Sandusky the day after tomorrow, & proceed thence, thro' Ohio, by Pittsburgh, & the Cumberland road, to Washington. I should have gone today, but it is necessary to send the means of transportation before us, to meet us there, as we shall travel abt. 80 miles thro' the wilderness, & rely only on what is to be forwarded from this place. Communicate this to Mr. Crawford & Mr. Graham, as it will not be in my power to write them by this mail.
>
> With very sincere regards yours, James Monroe[13]

The letter reflects the extensive travel preparations necessary in the early nineteenth century. Without an adequate road to Ohio, for which Detroit's residents lobbied, Monroe had to sail south across Lake Erie to Sandusky Bay. From there, he planned a more arduous return east, by land through Ohio and Pennsylvania, than his journey west across Lake Erie from Buffalo. In total, he spent six days in Michigan Territory, comparable to other stops on his tour. When he left on August 18, he could rest satisfied that his visit had brought encouragement to its residents and proved his commitment to unifying the entire country.

The visit did not receive such positive reviews in the East. The disdain that easterners had for the frontier was evident in a letter sent to William Woodbridge, the Detroit officer of customs, shortly after Monroe's departure:

> We have not heard that the President had reached Detroit but soon expect to hear of much pomp, the erection of triumphant arches, [illegible] crowns, etc. & I think If I have not heretofore been mistaken in Mr. Monroe, he will be glad when he gets into Virginia where he will be treated like a good private citizen. The people at the Northward appear to think it a wonderful condensension on the part of Mr. Monroe to come so low as to mix with the sovereign people.[14]

The letter lampooned the elaborate preparations that a place like Detroit made for a presidential visit. Such a production appeared silly and almost pathetic in the eyes of an easterner. In 1818, a published narrative of Monroe's tour by Samuel Waldo Putnam was released. Putnam, too, expressed condescension toward Detroit by implying that Monroe resented visiting the frontier outpost: "The President left this interesting section of our country [Buffalo] for *Detroit*, with feelings not to be described."[15] The statement likely says more about Putnam's sentiments than it does about Monroe's. Before summarizing the president's activities in Detroit, the narrative recounts the fort's poor performance in the War of 1812, mostly focusing on Hull's surrender. Putnam describes the capitulation as "humiliating," "excruciating in the extreme," and "a suffering . . . more poignant than death and torture." Evidently, Monroe's visit to Detroit and the accompanying public relations campaign by local residents did not fully reverse the town's national reputation.[16]

The people of Michigan Territory, however, still looked favorably upon the president's visit. They could point to several positive developments in the immediate period after the tour. Of the residents' primary concerns, the biggest success was having more property for sale. Within a year of Monroe's visit, there was a government land office in Detroit, and a large amount of property in the area soon went on the market.[17] The other main concern, a road to Ohio through the Black Swamp, took much longer. In November 1817, Cass wrote to acting Secretary of War George Graham to inquire about the road and referenced the president's visit: "It [the request] is forwarded in consequence of an intimation, which fell from the President during his tour through this country."[18] Cass's attempt was in vain. The construction of a road through the Black Swamp was not undertaken in any serious way until nearly thirty-five years after Monroe's trip to Detroit. Although the lack of action upset residents, the development of steamboats helped to ease the transportation problem. On August 27, 1818, a little more than a year after the president's visit, *Walk-in-the-Water* became the first steamboat to operate on the upper Great Lakes. Steamboats dramatically improved travel to and from the frontier town in a way that a road could not.[19]

The final major local concern underlying President's Monroe's visit was Michigan Territory's lack of national political representation. It took twenty years after Monroe's encouraging tour for Michigan to become a state. As president, though, there was nothing Monroe could have done directly to assist in the process of reaching statehood. The guidelines for that process were set forth in the Northwest Ordinance of 1787. After being ruled by a governor and judges appointed by Congress, a territory could form a legislature after it had 5,000 free male inhabitants, and the legislature could send a nonvoting delegate to Congress. Finally, after reaching a population of 60,000, a territory could write a constitution and apply to Congress for statehood. In 1818, Michigan reached the second stage on the road to statehood, and William Woodbridge served as its first delegate in Congress the following year. Although there is no evidence that Monroe lobbied for Michigan Territory to reach delegate status, his visit and speech gave residents important assurances of their future role in the Union.

A final legacy of Monroe's visit is the city and county named after him: Monroe, Michigan. Before changing its name in 1824, the community was known as Frenchtown, after the French settlers who migrated south from Detroit to live near the River Raisin in the 1780s. The combination of Monroe's support for the community during the War of 1812 and his visit to the region in 1817 led residents to apply for the name change. The national government rejected the request several times before finally agreeing. On May 1, 1824, John McLean, the postmaster general of the United States, explained the rejection to Charles Noble, the postmaster of Frenchtown: "Your place has been so long known by the name of Frenchtown that it appears to me a change is not advisable at present, particularly as the name which you propose [Monroe] is already applied to nearly 20 post offices."[20] The residents of Frenchtown persisted. In July 1824, their efforts were finally rewarded, as McLean delivered the good news: "I have changed the name of your office on the books of this Department from French town to that of Monroe in Michigan Territory."[21] The official name change took place on July 24, 1824, permanently linking the town on the River Raisin with the fifth president of the United States.[22]

Monroe's visit to Detroit in 1817 was a turning point for connecting the region to the nation. Despite eastern critiques, the town demonstrated that it was worthy of hosting the country's leader. From the president's review of the troops at the fort to the ceremony honoring General Macomb, residents could take pride in the region's contributions to the nation. The visit also led to concrete accomplishments, particularly the opening of a government land office in Michigan Territory. But the most significant effect was symbolic. For Monroe, journeying to the frontier demonstrated his commitment to national unity without the distraction of party politics. For local residents, the visit provided a chance to envision their region's future place in the Union.

NOTES

1 George Dangerfield, *The Awakening of American Nationalism, 1815-1828* (New York: Harper & Row, 1965), 35.

2 For Monroe's full 1817 tour, see S.A. Mitchell and H. Ames, *A Narrative of a Tour of Observation, Made during the Summer of 1817* (Philadelphia: Clark & Raser, 1818); and Samuel P. Waldo, *The Tour of James Monroe, President of the United States, in the Year 1817* (Hartford: F.D. Bolles & Co., 1818). For an overview of events in Detroit, see Henry D. Brown, *Detroit Entertains a President* (Detroit: Wayne University Press, 1954). For Monroe's presidency, see Noble E. Cunningham, *The Presidency of James Monroe* (Lawrence: University Press of Kansas, 1966); and Harry Ammon, *James Monroe: The Quest for National Identity* (New York: McGraw-Hill, 1971).

3 For the battles at the River Raisin and their aftermath, see Ralph Naveaux, *Invaded on All Sides: The Story of Michigan's Greatest Battlefield Scene of the Engagements at Frenchtown and the River Raisin in the War of 1812* (Marceline, MO: Walsworth, 2008); Dennis M. Au, *War on the Raisin: A Narrative Account of the War of 1812 in the River Raisin Settlement, Michigan Territory* (Monroe, MI: Monroe County Historical Commission, 1981); and the essays in this volume by Carly Campbell, Scott A. Jankowski, and Timothy Marks.

4 Diary of John Montieth, August 13, 1817, D5:1808-1819, p. 34, John Montieth Papers, BHC.

5 "Arrival of the President," *Detroit Gazette*, August 16, 1817.

6 "Arrival of the President."

7 James Monroe to [?], August 30, 1812, Folder 1, James Monroe Papers, BHC.

8 Lewis Cass to Solomon Sibley, August 1817, Box 43, Solomon Sibley Papers, BHC.

9 "Arrival of the President."

10 "Arrival of the President"; Brown, 11-12. Donald R. Hickey argues that Macomb's exploits at the Battle of Plattsburg have been exaggerated (*Don't Give Up the Ship! Myths of the War of 1812* [Urbana: University of Illinois Press, 2006], 75-77). The point is well taken, but does not change the fact of Macomb's fame at the time.

11 Mitchell and Ames, 203. For the Steamboat Hotel, see the essay in this volume by Kristen Harrell.

12 "Arrival of the President."

13 James Monroe Letter to [?], August 16, 1817, Monroe Papers.

14 [?] to William Woodbridge, August 29, 1817, Box 14, p. 5, William Woodbridge Papers, BHC.

15 Waldo, 234.

16 Waldo, 235.

17 Brown, 15-16.

18 Lewis Cass to George Graham, November 27, 1817, Box 3, Lewis Cass Papers, BHC.

19 Arthur M. Woodford, *This Is Detroit, 1701-2001* (Detroit: Wayne State University Press, 2001), 49-50.

20 John McLean to Charles Noble, May 1, 1824, Box 1, Charles Noble Correspondence Collection, Monroe County Historical Museum Archives, Monroe, MI.

21 John McLean to Charles Noble, July 1, 1824, Box 1, Charles Noble Correspondence Collection.

22 Walter Romig, *Michigan Place Names: The History of the Founding and the Naming of More Than Five Thousand Past and Present Michigan Communities* (Detroit: Wayne State University Press, 1986), 338.

Portrait of John R. Williams
Artist unknown, c. 1830. Oil on canvas. Detroit Historical Society Collection.

"I have been a great looser":
John R. Williams and the War of 1812
Matthew R. Thick

In April 1812, prominent Detroit merchant John R. Williams received a letter telling him to be wary of a potential Indian uprising near Detroit. The letter was from an acquaintance of his who lived near Fort Defiance, Ohio: "From what I have seen in this place of the few Indians that have been here since my arrival I have noticed a very hostile disposition & threatening temper towards us[.] [W]e have I sincerely believe something serious to apprehend especially in the event of War with England [and] every disposition is making to insure the capture of this place by the United forces of The English & Savages." Williams's friend had evidence to support his claim: a chilling tale of murder. An Indian man was recently seen roaming house to house, asking for food and water. Those who refused were found dead the next morning, "killed with an axe or a tomahawk."[1] Williams reacted to the news by arming the local militia with muskets, powder, and ball from his own stores, and he joined the local artillery regiment. He fed and paid men with his own money under the presumption that the United States government would compensate him. Once Detroit was overrun by British forces and their Indian allies soon after the War of 1812 erupted, Williams moved himself, his family, and his store to the relative safety of Albany, New York, where his fight for reimbursement began.[2]

Born in 1785, Williams grew to become an influential figure in early nineteenth-century Detroit. He was a successful merchant and held several public positions, including justice of the peace, town clerk of Hamtramck, and trustee of the town of Detroit. In about 1807, Williams added an "R" to his name to distinguish himself from another Detroiter named John Williams – a sign he cared about his reputation. After the war, John R. became the city of Detroit's first mayor under its amended charter of 1824. He was educated, fluent in French and English, and often taught local children at an individual rate of $1 per month. Williams's financial success most likely stemmed from his familial ties with the Campaus, other well-established merchants in Detroit. His father, Thomas Williams, was also notable in the region, a staunch loyalist during the American revolutionary era when Detroit was under British control. In 1804, John R. married Mary Mott, and the couple had ten children together.[3]

The War of 1812 touched off a series of misfortunes for Williams. When he decided to move to Albany, his family packed household items into two large trunks and boarded the British schooner *Caledonia*, which sailed under a flag of truce. Before leaving Detroit, Williams wrote to British Colonel Henry Procter, asking for safe passage on the Great Lakes and received a scribbled reply: "It is impossible at this time to assure you any specific conveyance, but no Objections will be made to your Embarking in a private vessel[.]"[4] The Williams family arrived at Buffalo via Lake Erie and disembarked for Albany. Williams had plans for the family's trunks to be delivered, but the U.S. Navy soon took the *Caledonia* at Buffalo. The navy treated the schooner as an enemy prize because it had been used in the earlier capture of General William Hull's papers on the Detroit River. During the transfer of the *Caledonia* to the Americans, Williams's goods were either lost or stolen. This misfortune led Williams to petition Congress for compensation.[5]

The effort lasted for years. Williams's quest shines a light on the character and drive that made him one of Detroit's most successful early leaders. Although mostly ignored by scholars,

Williams's hardships reveal several larger challenges that residents of Michigan Territory faced before statehood. First, his struggle shows that the costs of war were not limited to casualty lists and land seizures. The war affected all facets of civilian life, including individual finances. Williams's experience also illustrates the difficulties one might have endured by not having sufficient representation in Congress. Michigan was still a territory without the population necessary (5,000 free male inhabitants) to even have a nonvoting delegate in Congress. Without his own representative, Williams petitioned representatives from New York while living in Albany and upon returning to Detroit. Despite his political connections, receiving compensation from the government was no easy task. Williams worked every channel at his disposal to accomplish his goal of being repaid for the losses he incurred during the war. When his claims were denied, he regrouped and tried another avenue. Williams was not alone in this fight. There were many other people in the Detroit River region in similar situations; their property was destroyed or confiscated, and they wished for the government to repay them.[6]

While living in New York between September 1812 and the summer of 1814, Williams wrote letters to government officials, including Representative John Lovett, Senator Obadiah German, both of New York, and Richard Rush, then comptroller of the U.S. Treasury. Williams did not write to each political figure at once; rather, he would normally write to one individual until that person absolved himself of any responsibility for the merchant's losses. After being denied, Williams then typically wrote one final letter prompting the official to pass his case onto another individual. For example, on May 31, 1813, he implored Senator German: "Should you think best to submit my claim to the House of Representatives, I beg you Sir, to leave the papers with the Hon.ble John Lovett."[7] Williams's desire was twofold: compensation for property lost on the *Caledonia* and forgiveness of interest payments on a land grant for territory in Detroit that was being held by the British. Along with his application was an itemized list of his losses, down to two tablespoons of pepper. This detail was indicative of Williams's nature. He was incredibly meticulous and organized, no doubt a reason for his success in business.[8]

As instructed, Senator German passed Williams's claim to Representative Lovett. In June 1813, Lovett wrote to Williams:

> Sir, without having it in my power to advise you of any certain beneficial interest secured by your two petitions forwarded to Congress, it may, nevertheless, be gratifying to you to know the disposition which has been made of them, and the probable course they may take. They were, yesterday, presented in the House of Representatives . . . [although] I think there is no probability that [they] will be acted upon at the present.[9]

The news did not gratify Williams. He replied with a sixteen-page letter of grievance addressed to Lovett. Williams probably thought that Lovett failed to completely understand his situation, especially since he was from Michigan Territory, not New York. In the lengthy letter, Williams traced events that had transpired well before the war, accusing the territory's leadership of being ineffective, beginning with Governor Hull and Judge Augustus B. Woodward. Williams closed by condemning the British occupation of Detroit. He had nowhere else to turn; Lovett *had* to help.[10]

Meanwhile, Williams incurred even more losses. After he received news from a friend that Detroit had been liberated in September 1813, he decided to reopen his store. It took some time, but Williams gathered goods to be sent to Detroit from Buffalo. In December, British forces, infuriated over the burning of York (today Toronto) the previous spring, marched on Buffalo and burned every structure but one. Williams's goods were either destroyed or plundered. Soon afterward, he added this event to his original petition to Congress, claiming that it was the responsibility of the government to protect the property of its citizenry. He was so upset that he journeyed to Washington to reiterate his claims in person. As with his letters, government officials passed responsibility for his case from one person to the next.[11]

The amount Williams petitioned for constantly grew. His first claim, for the items lost on the *Caledonia*, was for $1,515. The exact amount that Williams requested for the interest on his land grants in Detroit is unclear from historical records, but he never dropped the claim. He also eventually added the cost of food and salaries for the companies of territorial militia that he supported immediately before the war. Williams further claimed that he should be repaid for property that American soldiers had used, such as his house, stoves, and horses, while they camped at Detroit. The loss of goods at Buffalo, Williams calculated, amounted to $1,600. In total, he argued that the U.S. government owed him more than $12,000, lamenting, "I have been a great looser by the events of the late war."[12]

Williams was still wealthy. He might have been a "great looser," but the war had not made him destitute like so many others in the Detroit River region. Principle, not financial gain, was his overriding motivation in seeking compensation. Although he privately estimated his losses at $12,000, Williams asked for only a portion of it: $1,600 for his losses at Buffalo, $1,515 for his losses on the *Caledonia*, forgiveness of interest from his Detroit land debts, and several hundred dollars that he had used to supply the militia. Unlike other Detroiters, Williams did not starve or lack shelter. From 1814 to 1820, his account in the Bank of Albany consistently hovered in the $60,000 range. His petitions showed that he was driven to fight for what he considered a just cause: "It is the purpose of a government to protect its Citizens." And despite the fact that one official after another turned down his requests, he did not give up.[13]

Williams petitioned Congress from 1812 to at least the early 1820s. One of the reasons why he kept up the fight for so long was that his claims were pushed aside or moved from one congressional committee to another. As hearings on his claims dragged on, some of the players changed. After elections, he had to begin anew. Also, Williams occasionally petitioned the wrong department. For example, in February 1814, the U.S. Committee on Claims declined his petition, explaining that his losses were an act of war and outside the committee's jurisdiction. Therefore, Williams petitioned higher government authorities, including Secretary of War William Crawford.[14]

After the war, Williams reentered politics. His struggles with congressmen outside of Michigan likely contributed to his rallying for the territory to have representation. In 1818, he signed Michigan's successful application for elevated territorial status, which led to an election of a nonvoting delegate to Congress. Williams made a bid for this position but fell short to William Woodbridge, who held multiple territorial, state, and national offices over a long career. In 1817, territorial Governor Lewis Cass appointed Williams as associate justice for Wayne County, a position he initially declined but ultimately accepted due to Cass's insistence. Williams stated that he was not qualified to be a judge and attempted to resign repeatedly. Cass refused each request. All the while, Williams continued to have his compensation claims rejected.[15]

His petitions finally began to subside in the 1820s. For all his work, Williams received a mere $10 in 1815 for the use of his stove during the war. As for his larger claims, it is not clear if he was ever paid. Either way, Williams displayed the tenacity evident in all his affairs. For more than ten years, he wrote consistently to a multitude of politicians. Although he often got the run-around, it did not stop him from pursuing all possible options. Williams was committed to principle in business and politics and, for this reason, did not give up easily. The same drive and motivation fueled his political career, as he was later noted for speaking out against government corruption. Despite losing the election for territorial delegate to Congress, Williams was later elected for several, nonconsecutive terms as mayor of Detroit, his last in 1846. He also served as president of the Bank of Michigan, having first been elected in 1818 and then reelected several times.

In 1829, he was appointed major-general of the Michigan militia. The following year, Williams worked to bring a printing press to Detroit. His efforts made possible the launch of the *Democratic Free Press and Michigan Intelligencer*, the forerunner of the *Detroit Free Press*. Williams's failure to be compensated for his losses incurred during the War of 1812 hardly deterred him from success in other areas of his life – a life grounded in principle.[16]

NOTES

1 [?] to John R. Williams, April 28, 1812, Folder 1812, Box 3, John R. Williams Papers, BHC.

2 John R. Williams to Richard Rush, March 22, 1813, Folder 1813, Box 3, Williams Papers.

3 M. Gertrude Ann Malloy, "Public Activities of John R. Williams, 1818-1830" (master's thesis, University of Detroit, 1943); John R. Williams, "Sketch of the Life of General John R. Williams," in *MPHC*, 29:491-96 (The author of this work is not the main figure of this essay; it was most likely authored by his grandson in the 1890s); Receipt for Teaching Services, Folder 1812, Box 3, Williams Papers. There is little biographical material on Williams. Malloy's thesis is the most extensive, providing some background on his life. Most sources that mention Williams deal only with his time as mayor, his influence on the Bank of Michigan, and his role in the writing of Detroit's City Charter. See Clarence M. Burton, *History of Detroit: 1780 to 1850: Financial and Commercial* (Detroit: Burton, 1917); and *City of Detroit*.

4 Henry Procter to John R. Williams, September 7, 1812, Folder 1812, Box 3, Williams Papers.

5 John R. Williams to John Lovett, November 22, 1813, Folder 1813, Box 3, Williams Papers. Williams's description of his losses and other correspondence pertaining to his compensation claim are reprinted in "War of 1812 – Williams Papers," in *MPHC*, 32:518-20. For the earlier capture of Governor William Hull's papers on the Detroit River, see the essay in this volume by Kerri Jansen.

6 The United States Committee on Claims reviewed applications for the war for more than a half-century, from 1812 to 1870. For claims in the Detroit River region, see Ralph Naveaux, *Invaded on All Sides: The Story of Michigan's Greatest Battlefield Scene of the Engagements at Frenchtown and the River Raisin in the War of 1812* (Marceline, MO: Walsworth, 2008); and the essays in this volume by Sharon Tevis Finch, Justin Wargo, and Meghan McGowan.

7 John R. Williams to Obadiah German, May 31, 1813, Folder 1813, Box 3, Williams Papers.

8 Williams to Lovett, November 22, 1813.

9 John Lovett to John R. Williams, June 9, 1813, Folder 1813, Box 3, Williams Papers.

10 Williams to Lovett, November 22, 1813.

11 John R. Williams to John Lovett, not dated; John Lovett to John R. Williams, December 17, 1814, Folder 1814, Box 4, Williams Papers. For British attacks on Buffalo, see Alan Taylor, *The Civil War of 1812: American Citizens, British Subjects, Irish Rebels, & Indian Allies* (New York: Knopf, 2010), 255-58.

12 John R. Williams to Richard Lee, October 22, 1817, Folder 1817 (July-Dec); John R. Williams, "Petition for the Goods that Were Lost," not dated, Folder 1818 (Nov-Dec); John R. Williams to Henry Baldwin, not dated, Folder 1818 (Jan-March), Box 5, Williams Papers (quote).

13 Williams to German, May 31, 1813 (quote); Williams to Lee, October 22, 1817; Williams, "Petition for the Goods that Were Lost."

14 Lovett to Williams, June 9, 1813; John R. Williams to William Crawford, no date, Folder 1816, Box 4, Williams Papers. Crawford served as secretary of war between August 1815 and October 1816.

15 Malloy, 14, 21; John R. Williams to Lewis Cass, January 12, 1817, Folder 1817 (Jan-June), Box 5, Williams Papers. In July 1816, Williams also faced harassment by a British naval vessel while aboard a merchant ship on the Detroit River. See the essay in this volume by James M. Shuryan.

16 Receipt of Payment of $10, no date, Folder 1815, Box 4, Williams Papers; Williams, "Sketch of the Life"; Williams to German, May 31, 1813. Williams died on October 20, 1854.

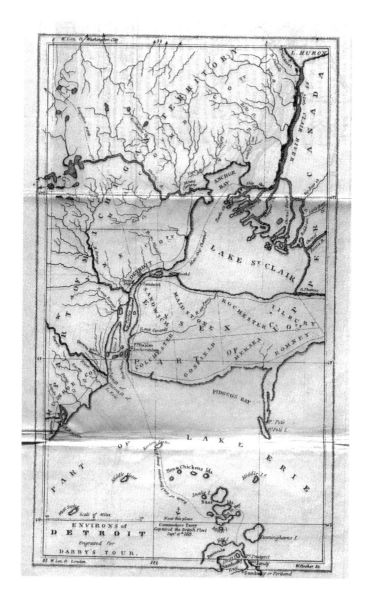

Environs of Detroit Engraved for Darby's Tour

Engraving by William Hooker. Published in William A. Darby, *A Tour from the City of New York to Detroit, in the Michigan Territory* (New York: Kirk & Mercein, 1819), facing 185.

Recasting Michigan's Image: The Darby Treatise
Charles Wilson Goode

Michigan languished for more than three decades in territorial status, the longest such term east of the Mississippi River. Geographically isolated, scorned in eastern circles, captured and ravaged during the War of 1812, the territory was not a choice destination for migrants. It long suffered from adverse publicity. In 1786, James Monroe wrote to Thomas Jefferson that the lands of the upper lakes "will not have a single bush on them, for ages" and predicted that the region "will perhaps never contain a sufficient number of Inhabitants to entitle them to membership in the confederacy."[1] Detroit expatriate John Gentle delivered a scathing assessment of the territory's political climate in 1807. In 1812, geographer Jedidiah Morse painted a desolate picture of the territory's edaphic potential. Surveyor General Edward Tiffin followed in 1815 by reporting that the land was not "worth the expenses of surveying it." He recommended that the United States "abandon the country," citing "extensive marshes . . . swamps beyond description . . . extreme sterility and barrenness of soil."[2]

In short, Michigan had image problems. Monroe's visit as president in 1817 served to enhance that image slightly, but Detroit's population remained appreciably unchanged as of 1819. Several authors identify the Erie Canal as instrumental in Michigan's advancements of the 1820s and 1830s, but it was not completed until 1825, five years after territorial land had begun to sell at a brisk pace. In an agrarian society, technological advancement and executive recognition were not sufficient to allay suspicion of infertile soils. Michigan needed a positive estimation of its potential from a learned and trusted source – someone with a scientific background, someone of solid national repute, someone without ulterior social or commercial interests. Someone like William Darby.[3]

When Darby's *A Tour from the City of New York to Detroit, in the Michigan Territory* was released in early 1819, the geographer's influence was at its peak. His treatise, map, and booklet on Louisiana warranted multiple printings, and the sprawling 1818 *Emigrant's Guide to the Western and Southwestern States and Territories* also fared well, commercially and critically. Concurrently, Darby entrenched himself in eastern social, professional, governmental, and commercial networks. Newspapers reviewed his works, published his letters, and provided information on his extensive public lectures. The populous East was obsessed with western migration, but nineteenth-century travelogues were rife with hucksterism, boosterism, and romantic invention. A positive report from a knowledgeable and dispassionate source could prove a boon to a frontier locale. Michigan needed just that – and Darby delivered, dispelling the myth of soil infertility, discounting climatic and health concerns, and describing a future in which Michigan would occupy the geographic center, not the fringe.[4]

Darby's 1818 trip to Detroit had a somewhat impulsive inception. The surveyor, part of a boundary-water expedition associated with the impending Rush-Bagot Treaty, grew weary of the tedious pace of the project, and set out for Detroit on his own. Darby kept a journal with assessments and predictions that were grounded in scientific observation, and he held no apparent attachment to Michigan Territory. Therefore, the appeal of Darby's report was twofold: It was meticulously constructed and free of selfish interest. In addition to mundane scientific observations – geography, geology, topography, limnology, and biology – Darby expounded on history, Indian relations, land markets, commerce, manufacturing, settlements, silviculture and lumbering, mining and metals, infrastructure development, agricultural science and production, transportation and communication, public opinion, safety, and American culture. Such observances emphasized connections between human conditions and the natural world. For instance, Darby challenged folk wisdom concerning inferred correlations between indigenous flora and the agricultural potential of native soils. Specifically, he dismissed the notion that a prevalence of conifers precluded substantial agricultural production. Rather, he asserted that the improving discipline of agronomics was developing formulas that facilitated "good husbandry." The northwest frontier was ripe for agricultural development.[5]

The large number of topics covered in Darby's treatise divided into three major categories: physical science, biological science, and social science. While his notes on the first domain were the most copious, the combination of disciplines provided a rich, multifaceted view of Michigan Territory. Reporting on the region's physiography fell into two subcategories, terrestrial and aquatic, each of which included a vast array of inventory. Darby's endorsement of Michigan's soil quality and its general suitability for farming provided sanction critical to potential migrants. His similarly optimistic evaluation of the territory's water quality and availability completed the agricultural equation – great lakes indeed.[6]

Darby limited his assessment of the biota of the Great Lakes region mainly to flora and the potential for its commercial development. His sole mention of fauna concerns a nonindigenous species: sheep. In a somewhat parenthetical reference, which might better be placed in the category of culture rather than biology, Darby identified sheep as an example of a resource that might help release Americans from their widespread allegiance to foreign-produced goods. He cited the high cost of raw materials as a reason for consumer Europhilia. Why not grow your own wool, thereby lowering that commodity's price and enhancing the appeal of a competing domestic product? Michigan's ample supply of grazing land and fresh water made the recipe simple – just add shears. Darby's accounts of the region's flora had greater potential impact. One botanical component of Michigan's indigenous ecosystem was unmistakable, even from a distance: forests. If wool production could be framed as a means to help wean Americans from their dedication to British goods, then development of timber, lumber, construction, and woodworking industries presented an even better opportunity to bolster the domestic economy. Darby's work included assessments of the territory's many navigable inland waterways and their logistical value to lumbering. Rivers with sufficient depth and current were perfect delivery venues, as they could be used to float log rafts to mills. Darby was also not shy about highlighting the ecological ramifications of the then-prevalent method of clear-cutting. Railing against the "imprudent" excesses of the American timber industry, he characterized clear-cutting as unnecessary and unscientific.

On other topics, Darby's socio-cultural views were no less pointed. He suggested that following the colonial and revolutionary eras, a third stage of America's cultural evolution was in order – a more unified, less parochial U.S. identity, manifested by economic growth, diversity, and self-sufficiency, and made possible by expanded trade and communication. Prior to the advent of the railroads, that sort of cultural cross-pollination was most feasible via nautical transportation. Darby stated that Michigan was ideally located to participate in such a paradigm shift, but in order to take advantage of its geographic blessings, the territory would need to develop economically in areas other than fur. Darby identified Michigan's climatic, edaphic, and aquatic qualities as the ideal elements for such development. All that was lacking was an adequate supply of industrious inhabitants. By the time Darby's Michigan treatise was published, Ohio, Indiana, and Illinois had achieved statehood.

The westward wave of immigration was bypassing Michigan, due to the territory's inaccessibility and broadly held misapprehensions regarding its desirability as a destination. Michigan was perceived as remote, cold, dangerous, and agriculturally barren. While Darby's impartial look at the territory was not intended to promote economic development, his analysis surely helped to overcome trepidation among easterners.

Darby addressed misinformation on Michigan's weather, asserting that Detroit's leeward location created a climate more temperate than Buffalo's. Since the towns share a similar latitude, the author's point was clear: A leeward site results in lesser fluctuations in weather than a windward or land-locked location. Darby cautiously extended his assurance only as far north as Fort Gratiot (today Port Huron, Michigan), but the message was encouraging. The climate of the lower peninsula's southeast quadrant was conducive to settlement and its growing season long enough for agricultural success. Moreover, the geographer's enthusiastic yet qualified evaluation of Michigan's soil quality served to refute the effects of Tiffin's bleak 1815 assessment, which concluded, "there would not be more than one acre out of a hundred, if there would be one out of a thousand that would in any case admit of cultivation."[7] While acknowledging the region's "varied" soils, and conceding that some portions of Michigan's flat terrain would be "subject to immersion in wet seasons," Darby concluded that the territory's soil characteristics were well-suited for grain and fruit production.[8]

The promise of a moderate, healthy climate and an abundance of fertile soils enhanced Michigan's attractiveness to potential settlers. Yet Darby also noted that the territory was rightly seen as sparsely populated place, geographically and culturally isolated from the rest of the U.S. His journals continually interweave observations on the geophysical characteristics of the upper lakes with notes on the region's social, cultural, and economic conditions. Much of Darby's analysis of frontier life entailed mundane matters, such as harbor suitability, roads, bridges, wharves, canals, mills, navigability, military works, settlement siting, and technology. Beyond his analysis of infrastructure, Darby played the role of social scientist by describing frontier demography, ethnography, history, trades, industries, artisans, shops, criminal justice systems, politics, schools, and literacy. The broad range of topics complemented his environmental inventory. The result was a holistic assessment of frontier life, which often countered (and occasionally reinforced) eastern perceptions of circumstances in the Old Northwest.

Darby most indulged eastern concerns by focusing on the security of the region. His journey included stops in Upper Canada, which he found tranquil. Darby saw Canada as a valuable trading partner, rather than a military adversary. He described Fort Amherstburg as "now in ruins . . . to be perhaps never repaired."[9] In contrast, the treatise presented favorable reports on Michigan's military installations (forts Detroit, Gratiot, and Mackinac), all of which were located at nautical pinch points nearby Canadian waters. The impending Rush-Bagot Treaty would strictly limit naval armaments on both sides of the border, further evidence of détente. But what of the Indians? Did they represent a significant threat to the safety of settlements? Darby depicted the progress in Indian affairs by territorial Governor Lewis Cass and other officials in glowing terms. As a result of their work, he wrote, "The savage tribes are retiring." Darby estimated that seven million acres of Native American land had been obtained in the area in exchange for annuities, creation of Indian reserves, and provision of land west of the Mississippi River. "The cessions are of great consequence to the frontiers of Ohio and Michigan, as it tends to remove the savages to a greater distance westward," he concluded. All was quiet on the western front.[10]

In August 1818, Darby spent twelve days in Detroit. His journal entries during the stay emphasized the town's economic potential. "Detroit is now a place of extensive commerce, with all the attributes of a seaport," Darby wrote. He viewed both banks of the Detroit River as "a fine picture of agricultural and commercial prosperity."[11] In addition, he lauded the town's social order, comparing its "high state of culture" to that of other American coastal areas: "The resident society of Detroit, has all the exterior features of a flourishing and cultivated community, as much so, equivalent to numbers, as any city of the United States."[12] Darby also acknowledged the most serious impediment to the territory's progress: geographic remoteness. Detroit remained isolated from the rest of the country by water and "an uncultivated waste," a reference to the Black Swamp, an expanse of land that had long served as a barrier to overland travel from Ohio to Michigan Territory. But here, too, he found encouraging signs, as Detroit was "daily becoming less distant . . . [to] the great body of the United States community." The geographer's message was comprehensive and unmistakable: Michigan Territory was a desirable destination for settlers. Soon after A Tour was published in early 1819, the region welcomed the first ripple of a generation-long wave of migrants. Darby's prominence in his field, extensive connections and exposure in the East, and rigorous methodology all served to hasten Michigan's development.[13]

Darby's was not the sole endorsement of the territory's potential. In 1803, Indian agent Charles Jouette submitted a favorable report to Secretary of War Henry Dearborn: "With respect to the soil, there is a great degree of similarity throughout this part of the country, dark, or rather black, light, and, wherever, with few exceptions, it has been cultivated productive."[14] In particular, Detroit's natural environment was heartily conducive to the growing of fruit, wheat, Indian corn, grass, and hemp. However, Jouette qualified his positive soil assessment for certain Detroit-area locales, including Grosse Pointe, Hog Island (today Belle Isle), the area surrounding the Rouge River, and Stony Island, which he declared agriculturally unproductive. He also disparaged the region's topographically limited surface drainage and the ignorance of local farmers, whose methods "exhausted" the soil. Finally, Jouette's report criticized public health in the region, deeming Grosse Pointe as "very unhealthy" and condemning the Milk River and Huron River (today the Clinton River) for "unhealthful effluvia." The Rouge River area received particular attention: "It has at all times the complexion and appearance of a pool; and its exhalations, in the summer months, are extremely unhealthful. The ague and fever are, in these seasons, very prevalent; and fevers sometimes of a more malignant nature, confine whole families to their beds for weeks together." Despite these considerable reservations, Jouette found more potential in the region than any other outside expert or government official until Darby.[15]

Along with Darby, two other outsiders praised aspects of Michigan Territory in 1818: New Hampshire attorney Estwick Evans, who visited while walking across the U.S., and New York businessman and agriculturalist Elkanah Watson. "The soil is fertile and the climate perfectly congenial," Evans noted. "A yankee farmer carrying with him to this place his knowledge of agriculture, and his industry, might soon acquire a very handsome estate." Yet the peripatetic New Englander had a less sanguine take than Darby on the state of the American-Canadian borderlands. Evans encouraged development in the Northwest to "outweigh the counter influence of those of the British in its neighbourhood." Moreover, a fear of Indians permeated his account. Claiming that the late war had not secured peace on the frontier, Evans recounted several frightening tales of native depredations. He confessed that apprehension caused him to abort the remainder of his plans to examine the interior of Michigan Territory – hardly a ringing endorsement for potential migrants.[16]

Watson averred that Michigan Territory was "blessed with a luxuriant soil." He was certainly qualified to know. Watson was a progenitor of the agricultural fair and the Erie Canal. His frequent correspondence with James Madison reflect Watson's keen interest in and understanding of agronomics, including a proposal to establish a "National Board of Agriculture," an idea that piqued Madison's imagination as well. Watson attained phenomenal success as a New York businessman and his connections to prominent figures, periodicals, and agricultural societies indicate that he was both famous and highly influential. So why should Darby receive the bulk of the credit for publicizing Michigan's agricultural potential among eastern audiences? Why not Jouette, Evans, or Watson?[17]

Jouette's endorsement came far too early to be of any real benefit to Michigan, which had not even secured separate territorial status in 1803. That year, Ohio achieved statehood, and land there was still cheap, plentiful, productive, reasonably secure, and accessible. Detroit was known, if at all, as a French-speaking, fur-trading, military outpost on a distant frontier – an "American oasis," in the words of the historian Alan Taylor. Furthermore, Jouette's missive probably amounted to nothing more than an interdepartmental memorandum, a perfunctory report disseminated to a small group of government officials. Finally, there was the problem of "ague" and "fever."[18]

Evans's approval of the soil and climate in Michigan Territory came at just the right time. He, Darby, and Watson visited Detroit in 1818, on the cusp of several events that would eventually transform Michigan. The year marked the opening of the Detroit land office, initiation of steamship service on Lake Erie, and continuation of Cass's impressive advocacy efforts on behalf of the territory. Work on the Erie Canal was underway, and Indiana and Illinois had garnered statehood. The westward push showed no sign of abatement or deceleration. However, *A Pedestrious Tour*, self-published in New Hampshire, unreviewed, and Evans's only book, likely reached only a very limited audience. Moreover, Evans lacked Darby's (or Watson's) scientific credentials; he was a self-described "obscure" lawyer. The book remains a delightful read, with long, rambling passages on Native

American culture, militia organization, and the general inferiority of the western environment. Compared to Darby's meticulous and methodological treatment, Evans's work is more travelogue than treatise. Darby measured current velocities and flow rates; Evans's dogs were killed by wolves. Ultimately, Evans's fear of Indian attack eclipsed his praise of Michigan's soil and climate.[19]

Watson did not share Evans's liabilities. A published author with impeccable agronomic credentials, the New Yorker became rich and famous as a banker. But his credibility was in question, since his daughter and son-in-law lived in Michigan Territory. He also owned large tracts of land in the Detroit area, particularly at Rouge River (perhaps he had not read Jouette's report). Additionally, Watson's biography states that "dubious lobbying" helped him receive the lucrative charter for the Bank of Albany in 1803. Despite his reputation as a scientist, Watson bore burdens that Darby did not – genuine skepticism regarding his objectivity and allegations of insider dealings. Those who knew Watson well enough to trust his horticultural expertise were likely aware of his Michigan associations. In addition, it appears that his notes on Detroit were not made public until his memoirs were printed in 1856, long after the settlement boom. As with Evans and Jouette, distribution of Watson's endorsement of Michigan Territory was in all probability limited in scope and effect.[20]

Darby suffered no such limitations. *A Tour* followed successful books on Louisiana and other western states and territories, and a year after its publication, his *Memoir of Florida* was released. Darby's books, maps, and booklets sold well, were favorably reviewed, and assiduously promoted. Moreover, his connections in New York, a font of emigration, certainly linked his works with potential settlers, investors, and speculators. Amid his nearly stultifying array of data on the upper lakes, he included information that countered Tiffin's geophysical slur, Jouette's qualms about health, and Evans's fear of the Indians and British. It was as if Cass himself had written the review, with one profound exception: Darby's connection to Michigan Territory was limited to the twelve days he spent there in 1818.

In the decade following Darby's assessment, the long-foundering territory finally experienced a substantial wave of settlement. Cass had addressed the region's problems concerning security, accessibility, and development. But the most significant catalyst was radical improvements in technology and infrastructure. The Erie Canal and the initiation and development of regular steamboat service on the Great Lakes revolutionized passenger and freight delivery from the East to the frontier. Transportation became far more reliable and exponentially cheaper. Steam power enlarged carrying capacities and reduced travel time, allowing lower rates and increased profits. *A Tour* reported on the August 1818 debut of *Walk-in-the-Water*, the first steamer to reach Detroit, and commented enthusiastically on the enormous potential of the new medium. Moreover, Darby's addenda included correspondence from Isaac Briggs, an engineer working on the then-nascent Erie Canal. Briggs reported that, although only 15 percent of the project was completed, it was already generating revenue and excitement. Darby's evaluation of the profound impact of the "grand canal" went beyond matters of cost and convenience. To the geographer, the eventual direct connection between the Atlantic world and the Great Lakes was a component in a grander schema that would link New York, Detroit, St. Louis, and New Orleans. The commercial benefits of such an arrangement were obvious, but Darby envisioned something more. Intersectional trade would foster national identity and socio-cultural cohesion. Connection between the Great Lakes and the Mississippi River would complete the arc, and Darby assessed several potential routes for such a linkage. He analyzed a Maumee River-Wabash River option (with a possible River Raisin shunt to avoid the rapids), as well as a Chicago River-Illinois River alternative, and judged each to be a viable connector. Either way, Michigan was square in the middle.[21]

Darby's treatise on Michigan was the most studious and available for eastern audiences before statehood. His objective and positive appraisal of the territory joined a confluence of developments – technological, demographic, and political – that ushered in an immediate and lasting wave of migrants to the port of Detroit. Darby's connections and reputation in the East enhanced the distribution of his report and its clout. He was known and respected in government, literary, and commercial spheres. While a number of circumstances fostered Michigan's ascendancy, Darby's dispassionate endorsement served as an essential component. His measured affirmation of Michigan's agricultural potential effectively refuted previous accounts and helped the territory to emerge from a generation of social and economic torpor.

NOTES

1 James Monroe to Thomas Jefferson, January 19, 1786, in *The Writings of James Monroe*, ed. Stanislaus M. Hamilton, 7 vols. (New York: G.P. Putnam's Sons, 1898-1903), 1:117. See also Roscoe C. Buley, *The Old Northwest: Pioneer Period, 1815-1840*, 2 vols. (Indianapolis: Indiana Historical Society, 1950), 1:20.

2 Edward Tiffin to Josiah Meigs, November 30, 1815, in *MPHC*, 10:62. Meigs was the commissioner of the General Land Office. Tiffin based his recommendation on a unanimous report submitted by a crew assigned to Michigan. The surveyors quit their work in the territory after "suffering incredible hardships" (61). As a result, two million acres of land in Michigan Territory, which was supposed to be distributed to war veterans, was ignored. For Gentle, see "Extract of a letter from a gentleman in Detroit to the Editor of the *Western Star*, dated Feb. 26th, 1807," *Pittsburgh Commonwealth*, May 6, 1807. For Morse and additional unfavorable coverage of Michigan Territory in eastern newspapers, see Frank B. Woodford, *Lewis Cass: The Last Jeffersonian* (New Brunswick, NJ: Rutgers University Press, 1950), 108-9.

3 For Monroe's visit in 1817, see the essay in this volume by Kaitlin Cooper.

4   William Darby, *A Tour from the City of New York to Detroit, in the Michigan Territory: Made between the 2ᵈ of May and the 22ᵈ of September, 1818* (1819; reprint, Chicago: Quadrangle Books, 1962). By 1819, Darby's credentials and connections were well established. In 1806, he was named deputy surveyor for the Western District for the Territory of New Orleans. During the War of 1812, he worked as a topographer for General Andrew Jackson, service that earned him a captaincy, a fort named in his honor, and a letter of commendation from the general. Philadelphia magnate John Melish published the first edition of *A Geographic Study of Louisiana* in 1816. In the fall of 1815, Pittsburgh publisher Robert Patterson commissioned Darby to write a geographic and cultural assessment of his city, results of which were included in the 1818 *Emigrant's Guide to the Western and Southwestern States and Territories*, published in New York by Kirk & Mercein. Apparently, the guide was well received, since Kirk & Mercein chose to publish *A Tour* the following year. In 1816, Darby married Elizabeth Tanner, sister of prominent Philadelphia engraver Benjamin Tanner. Upon moving to New York in 1817, the geographer was elected to the New York Historical Society, where his network expanded to include luminaries such as Governor DeWitt Clinton, Robert Fulton, John Jay, and Stephen Van Renssalaer. Numerous eastern periodicals provided correspondence from and review of Darby, including Philadelphia's *National Gazette*, Baltimore's *Niles' Weekly Register*, the *New York Columbian*, *Analectic Magazine*, the *North American Review*, and the *American Monthly Magazine and Critical Review*. He was further exposed to eastern audiences through a press tour and an extensive series of lectures in 1819. A general consensus exists amongst the reviewers of Darby's various works: Although the author's style may have been dry, the content was thoughtful, unbiased, and valuable. Darby biographer J. Gerald Kennedy specifies the importance of the edaphic component of Darby's works, claiming that the author's reports helped to dispel misinformation about supposedly poor soils. Kennedy, *The Astonished Traveler: William Darby, Frontier Geographer and Man of Letters* (Baton Rouge: Louisiana State University Press, 1981).

5   Darby, *Tour from the City of New York*. There are few references to Darby in the secondary literature on Michigan Territory, which can be explained in part by the enormous chronological gap between the original release of *A Tour* in 1819 and its reprinting in 1962. Woodford includes two sentences on the cartographer (109), and Buley provides three sentences (1:51). For an exception, see Brian L. Dunnigan, *Frontier Metropolis: Picturing Early Detroit, 1701-1838* (Detroit: Wayne State University Press, 2001), 154-55, 174. Dunnigan includes a map and quotes from Darby's tour of Michigan Territory. For the Rush-Bagot Treaty, see the essay in this volume by James M. Shuryan.

6   Darby, *Tour from the City of New York*.

7   Tiffin to Meigs, November 30, 1815, 10:62.

8   Darby, *Tour from the City of New York*, x ("varied"); 199 ("subject to immersion").

9   Darby, *Tour from the City of New York*, 193. For Fort Amherstburg, see the essay in this volume by Joshua Zimberg.

10 Darby, *Tour from the City of New York*, 188 ("savage tribes"); 196 ("cessions"). For Indian treaties, see the essay in this volume by Steve Lyskawa.

11 Darby, *Tour from the City of New York*, 190 ("Detroit is now"); 194 ("a fine picture").

12 Darby, *Tour from the City of New York*, 194 ("high state"); 190 ("The resident society").

13 Darby, *Tour from the City of New York*, 188.

14 Charles Jouette to Henry Dearborn, July 25, 1803, in *American State Papers: Documents, Legislative and Executive, of the Congress of the United States.* Public Lands, vol. 1 (Washington, DC: Gales and Seaton, 1832), 190-93; 191 (quote).

15 Jouette to Dearborn, July 25, 1803, 192.

16 Estwick Evans, *A Pedestrious Tour, of Four Thousand Miles: Through the Western States and Territories* (Concord, NH: Joseph C. Spear, 1819), 118 ("The soil" and "A yankee"); 117 ("outweigh"). See also Floyd R. Dain, *Detroit and the Westward Movement* (Detroit: Wayne University Press, 1951), 74-75.

17 Winslow C. Watson, ed., *Men and Times of the Revolution; or, Memoirs of Elkanah Watson* (New York: Dana and Co., 1856), 495. For Watson's background, see Dain, 74-75; and "Elkanah Watson Papers, 1773-1884," New York State Library, www.nysl.nysed.gov/msscfa/sc13294.htm (accessed April 30, 2012).

18 Alan Taylor, *The Civil War of 1812: American Citizens, British Subjects, Irish Rebels, & Indian Allies* (New York: Knopf, 2010), 153.

19 Evans, *Pedestrious Tour.*

20 "Elkanah Watson Papers, 1773-1884."

21 Darby, *Tour from the City of New York*, 173, 207, addenda (lxi-lxiii). For the emergence of growth in Michigan Territory in the 1820s, see Dunnigan, 148-50; Willis F. Dunbar, *Lewis Cass* (Grand Rapids: Eerdmans, 1970), chap. 3; and issues of the *Detroit Gazette* between May 10, 1822, and May 2, 1823. In 1822, the flow of immigrants became substantial. By 1823, the floodgates had opened, prompting the *Gazette* to declare a moratorium on its public relations campaign.

Selected Bibliography

Manuscripts

Archives of Michigan, Lansing
Edwin J. Benson Papers
Historical Commission Papers
Map Collection
University of Wisconsin Collection on the Detroit Fur Trade
Wayne County Probate Court Records

Bentley Historical Library, University of Michigan, Ann Arbor
John Anderson and Family Papers
Elijah Brush Papers
Campau Family Papers
Detroit, Michigan, Papers
Michigan River Raisin Monument Commission Records
Pattengill Family Papers
Sault Sainte Marie Collection
Ste. Anne's Church Records
United States Bureau of Customs, District of Michilimackinac
    Impost Book

Burton Historical Collection, Detroit Public Library

James Abbott Papers
Julia Larned Allen Papers
Fanny Johnston Anderson Papers
John Anderson Correspondence
George C. Anthon Papers
John Askin Papers
Baby Family Papers
Elizabeth Abbott Baby Papers
Joseph E. Bayliss Papers
Henry Berthelet Papers
Henry Bird Papers
Levi Bishop Papers
Lewis Bond Papers
Joriah Brady Papers
William Burnett Papers
Clarence M. Burton Papers
Clarence M. Burton Works

Campau Family Papers
Jacques Campau Papers
John Campbell Papers
Canadian Archives
Lewis Cass Papers
George B. Catlin Papers
Chêne Family Papers
Edward V. Cicotte Papers
Green Clay Papers
Christian Clemens Papers
Leonard Covington Papers
Jean Baptiste Crête Papers
Christian Denissen Papers
Detroit Archives
Detroit Historical Society Records
Ennis Duncan Jr. Papers
John Edgar Papers

William Edgar Papers
Benjamin F. Emery Papers
Matthew Ernest (Ernst) Papers
John Farmer Papers
Silas Farmer Papers
Otto O. Fisher Papers
Alexander Fraser Papers
Susan Burnham Greeley Papers
Stanley Griswold Correspondence
Gabriel J. Godfroy Papers
Alexander Grant Papers
William Henry Harrison Papers
Alexander Harrow Family Papers
James Henry Papers
J. Heward Papers
Harris H. Hickman Papers
Jacob M. Howard Papers
Nancy Hubbard Howard Papers
William Hull Papers
George Hunt Papers
Indians of North America
Thomas Jefferson Papers
Jacob Kingsbury Papers
William Kirby Papers
Labadie Family Papers
Charles Larned Papers
Joseph H. Larwill Papers
Benson J. Lossing Papers
Lyon Family Papers
George F. MacDonald Papers
Macomb Family Papers
Alexander Macomb Papers
John Mason Papers
Duncan McArthur Papers
George McDougall Papers
Alexander McKee Papers
George Meldrum Papers
Meldrum & Park Papers
Michigan Territory Papers
Miscellany by Date
James Monroe Papers
John Montieth Papers
Moran Family Papers

Charles Moran Papers
J. Bell Moran Papers
George Morgan Papers
Daniel Morison Papers
Francis (François) Navarre Papers
Robert Navarre Papers
George Paré Papers
William Park Papers
Oliver C. Pope Papers
Augustus S. Porter Papers
Pierre Potier Papers
Henry Procter Papers
Lawrence Reynolds Papers
Gabriel Richard Papers
Rivard Family Papers
William Robertson Papers
John Robinson Papers
Robison Family Papers
Robert Sanders Papers
Winthrop Sargent Papers
Henry Schoolcraft Papers
William M. Scott Papers
Isaac Shelby Papers
Solomon Sibley Papers
Arthur Sinclair Papers
John Smith Jr. Papers
Thomas Smith Papers
Arthur St. Clair Papers
Harold E. Stoll Papers
Stuart Family Papers
James Taylor Papers
Charles C. Trowbridge Papers
Christopher Tuttle Papers
United States Archives
Jeremiah Van Rensselaer Papers
Charles I. Walker Papers
War of 1812 Sesquicentennial
    Celebration Committee
Wayne County, Indiana Territory,
    Papers
Wayne County, Northwest
    Territory, Papers
John Wilkins Papers

John R. Williams Papers
Thomas Williams Papers
General James Winchester Papers
Benjamin F. H. Witherell Papers
Lucile Oughtred Woltz Papers

Dudley Woodbridge Papers
William Woodbridge Papers
Augustus B. Woodward Papers
Woolsey Family Papers
Samuel Zug Papers

William L. Clements Library, University of Michigan, Ann Arbor
Randolph Adams Papers
British North America Collection
Lewis Cass Papers
Isaac Chauncey Papers
Iconography of Detroit Notebooks
William Knox Papers
Michigan Collection
Abbé Montesquiou Journal
Native American History Collection
James Patten Papers
Quaker Collection
Alexander Thompson Papers
George Thompson Papers
Wilson Family Papers
Woods Family Papers

Clarke Historical Library, Central Michigan University, Mount Pleasant
Robert Cockerton Correspondence
Edith L. Flack, The Escape from the River Raisin Massacre, 1812
Whitmore Knaggs Collection
Tecumseh Vertical Files

Detroit Archdiocesan Archives
Parish Records

Elmwood Cemetery Records, Detroit
Burial Book A

Fort Malden National Historic Site of Canada, Amherstburg, Ontario
Sheridan Alder, "The American Occupation of the Western District"
    (unpublished paper)
Matthew Elliott Collection
R. Frajolah Collection
Alexander McKee Family Genealogical File

Marsh Collection Society, Amherstburg, Ontario
Gregor McGregor Papers
Historic Landscape Conservation Study, Fort Malden

Monroe County Historical Museum Archives, Monroe, Michigan
Russell E. Bidlack's Notes
Bower Papers
Couture Papers
Durocher Papers
Knaggs Papers
Letters of Capt. John McCalla
Mommini Papers
Navarre Papers
Charles Noble Correspondence Collection
Obituaries, Newspaper Clipping Files, Family & Small Collections

Ohio Historical Society, Columbus
Return Jonathan Meigs Papers
Winthrop Sargent Papers

State Historical Society of Wisconsin, Madison
Lyman Copeland Draper Manuscript Collection

Windsor's Community Museum, Windsor, Ontario
Baby Family Papers
Tom Davies, "Ontario Heritage Foundation – A Report for the
    Heritage Trust – The Duff-Baby House" (unpublished paper)
Western District Records
Windsor's Community Museum Directory of Holdings

Published Primary

American State Papers, Documents, Legislative and Executive, of the Congress of the United States. 38 vols. Washington, DC: Gales and Seaton, 1832-61.

American State Papers, Indian Affairs. 2 vols. Washington, DC: Gales and Seaton, 1832-34.

Anthony Wayne Parkway Board. *Papers on the War of 1812 in the Northwest*. 7 vols. Columbus: Ohio State Museum, 1958-61.

Atherton, William. *Narrative of the Suffering and Defeat of the North-Western Army under General Winchester*. Frankfort, KY: A.G. Hodges, 1842.

Baby, William L. *Souvenirs of the Past: Giving a Correct Account of the Customs and Habits of the Pioneers of Canada and the Surrounding Country*. Windsor, ON: n.p., 1896.

Bacon, Lydia B. Stetson. *Biography of Mrs. Lydia B. Bacon*. Boston: Massachusetts Sabbath School Society, 1856.

Bamford, Don, and Paul Carroll, eds. *Four Years on the Great Lakes, 1813-1816: The Journal of Lieutenant David Wingfield, Royal Navy*. Toronto: Natural Heritage Books, 2009.

Bibeau, Claudette Piquette et al., eds. *Mariages St-Jean-Baptiste d'Amherstburg, 1802-1985*. Ottawa: Société Franco-Ontarienne d'Histoire et de Généalogie, 1987.

Blume, William W., ed. *Transactions of the Supreme Court of the Territory of Michigan*. 6 vols. Ann Arbor: University of Michigan Press, 1935-40.

Boehm, Robert B., and Randall L. Buchman, eds. *Journal of the Northwestern Campaign of 1812-13: Under Major-General William H. Harrison*. Defiance, OH: Defiance College Press, 1975.

Brannan, John, ed. *Official Letters of the Military and Naval Officers of the United States during the War with Great Britain in the Years 1812, 13, 14, & 15*. Washington, DC: Wax & Gideon. 1823. Reprint, New York: Arno Press, 1971.

Brunson, Alfred. *A Western Pioneer*. Cincinnati: Hitchcock and Walden, 1872.

Burton, M. Anges, and Clarence M. Burton, eds. *Governor and Judges Journal: Proceedings of the Land Board of Detroit*. Detroit: Michigan Territory Commission on Land Titles, 1915.

———, eds. *Manuscripts from the Burton Historical Collection*. 8 vols. Detroit: Burton, 1916-18.

Burton, Clarence M., ed. *Corporation of the Town of Detroit. Act of Incorporation and Journal of the Board of Trustees, 1802-1805*. Detroit: Detroit Public Library, 1922.

Casselman, Alexander C., ed. *The War of 1812*. 1842. Reprint, Toronto: Musson Book, 1902.

Carter, Clarence E., and John P. Bloom, eds. *The Territorial Papers of the United States*. 27 vols. Washington, DC: Department of State and National Archives and Records Service, 1934-69.

Colquhoun, Arthur H.U., ed. *Tecumseh and Richardson. The Story of a Trip to Walpole Island and Port Sarnia*. Toronto: Ontario Book Co., 1924.

Cook, Samuel P. *Laws of the Territory of Michigan*. 4 vols. Lansing: W.S. George, 1871-84.

Coyne, James H., ed. *The Talbot Papers*. 2 vols. Ottawa: Royal Society of Canada, 1908-10.

Crawford, Mary M., ed. "Mrs. Lydia B. Bacon's Journal, 1811-1812." *Indiana Magazine of History* 40 (1944): 367-86; 41 (1945): 59-79.

Cruikshank, E.A., ed. *Documents Relating to the Invasion of Canada and the Surrender of Detroit, 1812*. 1912. Reprint, New York: Arno Press, 1971.

Dalliba, James. *A Narrative of the Battle of Brownstown*. New York: David Longworth, 1816.

Darby, William. *A Tour from the City of New York to Detroit, in the Michigan Territory: Made between the 2^d of May and the 22^d of September, 1818*. 1819. Reprint, Chicago: Quadrangle Books, 1962.

Dawson, Moses. *A Historical Narrative of the Civil and Military Services of Major-General William H. Harrison*. Cincinnati: M. Dawson, 1824.

Denissen, Christian et al., eds. *Genealogy of the French Families of the Detroit River Region, 1701-1936*. 2 vols. 1976. Reprint, Detroit: Society for Genealogical Research, 1987.

Detroit Public Library. *Burton Historical Collection Leaflet*. 11 vols. Detroit: Detroit Public Library, 1922-31.

Dudley, Thomas P. *Battle and Massacre at Frenchtown, Michigan, January, 1813*. 1813. Reprint, Cleveland: Western Reserve Historical Society, 1870.

Dudley, William S. et al., eds. *The Naval War of 1812: A Documentary History*. 3 vols. Washington, DC: Naval Historical Center, 1985-2002.

Fay, H.A., ed. *Collection of the Official Accounts, in Detail, of all the Battles Fought by Sea and Land*. New York: E. Conrad, 1817.

Fredriksen, John C., ed. *Surgeon of the Lakes: The Diary of Dr. Usher Parsons, 1812-1814*. Erie, PA: Erie County Historical Society, 2000.

Gellner, John, ed. *Recollections of the War of 1812: Three Eyewitnesses' Accounts*. Toronto: Baxter, 1964.

Graves, Donald E., ed. *Merry Hearts Make Light Days: The War of 1812 Journal of Lieutenant John Le Couteur, 104th Foot*. Ottawa: Carleton University Press, 1993.

Hosmer, Hezekiah L. *Early History of the Maumee Valley*. Toledo: Hosmer & Harris, 1858.

Hull, William. *Defence of Brigadier General W. Hull: Delivered before the General Court Martial*. Boston: Wells and Lilly, 1814.

———. *Memoirs of the Campaign of the North Western Army of the United States, A.D. 1812*. Boston: True & Greene, 1824.

Kappler, Charles J., ed. *Indian Affairs. Laws and Treaties*. 7 vols. Washington, DC: Government Printing Office, 1904-79.

Kelley, Sharon A. et al., eds. *Marriage Records, Ste. Anne Church, Detroit, 1701-1850*. Detroit: Detroit Society for Genealogical Research, 2001.

Kershaw, Kenneth A., ed. *Early Printed Maps of Canada*. 4 vols. Ancaster, ON: Kershaw, 1993-98.

Klinck, Carl F., ed. *Tecumseh: Fact and Fiction in Early Records*. 1961. Reprint, Ottawa: Tecumseh Press, 1978.

Klinck, Carl F. et al., eds. *The Journal of Major John Norton, 1816*. 1970. Reprint, Toronto: Champlain Society, 2011.

Knopf, Richard C., ed. *A Short History of the Life of John Anderson*. Columbus, OH: Anthony Wayne Parkway Board, 1956.

———, ed. *Document Transcriptions of the War of 1812 in the Northwest*. 10 vols. Columbus: Ohio Historical Society, 1957-62.

Lajeunesse, Ernest J., ed. *The Windsor Border Region, Canada's Southernmost Frontier; a Collection of Documents*. Toronto: Champlain Society, 1960.

Mallary, Timothy, and John Davenport, eds. *A Journal Containing an Interesting and Accurate Account of the Hardships, Sufferings, Battles, Defeat, and Captivity of Those Heroic Kentucky Volunteers*. 1854. Reprint, New York: William Abbatt, 1914.

Michigan Pioneer and Historical Society. *Michigan Pioneer and Historical Collection*. 40 vols. Lansing: Michigan Historical Commission, 1877-1929.

Michigan Works Progress Administration, Vital Records Project. *Early Land Transfers, Detroit and Wayne County, Michigan*. 54 vols. Detroit: Louisa St. Clair Chapter, Daughters of the American Revolution, 1936-40.

Mitchell, S.A., and H. Ames. *A Narrative of a Tour of Observation, Made during the Summer of 1817*. Philadelphia: Clark & Raser, 1818.

Monroe County Community College, eds. *Laurent Durocher's Account of the Battles & Massacre of the River Raisin, January 18, 22 & 23, 1813*. Monroe, MI: Monroe County Community College, 1987.

Noël, Françoise, ed. *Family Life and Sociability in Upper and Lower Canada, 1780-1870: A View from Diaries and Family Correspondence*. Montreal: McGill-Queen's University Press, 2003.

Ohde, James, ed. *The Journal of Nathen Newsom*. Columbus, OH: Anthony Wayne Parkway Board, 1957.

Osawamick, Sam. "A Battle in the War of 1812." In *Odawa Language Project: Second Report*. Edited by Glyne L. Piggott and Jonathan Kaye. Toronto: Centre for Linguistic Studies, University of Toronto, 1973.

Parish, John C., ed. *The Robert Lucas Journal of the War of 1812 during the Campaign under General William Hull*. Iowa City: State Historical Society of Iowa, 1906.

Price, Wilma B., ed. *The Battle and Massacre of the River Raisin (Battle of French Town)*. Monroe, MI: Monroe County Historical Society and Monroe County Library System, 1981.

Quaife, Milo M., ed. *The John Askin Papers*. 2 vols. Detroit: Detroit Library Commission, 1928-31.

———, ed. *War on the Detroit: The Chronicles of Thomas Verchères de Boucherville and the Capitulation, by an Ohio Volunteer*. Chicago: Lakeside Press, 1940.

Richardson, John. *The Canadian Brothers, or, the Prophecy Fulfilled: A Tale of the Late American War*. 1840. Reprint, edited by Donald Stevens. Ottawa: Carleton University Press, 1992.

———. *Richardson's War of 1812: With Notes and a Life of the Author*. Edited by Alexander C. Casselman, 1902. Reprint, Toronto: Coles Publishing Co., 1974.

Russell, Donna Valley, ed. *Michigan Censuses, 1710-1830, under the French, British, and Americans*. Detroit: Detroit Society for Genealogical Research, 1982.

Tupper, Ferdinand Brock, ed. *The Life and Correspondence of Major-General Sir Isaac Brock*. London: Simpkin, Marshall, 1845.

United States Congress. *Barbarities of the Enemy, Exposed in a Report of the Committee of the House of Representatives*. Worcester, MA: Isaac Sturtevant, 1814.

Vail, R.W.G., ed. *A Narrative of the Captivity and Sufferings of James Van Horn on the Plains of Michigan*. 1817. Reprint, Middleboro, MA: L.B. Romaine, 1956.

Vexler, Robert I., ed. *Detroit: A Chronological and Documentary History, 1701-1976*. Dobbs Ferry, NY: Oceana Publications, 1977.

Waldo, Samuel P. *The Tour of James Monroe, President of the United States, in the Year 1817*. Hartford: F.D. Bolles & Co., 1818.

Walker, Adam. *A Journal of Two Campaigns of the Fourth Regiment of the U.S. Infantry in the Michigan and Indiana Territories*. Keene, NH: Sentinel Press, 1816.

White, Virgil D., ed. *Index to War of 1812 Pension Files*. 3 vols. Waynesboro, TN: National Historic Pub. Co., 1989.

Winchester, James. *Historical Details Having Relation to the Campaign of the North-Western Army*. Lexington, KY: Worsley & Smith, 1818.

Wood, Eleazer D. et al., eds. *Journal of the Northwestern Campaign of 1812-13: Under Major-General William H. Harrison*. Defiance, OH: Defiance College Press, 1975.

Wood, William C.H., ed. *Select British Documents of the Canadian War of 1812*. 3 vols. 1920-28. Reprint, New York: Greenwood Press, 1968.

Wright, Richard J., ed. *The John Hunt Memoirs: Early Years of the Maumee Basin, 1812-1835*. Maumee, OH: Maumee Valley Historical Society, 1978.

Secondary Sources

Adelman, Jeremy, and Stephen Aron. "From Borderlands to Borders: Empires, Nation-States and the Peoples in between in North American History." *American Historical Review* 104 (1999): 814-41.

Altoff, Gerard T. *Deep Water Sailors, Shallow Water Soldiers: Manning the United States Fleet on Lake Erie, 1813*. Put-in-Bay, OH: Perry Group, 1993.

———. *Amongst My Best Men: African-Americans and the War of 1812*. Put-in-Bay, OH: Perry Group, 1996.

Amherstburg Bicentennial Book Committee. *Amherstburg, 1796-1996: The New Town on the Garrison Grounds*. Amherstburg, ON: Amherstburg Bicentennial Book Committee, 1996.

Anderson, Robert T. et al., eds. *American Indian Law: Cases and Commentary*. St. Paul, MN: Thomson/West, 2008.

Antal, Sandy. *A Wampum Denied: Procter's War of 1812*. Ottawa: Carleton University Press, 1997.

———. *Invasions: Taking and Retaking Detroit and the Western District during the War of 1812 and Its Aftermath*. Windsor, ON: Essex County Historical Society, 2011.

Au, Dennis M. *War on the Raisin: A Narrative Account of the War of 1812 in the River Raisin Settlement, Michigan Territory*. Monroe, MI: Monroe County Historical Commission, 1981.

Bald, Frederick C. *Detroit's First American Decade, 1796-1805*. Ann Arbor: University of Michigan Press, 1948.

———. *Michigan in Four Centuries: Line Drawings by William Thomas Woodward*. New York: Harper, 1954.

Bamford, Don. *Freshwater Heritage: A History of Sail on the Great Lakes, 1670-1918*. Toronto: Natural Heritage Books, 2007.

Barr, Daniel P., ed. *The Boundaries between Us: Natives and Newcomers along the Frontiers of the Old Northwest Territory, 1750-1850*. Kent, OH: Kent State University Press, 2006.

Barry, James P. *Old Forts of the Great Lakes: Sentinels in the Wilderness*. Lansing, MI: Thunder Bay Press, 1994.

Bartolo, Ghislaine Pieters, and Lynn Waybright Reaume, eds. *The Cross Leads Generations On: A Bicentennial Retrospect, St. Mary of the Immaculate Conception Formerly Known as St. Antoine at the River Raisin, Monroe, Michigan, 1788-1988*. Tappan, NY: Custombook, 1988.

Berton, Pierre. *The Invasion of Canada, 1812-1813*. Boston: Little, Brown, 1980.

———. *Flames across the Border: the Canadian-American Tragedy, 1813-1814*. Boston: Little, Brown, 1981.

Bidlack, Russell E. *The Yankee Meets the Frenchman: River Raisin, 1817-1830, Social, Political, Military*. Ann Arbor: Historical Society of Michigan, 1965.

Bird, Harrison. *War for the West, 1790-1813*. New York: Oxford University Press, 1971.

Bond, Beverley W. *The Civilization of the Old Northwest: A Study of Political, Social and Economic Development, 1788-1812*. New York: Macmillan, 1934.

Bourinot, John G. *Canada under British Rule, 1760-1900*. Cambridge: Cambridge University Press, 1900.

Bowes, John P. *Exiles and Pioneers: Eastern Indians in the Trans-Mississippi West*. New York: Cambridge University Press, 2007.

Boyea, Earl. *Gabriel Richard: Servant of God*. Ann Arbor, MI: University Litho, 2001.

Brady, Cyrus T. *Border Fights and Fighters: Stories of the Pioneers between the Alleghenies and the Mississippi and in the Texan Republic*. New York: McClure, Phillips, 1902.

Bragg, Amy Elliot. *Hidden History of Detroit*. Charleston, SC: History Press, 2011.

Brown, Elizabeth Gaspar. "Frontier Justice: Wayne County 1796-1836." *The American Journal of Legal History* 16 (1972): 126-53.

Brown, George W. et al., eds. *Dictionary of Canadian Biography*. 15 vols. Toronto: University of Toronto Press, 1965-2005.

Brown, Henry D. *Detroit Entertains a President*. Detroit: Wayne University Press, 1954.

Brune, Nick et al., eds. *Defining Canada: History, Identity, and Culture*. Toronto: McGraw-Hill Ryerson, 2003.

Brunsman, Denver, and Joel Stone, eds. *Revolutionary Detroit: Portraits in Political and Cultural Change, 1760-1805*. Detroit: Detroit Historical Society, 2009.

Bukowczyk, John J. et al. *Permeable Border: The Great Lakes Basin as Transnational Region, 1650-1990*. Pittsburgh: University of Pittsburgh Press, 2005.

Buley, Roscoe C. *The Old Northwest: Pioneer Period, 1815-1840*. 2 vols. Indianapolis: Indiana Historical Society, 1950.

Burns, Virginia. *Lewis Cass, Frontier Soldier*. Bath, MI: Enterprise Press, 1980.

Burton, Clarence M. *History of Detroit: 1780 to 1850: Financial and Commercial*. Detroit: Burton, 1917.

———. *The City of Detroit Michigan, 1701-1922*. 5 vols. Detroit and Chicago: S.J. Clarke, 1922.

———. "The Courts of Early Detroit." *Bench and Bar* 3 (1923): 2; 11.

Callahan, James M. "Agreement of 1817 – Reduction of Naval Forces upon the American Lakes." In *Annual Report of the American Historical Association for the Year 1895*, 367-92. Washington, DC: Government Printing Office, 1896.

Calloway, Colin G. "The End of an Era: British-Indian Relations in the Great Lakes Region after the War of 1812." *Michigan Historical Review* 12 (1986): 1-20.

———. *The Shawnees and the War for America*. New York: Viking, 2007.

Campbell, James V. *Outlines of the Political History of Michigan*. Detroit: Schober, 1876.

Campbell, Maria, Abraham Lincoln et al., eds. *Revolutionary Services and Civil Life of General William Hull*. New York: D. Appleton, 1848.

Canniff, William. *History of the Settlement of Upper Canada (Ontario)*. Toronto: Dudley & Burns, 1869.

Carter-Edwards, Dennis. "The War of 1812 along the Detroit Frontier: A Canadian Perspective." *Michigan Historical Review* 13 (1987): 25-50.

Caruso, John A. *The Great Lakes Frontier: An Epic of the Old Northwest*. Indianapolis: Bobbs-Merrill, 1961.

Catlin, George B. *The Story of Detroit*. Detroit: The Detroit News, 1923.

———. *The Siege of Detroit*. Detroit: The Detroit News, 1926.

Catlin, George B., ed. *Local History of Detroit and Wayne County*. Dayton, OH: National Historical Association, 1928.

Cayton, Andrew R.L., and Fredrika J. Teute, eds. *Contact Points: American Frontiers from the Mohawk Valley to the Mississippi, 1750-1830*. Chapel Hill: University of North Carolina Press, 1998.

Chiasson, Germaine et al., eds. *Mariages, Paroisse L'Assomption de Windsor, Ontario, 1700-1985*. 2 vols. Ottawa: Société Franco-Ontarienne d'Histoire et de Généalogie, 1985.

Clarke, John. *Land, Power, and Economics on the Frontier of Upper Canada*. Montreal: McGill-Queen's University Press, 2001.

Clarke, Peter D. *The Origin and Traditional History of the Wyandotte, and Sketches of Other Indian Tribes of North America*. Toronto: Hunter, Rose, 1870.

Cleland, Charles E. *Rites of Conquest: The History and Culture of Michigan's Native Americans*. Ann Arbor: University of Michigan Press, 1992.

Clift, G. Glenn. *Remember the Raisin! Kentucky and Kentuckians in the Battles and Massacre at Frenchtown, Michigan Territory, in the War of 1812*. Frankfort: Kentucky Historical Society, 1961.

Coffin, William F. *1812: the War, and its Moral: A Canadian Chronicle*. Montreal: John Lovell, 1864.

Cohen, Andrew. *The Unfinished Canadian: The People We Are*. Toronto: McClelland & Stewart, 2007.

Cooper, Afua. "The Fluid Frontier: Blacks and the Detroit River Region: A Focus on Henry Bibb." *Canadian Review of American Studies* 30 (2000): 129-49.

Corey, Albert B. *Canadian-American Relations along the Detroit River*. Detroit: Wayne State University Press, 1957.

Craig, Gerald M. *Upper Canada: The Formative Years, 1784-1841*. New York: Oxford University Press, 1963.

Crawford, Kim. *The Daring Trader: Jacob Smith in the Michigan Territory, 1802-1825*. East Lansing: Michigan State University Press, 2012.

Cruikshank, E.A. *Harrison and Procter: The River Raisin*. Ottawa: Royal Society of Canada, 1911.

———. *A Study of Disaffection in Upper Canada in 1812-15*. Ottawa: Royal Society of Canada, 1912.

Cuthbertson, George A. *Freshwater: A History and a Narrative of the Great Lakes*. New York: Macmillan, 1931.

Dain, Floyd R. *Detroit and the Westward Movement*. Detroit: Wayne University Press, 1951.

———. *Every House a Frontier: Detroit's Economic Progress, 1815-1825*. Detroit: Wayne State University Press, 1956.

Dale, Ronald J. *The Invasion of Canada: Battles of the War of 1812*. Toronto: J. Lorimer, 2001.

Davidson, Carlisle G., ed. *Heritage of Faith: Detroit's Religious Communities, 1701-1976*. Detroit: Detroit's Religious Bicentennial Task Force, 1976.

Douglas, R. Alan. *Mansion to Museum: The François Baby House and Its Times*. Windsor, ON: Essex County Historical Society, 1989.

———. *Uppermost Canada: The Western District and the Detroit Frontier, 1800-1850*. Detroit: Wayne State University Press, 2001.

Dowd, Gregory E. *A Spirited Resistance: The North American Indian Struggle for Unity, 1745-1815*. Baltimore: Johns Hopkins University Press, 1992.

Drake, Benjamin. *Life of Tecumseh and His Brother the Prophet; with a Historical Sketch of the Shawanoe Indians*. Cincinnati: E. Morgan, 1841.

DuLong, John P. *French Canadians in Michigan*. East Lansing: Michigan State University Press, 2001.

Dumont, Julia L., and Sandra Parker. *Tecumseh and Other Stories of the Ohio River Valley*. Bowling Green, OH: Bowling Green State University Popular Press, 2000.

Dunbar, Willis F. *Lewis Cass*. Grand Rapids: Eerdmans, 1970.

Dunnigan, Brian L. *The British Army at Mackinac, 1812-1815*. Lansing: Mackinac Island State Park Commission, 1980.

————. *Frontier Metropolis: Picturing Early Detroit, 1701-1838*. Detroit: Wayne State University Press, 2001.

————. *Garrison Town: Detroit's Strategic Location Gave Its Early Years a Definitive Military Flavor*. Detroit: Wayne State University Press, 2001.

————. *The Prettiest Settlement in America: A Select Bibliography of Early Detroit through the War of 1812*. Mount Pleasant: Central Michigan University, 2001.

————. *A Picturesque Situation: Mackinac before Photography, 1615-1860*. Detroit: Wayne State University Press, 2008.

Dutton, Charles J. *Oliver Hazard Perry*. New York: Longmans, Green and Co., 1935.

Eckert, Allan W. *A Sorrow in Our Heart: The Life of Tecumseh*. New York: Bantam, 1992.

Edmunds, R. David. *The Potawatomis: Keepers of the Fire*. Norman: University of Oklahoma Press, 1978.

————. *The Shawnee Prophet*. Lincoln: University of Nebraska Press, 1983.

————. *Tecumseh and the Quest for Indian Leadership*. Boston: Little, Brown, 1984.

————. *Enduring Nations: Native Americans in the Midwest*. Urbana: University of Illinois Press, 2008.

Ermatinger, Charles O. *The Talbot Regime: or, the First Half Century of the Talbot Settlement*. St. Thomas, ON: Municipal World, 1904.

Farmer, Silas. *The History of Detroit and Michigan: Or the Metropolis Illustrated*. Detroit: S. Farmer, 1884.

————. *History of Detroit and Wayne County and Early Michigan: A Chronological Cyclopedia of the Past & Present*. 1890. Reprint, Detroit: Gale Research, 1969.

Farmer, Silas et al., eds. *The Bi-Centenary of the Founding of City of Detroit 1701-1901, Being the Official Report of the Celebration of July 24, 25, 26, 1901*. Detroit: C.M. Rousseau, 1902.

Finkelman, Paul et al., eds. *The History of Michigan Law*. Athens: Ohio University Press, 2006.

Fitzgibbon, John. "King Alcohol: His Rise, Reign, and Fall in Michigan." *Michigan History* 2 (1918): 737-80.

Franck, Michael. *Elmwood Endures: History of a Detroit Cemetery*. Detroit: Wayne State University Press, 1996.

Fredriksen, John C. *The United States Army in the War of 1812: Concise Biographies of Commanders and Operational Histories of Regiments, with Bibliographies of Published and Primary Resources*. Jefferson, NC: McFarland, 2009.

Fuller, George N. "Settlement of Michigan Territory." *Mississippi Valley Historical Society* 2 (1915): 25-55.

———. *Economic and Social Beginnings of Michigan: A Study of the Settlement of the Lower Peninsula during the Territorial Period, 1805-1837.* Lansing: Wynkoop Hallenbeck Crawford, 1916.

Gilpin, Alec R. "General William Hull and the War on Detroit in 1812." PhD diss., University of Michigan, 1949.

———. *The War of 1812 in the Old Northwest.* East Lansing: Michigan State University Press, 1958.

———. *The Territory of Michigan.* East Lansing: Michigan State University Press, 1970.

Gold, Susan Dudley. *Indian Treaties.* New York: Twenty-First Century Books, 1997.

Goldowsky, Seebert J. *Yankee Surgeon: The Life and Times of Usher Parsons, 1788-1868.* Boston: Francis A. Countway Library of Medicine, 1988.

Goodrich, Calvin. *The First Michigan Frontier.* Ann Arbor: University of Michigan Press, 1940.

Gough, Barry. *Fighting Sail on Lake Huron and Georgian Bay: The War of 1812 and Its Aftermath.* Annapolis, MD: Naval Institute Press, 2002.

Gray, William M. *Soldiers of the King: The Upper Canadian Militia, 1812-1815.* Erin, ON: Boston Mills Press, 1995.

Greenman, Emerson F. *The Indians of Michigan.* Lansing: Michigan Historical Commission, 1961.

Grenier, John. *The First Way of War: American War Making on the Frontier, 1607-1814.* New York: Cambridge University Press, 2005.

Hamil, Fred C. *The Valley of the Lower Thames, 1640 to 1850.* Toronto: University of Toronto Press, 1951.

———. *Michigan in the War of 1812.* Lansing: Michigan Historical Commission, 1960.

Haring, Sidney L. *White Man's Law: Native People in Nineteenth-Century Canadian Jurisprudence.* Toronto: University of Toronto Press, 1998.

Harris, Richard C. et al., eds. *Historical Atlas of Canada.* 3 vols. Toronto: University of Toronto Press, 1987-93.

Hatcher, Harlan H. *Lake Erie.* Indianapolis: Bobbs-Merrill, 1945.

Hele, Karl S. *Lines Drawn upon the Water: First Nations and the Great Lakes Borders and Borderlands.* Waterloo, ON: Wilfrid Laurier University Press, 2008.

Herndon, Nell. "Detroit under British Rule, 1812-13." MA thesis, Wayne University, 1933.

Hickey, Donald R. *The War of 1812: A Forgotten Conflict.* Urbana: University of Illinois Press, 1989.

———. *Don't Give Up the Ship! Myths of the War of 1812.* Urbana: University of Illinois Press, 2006.

Hill, Daniel G. *The Freedom Seekers: Blacks in Early Canada*. Agincourt, ON: Book Society of Canada, 1981.

Horsman, Reginald. *Frontier Detroit: 1760-1812*. Detroit: Michigan in Perspective Conference, 1964.

———. *Matthew Elliott, British Indian Agent*. Detroit: Wayne State University Press, 1964.

———. *The Frontier in the Formative Years, 1783-1815*. New York: Holt, Rinehart, and Winston, 1970.

———. *The Origins of Indian Removal, 1815-1824*. East Lansing: Michigan State University Press, 1970.

———. *Expansion and American Indian Policy, 1783-1812*. 1967. Reprint, Norman: University of Oklahoma Press, 1992.

Jacobson, Judy. *Detroit River Connections: Historical and Biographical Sketches of the Eastern Great Lakes Border Region*. Baltimore: Clearfield, 1994.

James, Charles C. *Early History of the Town of Amherstburg: A Short, Concise, and Interesting Sketch, with Explanatory Notes*. Amherstburg, ON: Echo, 1902.

Jenks, William L. *St. Clair County, Michigan, Its History and Its People*. 2 vols. Chicago: Lewis, 1912.

———. *The First Bank in Michigan: The Detroit Bank*. Port Huron, MI: First National Exchange Bank, 1916.

Johnson, J.K. *Becoming Prominent: Regional Leadership in Upper Canada, 1791-1841*. Kingston, ON: McGill-Queen's University Press, 1989.

Johnson, J.K., and Bruce G. Wilson, eds. *Historical Essays on Upper Canada: New Perspectives*. Ottawa: Carleton University Press, 1989.

Keffer, Marion C. *Migrations to/from Canada*. Ann Arbor, MI: Genealogical Society of Washtenaw County, 1982.

Kennedy, J. Gerald. *The Astonished Traveler: William Darby, Frontier Geographer and Man of Letters*. Baton Rouge: Louisiana State University Press, 1981.

Klunder, Willard C. *Lewis Cass and the Politics of Moderation*. Kent, OH: Kent State University Press, 1996.

Kneip, Therese A. "Slavery in Early Detroit." MA thesis, University of Detroit, 1938.

Kooker, Arthur R. "The Antislavery Movement in Michigan 1796-1840: A Study in Humanitarianism on an American Frontier." PhD diss., University of Michigan, 1941.

Krog, Carl E. "The British Great Lakes Forts." *Inland Seas* 42 (1986): 252-60.

Landon, Fred. *Western Ontario and the American Frontier*. 1941. Reprint, New York: Russell and Russell, 1970.

Larrie, Reginald R. *Makin' Free: African-Americans in the Northwest Territory*. Detroit: B. Ethridge Books, 1981.

Leasher, Evelyn M., ed. *Native Americans in Michigan: A Bibliography of the Material in the Clarke Historical Library*. Mount Pleasant: Clarke Historical Library, Central Michigan University, 1996.

Lebel, E.C. "History of Assumption, the First Parish in Upper Canada." *Report of the Canadian Catholic Historical Association* 21 (1954): 23-37.

Leeson, Michael A. et al., eds. *History of Macomb County, Michigan*. Chicago: Leeson, 1882.

Lossing, Benson J. *The Pictorial Field-Book of the War of 1812*. New York: Harper, 1869.

———. *Hull's Surrender of Detroit*. Philadelphia: J.E. Potter, 1875.

Louisville Free Public Library. *Books and Magazine Articles on Battle of Tippecanoe, Battle of the River Raisin, Battle of the Thames*. Louisville, KY: Louisville Free Public Library, 1913.

MacGregor, Roy. *Canadians: A Portrait of a Country and Its People*. Toronto: Viking Canada, 2007.

Magnaghi, Russell M. "Michigan's Indian Factory at Detroit, 1802-1805." *Inland Seas* 38 (1982): 171-78.

———. "Michigan's Indian Factory at Mackinac, 1808-1812." *Inland Seas* 39 (1983): 22-30.

Malcomson, Robert. *Warships of the Great Lakes, 1754-1834*. Annapolis, MD: Naval Institute Press, 2001.

———. "'Not Very Much Celebrated': The Evolution and Nature of the Provincial Marine, 1755-1813." *Northern Mariner* 11 (2001): 25-38.

Mason, Philip P., ed. *After Tippecanoe: Some Aspects of the War of 1812*. 1963. Reprint, East Lansing: Michigan State University Press, 2011.

Mast, Dolorita. *Always the Priest: The Life of Gabriel Richard, S.S*. Baltimore: Helicon, 1965.

McRae, Norman. "Early Blacks in Michigan, 1743-1800." *Detroit in Perspective: A Journal of Regional History* 2 (1976): 159-75.

———. "Blacks in Detroit, 1736-1833: The Search for Freedom and Community and Its Implications for Educators." PhD diss., University of Michigan, 1982.

Mika, Nick, and Helma Mika. *United Empire Loyalists: Pioneers of Upper Canada*. Belleville, ON: Mika, 1976.

Monroe County Historical Commission. *An Historical and Archaeological Investigation of the River Raisin Battle Site of 1813*. Monroe, MI: Monroe County Historical Commission, 1977.

Moore, Charles. *Governor, Judge, and Priest. Detroit, 1805-1815. A Paper Read before the Witenagemote, on Friday Evening, October the Second, 1891*. New York: DeVinne Press, 1891.

Moore, David R. "Canada and the United States, 1815-1830." PhD diss., University of Chicago, 1910.

Moran, J. Bell. *The Moran Family: 200 Years in Detroit.* Detroit: Alved, 1949.

Mull, Carol E. *The Underground Railroad in Michigan.* Jefferson, NC: McFarland, 2010.

Naveaux, Ralph. *Invaded on All Sides: The Story of Michigan's Greatest Battlefield Scene of the Engagements at Frenchtown and the River Raisin in the War of 1812.* Marceline, MO: Walsworth, 2008.

Neal, Frederick, ed. *The Township of Sandwich, Past and Present.* 1909. Reprint, Windsor: Essex County Historical Society and Windsor Public Library Board, 1979.

Nursey, Walter R. *The Story of Isaac Brock: Hero, Defender and Saviour of Upper Canada, 1812.* 1908. Reprint, Toronto: W. Briggs, 1909.

Owens, Robert M. *Mr. Jefferson's Hammer: William Henry Harrison and the Origins of American Indian Policy.* Norman: University of Oklahoma Press, 2007.

Palmer, Friend et al. *Early Days in Detroit.* Detroit: Hunt & June, 1906.

Paré, George. *The Catholic Church in Detroit, 1701-1888.* 1951. Reprint, Detroit: Wayne State University Press, 1983.

Pargellis, Stanley M. *Father Gabriel Richard.* Detroit: Wayne University Press, 1950.

Parkins, Almon E. *The Historical Geography of Detroit.* 1918. Reprint, Port Washington, NY: Kennikat, 1970.

Peterson, Jacqueline. "Prelude to Red River: A Social Portrait of the Great Lakes Métis." *Ethnohistory* 25 (1978): 41-67.

Peterson, Jacqueline, and Jennifer S.H. Brown, eds. *The New Peoples: Being and Becoming Métis in North America.* Winnipeg: University of Manitoba Press, 1985.

Pflug, Melissa A. "Politics of Great Lakes Indian Religion." *Michigan Historical Review* 18 (1992): 15-31.

Pickens, Buford L. *Early City Plans for Detroit, a Projected American Metropolis.* Detroit: Detroit Institute of Arts, 1943.

Pittman, Philip, and George M. Covington. *Don't Blame the Treaties: Native American Rights and the Michigan Indian Treaties.* West Bloomfield, MI: Altwerger and Mandel, 1992.

Prucha, Francis P. *Lewis Cass and American Indian Policy.* Detroit: Wayne State University Press, 1967.

———. *The Sword of the Republic: The United States Army on the Frontier 1783-1846.* New York: Macmillan, 1969.

Pryke, K.G., and L.L. Kulisek, eds. *The Western District: Papers from the Western District Conference.* Windsor, ON: Essex County Historical Society, 1983.

Quaife, Milo M. *Chicago and the Old Northwest, 1673-1835.* 1913. Reprint, Urbana: University of Illinois Press, 2001.

Quaife, Milo M., ed. "From Marietta to Detroit in 1815." *Historical*

Society of Northwestern Ohio, Quarterly Bulletin 4 (1942): 134-55.

Rau, Louise. "John Askin: Early Detroit Merchant." *Bulletin of the Business Historical Society* 10 (1936): 91-94.

Read, David B. *Life and Times of Major-General Sir Isaac Brock.* Toronto: W. Briggs, 1894.

Reps, John W. "Planning in the Wilderness: Detroit, 1805-1830." *Town Planning Review* 25 (1955): 240-50.

Resnick, Philip. *The European Roots of Canadian Identity.* Peterborough, ON: Broadview Press, 2005.

Rich, E.E. *The Fur Trade and the Northwest to 1857.* Toronto: McClelland and Stewart, 1967.

Ricketts, Shannon. *The Duff-Baby House, 221 Mill Street, Windsor, Ontario.* Ottawa: Historic Sites and Monuments Board of Canada, 1990.

Riddell, William R. *The First Judge at Detroit and His Court.* Lansing: Michigan State Bar Association, 1915.

———. *The Legal Profession in Upper Canada in Its Early Periods.* Toronto: Law Society of Upper Canada, 1916.

———. "The Slave in Upper Canada." *The Journal of Negro History* 4 (1919): 372-95.

———. "Slavery in Canada." *The Journal of Negro History* 5 (1920): 262-377.

———. *John Richardson.* Toronto: Ryerson Press, 1923.

———. "A Negro Slave in Detroit When Detroit Was Canadian." *Michigan History* 18 (1934): 48-52.

Roberts, Julia. *In Mixed Company: Taverns and Public Life in Upper Canada.* Vancouver: University of British Columbia Press, 2009.

Roosevelt, Theodore. *The Naval War of 1812, or, the History of the United States Navy during the Last War with Great Britain.* 1894. Reprint, Annapolis, MD: Naval Institute Press, 1987.

Ross, Robert B. *History of the Knaggs Family of Ohio and Michigan. Historical, Biological, and Genealogical.* Detroit: C.M. Burton, 1902.

Ross, Robert B., and George B. Catlin. *Landmarks of Detroit: A History of the City.* Detroit: Evening News Association, 1898.

———. *The Early Bench and Bar of Detroit from 1805 to the End of 1850.* Detroit: Richard P. Joy and Clarence M. Burton, 1907.

Ross, Victoria J. *Detroit's Historic Drinking Establishments.* Charleston, SC: Arcadia, 2008.

Russell, Nelson V. *The British Régime in Michigan and the Old Northwest, 1760-1796.* 1939. Reprint, Philadelphia: Porcupine Press, 1978.

Sheldon, Electra M. *Early History of Michigan from the First Settlement to 1815.* New York: A.S. Barnes, 1856.

Sheppard, George. *Plunder, Profit, and Paroles: A Social History of the War of 1812 in Upper Canada.* Montreal: McGill-Queen's University Press, 1994.

Sherer, Tim. "Surviving in Frontier Detroit." *The Great Lakes Review* 8 (1982): 11-19.

Silver, Peter. *Our Savage Neighbors: How Indian War Transformed Early America*. New York: Norton, 2007.

Sioui, Georges E. *Huron-Wendat: The Heritage of the Circle*. Translated by Jane Brierley. East Lansing: Michigan State University Press, 1999.

Skaggs, David C., and Larry L. Nelson, eds. *The Sixty Years' War for the Great Lakes, 1754-1814*. East Lansing: Michigan State University Press, 2001.

Sleeper-Smith, Susan, ed. "Forum: The Middle Ground Revisited." *William and Mary Quarterly* 63 (2006): 3-96.

Smith, W.L.G. *The Life and Times of Lewis Cass*. New York: Derby & Jackson, 1856.

St-Denis, Guy. *Tecumseh's Bones*. Montreal: McGill-Queen's University Press, 2005.

Stone, Joel. "Taverns of Early Detroit." *Michigan History* 92 (2008): 46-51.

Sugden, John. *Tecumseh's Last Stand*. Norman: University of Oklahoma Press, 1985.

———. *Tecumseh: A Life*. New York: Henry Holt and Co., 1998.

Tanner, Helen Hornbeck et al., eds. *Atlas of Great Lakes Indian History*. Norman: University of Oklahoma Press, 1986.

Taylor, Alan. "The Late Loyalists: Northern Reflections of the Early American Republic." *Journal of the Early Republic* 27 (2007): 1-34.

———. *The Civil War of 1812: American Citizens, British Subjects, Irish Rebels, & Indian Allies*. New York: Knopf, 2010.

Teasdale, Guillaume. "Separate Destinies: the French of the Detroit River Region and Their Indian Neighbours, 1763-1815." *Recherches amerindiennes au Quebec* 39 (2009): 23-45, 186.

———. "The French of Orchard Country: Territory, Landscape, and Ethnicity in the Detroit River Region, 1680s-1810s." PhD diss., York University, 2010.

Tucker, Glenn. *Tecumseh: Vision of Glory*. Indianapolis: Bobb-Merrill, 1956.

Turner, Wesley B. *The War of 1812: The War That Both Sides Won*. Toronto: Dundurn Press, 1990.

———. *The Astonishing General: The Life and Legacy of Sir Isaac Brock*. Toronto: Dundurn Press, 2011.

Utley, Henry M. et al. *Michigan as a Province, Territory, and a State, the Twenty-Sixth Member of the Federal Union*. 4 vols. New York: Publishing Society of Michigan, 1906.

Vorderstrasse, Alfred B. *Detroit in the War of 1812*. Detroit: Wayne University Press, 1951.

Wade, Mason. *The French Canadians, 1760-1967*. 2 vols. Toronto: Macmillan, 1968.

Welsh, William J., and David C. Skaggs, eds. *War on the Great Lakes: Essays Commemorating the 175th Anniversary of the Battle of Lake Erie*. Kent, OH: Kent State University Press, 1991.

Wheeler-Voegelin, Erminie. *An Ethnohistorical Report on the Wyandot, Potawatomi, Ottawa, and Chippewa of Northwest Ohio*. New York: Garland, 1974.

White, Richard. *The Middle Ground: Indians, Empires, and Republics in the Great Lakes Region, 1650-1815*. New York: Cambridge University Press, 1991.

Widder, Agnes Haigh. "The John Askin Family Library: A Fur-Trading Family's Books." *Michigan Historical Review* 33 (2007): 27-57.

Wigmore, Gregory. "Before the Railroad: From Slavery to Freedom in the Canadian-American Borderland." *Journal of American History* 98 (2011): 437-54.

Willig, Timothy D. *Restoring the Chain of Friendship: British Policy and the Indians of the Great Lakes, 1783-1815*. Lincoln: University of Nebraska Press, 2008.

Wing, Talcott E. *History of Monroe County, Michigan*. New York: Munsell, 1890.

Woodford, Arthur M. *This is Detroit, 1701-2001*. Detroit: Wayne State University Press, 2001.

Woodford, Frank B. *Lewis Cass, the Last Jeffersonian*. 1950. Reprint, New York: Octagon Books, 1973.

———. *Yankees in Wonderland*. Detroit: Wayne University Press, 1951.

———. *Mr. Jefferson's Disciple: A Life of Justice Woodward*. East Lansing: Michigan State College Press, 1953.

———. *Gabriel Richard, Frontier Ambassador*. Detroit: Wayne State University Press, 1958.

Woodford, Frank B., and Arthur M. Woodford. *All Our Yesterdays: A Brief History of Detroit*. Detroit: Wayne State University Press, 1969.

Yanik, Anthony J. *The Fall and Recapture of Detroit in the War of 1812: In Defense of William Hull*. Detroit: Wayne State University Press, 2011.

Zeisler, Karl. "The Battle of the River Raisin." *Bulletin of the Detroit Historical Society* 18 (1962): 4-10.

Websites

Canada Gen Web Cemetery Project. "Assumption Roman Catholic Cemetery." http://cemetery.canadagenweb.org/ON/ONA15634.

Canadiana.org. "Early Canadiana Online." www.canadiana.ca/en/home.

The Discriminating General. "The War of 1812 Website." www.warof1812.ca.

Friends of the River Raisin Battlefield. "River Raisin Battlefield: 'Remember the Raisin.'" www.riverraisinbattlefield.org.

The Library of Michigan and Archives of Michigan. "Seeking Michigan." http://seekingmichigan.org.

The Monroe County Library System and the Monroe County Historical Commission. "War of 1812 Digital Collection: Footsteps to the Battlefield." http://monroe.lib.mi.us/war_of_1812/main.htm.

National Park Service. "'Best Troops in the World': The Michigan Territorial Militia in the Detroit River Theater during the War of 1812," by Dennis M. Au. www.nps.gov/history/history/online_books/gero/papers/1991-1992/sec7.htm.

———. "Perry's Victory & International Peace Memorial." www.nps.gov/pevi/index.htm.

———. "River Raisin National Battlefield Park." www.nps.gov/rira/index.htm.

Ohio Historical Society. "Ohio Fundamental Documents." www.ohiohistory.org/resource/database/funddocs.html.

Ohio History Central. "Ohio History Central: An Online Encyclopedia of Ohio History." www.ohiohistorycentral.org.

University of Michigan. "Michigan County Histories and Atlases Digitization Project." http://quod.lib.umich.edu/m/micounty/.

University of Toronto. "Dictionary of Canadian Biography Online." www.biographi.ca.

Yale Law School. "The Avalon Project: Documents in Law, History, and Diplomacy." http://avalon.law.yale.edu.